Advertising and a Democratic Press

☆

C. EDWIN BAKER

PRINCETON UNIVERSITY PRESS

PRINCETON, NEW JERSEY

Copyright © 1994 by Princeton University Press
Published by Princeton University Press, 41 William Street,
Princeton, New Jersey 08540
In the United Kingdom: Princeton University Press, Chichester, West Sussex
All Rights Reserved

Library of Congress Cataloging-in-Publication Data

Baker, C. Edwin
Advertising and a democratic press / C. Edwin Baker.
p. cm.
Includes bibliographical references and index.
ISBN 0-691-03258-0
ISBN 0-691-02116-3 (pbk.)
1. Advertising—Political aspects—United States. 2. Pressure groups—United States.
3. Censorship—United States. 4. Manipulative behavior—United States.
5. Freedom of the press—United States. 6. Advertising—Taxation—United States.
7. Advertising law—United States.—I. Title.
HF5813.U6B29 1993
659.1'0973—dc20   93-2177   CIP

This book has been composed in Adobe Galliard

Princeton University Press books are
printed on acid-free paper and meet the guidelines
for permanence and durability of the Committee
on Production Guidelines for Book Longevity
of the Council on Library Resources

Second printing, and first paperback printing, 1995

Printed in the United States of America by Princeton Academic Press

3   5   7   9   10   8   6   4   2

FOR

NANCY, MARY, KIRA, AND KAITLYN

☆

☆ *Contents* ☆

☆ *Preface* ☆

I ARGUE in this book that advertising seriously distorts and diminishes the mass media's contribution to a free and democratic society—and then consider policy responses. Here I want to respond to two possible reasons for doubting the practical relevance of such an argument.

First, folk wisdom holds: "If it ain't broke, don't fix it." Thus, when I argue for government interventions, for "repairs," that would affect press production, it is worth wondering whether my exercise is not best ignored—or even more wisely, emphatically rejected. Our press, or at least its print media, is respected around the world. Moreover, history is filled with recurrent instances of various governments censoring the press—often with their interventions justified in good faith as purportedly promoting the public good. But time after time these arguments and the resulting censorship were seen in retrospect to have been misguided. Caution recommends a firm stand against proposals for government intervention. This caution is especially wise if the press is basically OK, even though surely each of us has a few complaints and would prefer a slightly different press.

As I await the early edition of the next day's *New York Times* each night at the newsstand, I have an almost reflexive reaction: "This isn't perfect but it is quite informative; surely, we've got it pretty good with respect to the press." Although there are always problems and lapses, the modern American press provides more and better information to the public than any previous institution. This impressive even if imperfect press arguably exists precisely because of its freedom from government restraint, freedom constitutionally guaranteed in this country. Any attempt by government to impose, for example, requirements of press responsibility would result in a loss of valuable freedom—this last point being central to First Amendment doctrine that I fully support.[1]

But is our satisfaction Pollyannish? How would we know if the press were "broke?" In our understanding of all but the day's most local events, we are largely the products of our press. It is awfully easy to adopt the Whiggish view that it is not broken precisely because "it" is largely "us." Not knowing information or viewpoints that we do not have, how would we know if the press is not supplying the information and opinion that it should?

Granted, over time the American press has laudably served freedom and enlightenment. But this can hardly mean that it could not have done better and does not have serious flaws. Those interested in democracy in this country should be concerned about the public's incredibly low levels of political knowledge and its depressing level of even the minimal political participation involved in voting. Could this country's press be partly responsible for these failings? Once we begin questioning, many other questions follow. Is Watergate a victory of an adversarial press or a rare example of one paper's stumbling onto and atypically pursuing an astonishing, politically sensitive story? Why do not other reports of government and corporate failures and corruption generate constituencies for needed fundamental change? For every initiative for which observers praise the press, are there other equally or more important initiatives or media campaigns that the press fails to undertake—and how would we know? In an interesting project, nationally recognized commentators annually attempt to identify each year's top ten "censored" stories—not stories censored by the government but stories that the press on its own failed to publicize.[2] But since this project publishes media references for each story, "censored" obviously refers not to complete suppression but to the inadequacies of the national news media's coverage despite the story's obvious importance. Insignificant coverage can effectively mute a story's significant political or democratic relevance. These questions suggest that without reflective inquiry, there is no hope of understanding either the extent or the causes of the press's not undertaking needed initiatives. Nor of understanding the conditions under which the media could best serve a democratic society.

Advertising and a Democratic Press begins this critical inquiry. Despite widespread comfort with much of the American press, the book suggests that to a troubling and surprising extent the press *is* "broke" or, at least, in need of a major tune-up. Thus, the apparent adequacy of the existing press does not justify ignoring the possible need for structural reforms. The book also shows that advertising plays a key role in undermining press performance and, therefore, that advertising should be a major focus in the consideration of structural reforms.

Second, this book's call for laws directed at the press and informed by explicit governmental media policies might seem so inconsistent with valued First Amendment guarantees that the project can only be "academic" in the bad sense of the term. No matter how factually or normatively persuasive, arguably the book can have little real relevance because of the American constitutional order.

Policy-oriented media scholarship in this country, particularly within the legal academy, is undeveloped—underdeveloped in comparison with scholarship in other countries and especially in relation to the significance of the topic. Ironically, the shadow of the First Amendment may be part of the problem. My own scholarship has centered on deepening our understanding of the First Amendment or, more specifically, on broadening and strengthening its reach.[3] Thus, for me, this tentative observation about the First Amendment is especially troubling. Still, the paucity of policy-oriented thinking about the press may reflect a tendency of Americans or, at least, of communications and legal scholars to assume that any government action focused on the press is likely to be unconstitutional—and, therefore, worth considering only in terms of how or why the intervention should be criticized.

Of course, this legalistic response seldom blocks inquiry when the inquiry is demanded by a powerful, influential constituency. The media themselves, a politically central "interest group," have gotten special postal subsidies, special access to government officials and files and proceedings, exemptions from some taxes, monetary support through "patronage" advertising, a limited exemption from antitrust laws, along with various other privileges and economic benefits. But the media business has not sought legislative responses to the problem described in this book, the corrosive effects of private power on press freedom. Such legislation is likely to be costly to many elements within two of our society's most influential interest groups—the corporate-owned press and the corporate-serving advertising industry. Even if scholarly media critics show that lack of structural reform seriously damages both political and cultural democracy, the public is unlikely to feel the injury acutely or to associate the injury with the structure of the press. Organized public pressure for change does not easily develop.*

Still, the first step is to make reform "thinkable"—for example, not to be improperly blinded by the First Amendment. Thus, I ask those readers who assume the American press is in fairly good shape to suspend judgment long enough to read the critique in the first three chapters. And I ask those with the strongest commitments to the First Amendment, among whom I count myself, still to consider the policy proposals offered in chapter 4. Finally, chapter 5 will directly address the First Amendment issue— and show that the book's policy proposals would not be part of the history

---

* Although I maintain hope that it is not crucial, media reform seems much more likely in countries with strong political parties that can play a leadership role in change.

of misguided censorship but instead would promote constitutional ideals while meeting constitutional standards.

．　．　．　．　．

Many people helped me in one way or another with this book, and although I cannot mention them all here, I do want especially to thank, without attributing any responsibility for mistakes, several people: Mike Fitts, Oscar Gandy, Jr., Douglas Halijan, Jason Isralowitz, Seth Kreimer, Erin Lynch, Michael Madow, Guillermo Margadant, Gerry Neuman, Ed Rock, and Carol Sanger, and my editor at Princeton, Malcolm DeBevoise. I should also note that this book is a somewhat revised, updated, and expanded version of an article of the same title published in June 1992 in the *University of Pennsylvania Law Review*, whose editors provided useful assistance.

Advertising and a Democratic Press

☆

✩ *Introduction* ✩

THE FIRST AMENDMENT guarantees the press freedom from "abridgment" by government. Adopted in the wake of the colonists' resistance to the British Stamp Act, which heavily taxed newspaper advertisements as well as newspapers themselves, and at a time of early Massachusetts printers' resistance to similar state levies,[1] this constitutional guarantee might plausibly be interpreted to prohibit all taxes or governmental regulations of the press. Government might be seen as the sole, relevant threat to freedom, and freedom of the press might mean at bottom a laissez-faire marketplace for the mass media industry.

The thesis of this book, however, is that this view of freedom is wrong. Despite the potential danger and occasional occurrence of governmental censorship, private entities in general and advertisers in particular constitute the most consistent and the most pernicious "censors" of media content. Of course, advertising operates as a "censor" only because the media content desired by advertisers is not the same as the content desired by media consumers. Chapters 1 and 2 describe a variety of ways in which this divergence is manifested. The book shows that existing structures and behavior of private power centers prevent the media from adequately serving the needs of a democratic society. Organized private power is today probably the most serious threat to a free and democratic press. Thus, although advertising can be viewed as the lifeblood of free media, paying most of its costs and thus making the media widely available, this book examines advertising as a threat to a free and democratic press.

Once advertising is seen as a powerful censor and influential taskmaster that systematically undermines a free and democratic press, a host of questions arise. Which of advertisers' relations with the media are objectionable? Do they violate existing laws? Are new regulations desirable? Constitutional? Would a tax on advertising in the mass media be desirable, for example, as a means to reduce the influence of advertisers over media content? Constitutional? Might answers depend on how broadly the tax is applied? Or on the use of the resulting tax revenue?

The Stamp Act was not the last tax on newspaper advertising. For good reasons or bad, advertising taxes are often proposed. During the Civil War, Congress raised revenue by taxing newspaper advertising.[2] Florida recently adopted a tax on various services, including advertising, but underestimated the power of the advertising lobby, which quickly forced repeal.[3]

The Bush administration proposed, but quickly abandoned, a plan to limit the deductibility of advertising expenses.[4] Academics have proposed a progressive tax on newspaper advertising as preferable to the Newspaper Preservation Act's "joint operating agreements" as a means of promoting newspaper competition.[5] Many states are currently considering extending existing taxes to either newspaper sales or newspaper advertising.[6]

Likewise, American history provides many examples of regulation of advertising. The Federal Trade Commission regulates "false and misleading" *commercial* advertising, though when the "product" is a politician, such misleading advertising is arguably the norm and is certainly constitutionally protected. Tobacco advertising is subject to various forms of regulation that would be impermissible if applied to noncommercial advocacy of unhealthful practices or policies. The many forms of regulation of commercial speech—some wise, some not so—were constitutionally unquestionable as long as the commercial speech was understood not to be protected by the First Amendment. Given recent Supreme Court decisions, these regulations may again be safe from effective constitutional challenge.[7] More theoretically, I have argued in another book that excluding commercial speech from constitutional protection is justified, either because the advertising of a market-oriented enterprise is an integral part of an instrumentalist exercise of power by participants in market exchange, or because the dictates of the market rather than human choice determine the message content of advertisements.[8]

Powerful policy arguments against taxes on advertising, as well as other government regulations of advertising, emphasize that advertising pays the largest part of the bill for our "free press."[9] By "subsidizing" the press, advertising makes mass media broadly available. This subsidy enables the media to engage in the expensive activities of gathering, shaping, and distributing news (and entertainment). Advertising is so important to the press that some democracies give it constitutional status. For example, Germany, which like many countries views only the print media and not broadcasting as the "real" press, gives constitutional protection to the print media's reliance on advertising.[10]

Still, could advertising also undermine a free press? Defenders of advertising's present role easily concede that, like most social practices, advertising has negative as well as positive aspects. On the positive side, advertising often provides useful information to consumers and promotes purchasing behavior that may stimulate the economy. But there is a darker side. Two of the greatest causes of premature death and of loss of work are tobacco and alcohol—hardly products whose use merits promotion. Nevertheless,

4

"in 1979, tobacco and liquor companies were [magazines'] two largest advertisers."[11] More generally, advertising often distorts facts. It promotes contested consumerist values and contested visions of social life, of women, and of men. Neither advertising's overt nor its implicit messages have unambiguously desirable consequences for social life. Arguably the government should deal with these negative effects, if at all, with regulations directed at specific objectionable contents found in some advertising—and these regulations should be permissible. But, of course, narrow regulation of specific, objectionable content may be inadequate if, as Michael Schudson suggests, the most objectionable feature of advertising relates to its pervasive role in creating an impoverished culture, what Schudson terms "capitalist realism," an art form or symbolic culture that shapes our values, flattens experience, simplifies, portrays satisfactions as inevitably private, and glorifies private life and material ambition.[12]

In this book, however, I want mostly to put aside issues concerning the good or bad of advertising's own content. There is likely to be a wide consensus that, whatever evils are associated with the content of advertising, one reason for caution in regulating advertising is that it supports the media's nonadvertising content. The assumption is that advertising plays a key structural role in maintaining a free and democratic press. The primary purpose of this book is to evaluate that assumption. Thus, chapters 1 and 2 will consider the effect of advertising on media's nonadvertising content and on the distribution of that media content. Chapter 3 will briefly consider the light that an economic efficiency analysis sheds on the observations of chapters 1 and 2. Each chapter deepens the critique of the current advertising-based system of supporting the mass media. Then chapter 4 begins the necessary task of designing responsive policy proposals. Since any legislation dealing with the press immediately raises First Amendment questions, the book concludes in chapter 5 with an evaluation of the constitutionality of the proposals described in chapter 4.

Of course, to criticize effects of advertising on the press implies some image of proper press performance. My evaluative standpoint will be that of creating or maintaining a democratic, free press.[13] The focus is on the role of the press in serving a democratic government and culture. This standpoint reflects what I assume is a central element of the constitutional justification for extending protection to the press as an institution rather than merely protecting the press as an element of the individual's right of self-expression. Of course, this democracy-serving justification for protection is instrumental—but then the value and significance of any institution must lie in how it serves human values and interests.[14] Here the policy concern is this: what type of press, what type of mass media, will adequately serve a free and democratic society?

Obviously, this evaluative perspective will be influenced by the evaluator's conception of democracy. An elitist conception may require most centrally a press that performs the "checking function," that is, a press capable of and oriented toward exposing abuse of power.[15] A more robust conception of "participatory" democracy would require additional press functions, possibly suggested by the slogan "the public's right to know."[16] Depending on whether the more broad-based conception of democracy emphasized a republican *common* dialogue or, alternatively, a diversity of groups each with its own concerns and dialogue, the nature of optimal press segmentation of audiences would vary.

How specific the description of either democracy or the corresponding vision of an ideal press must be depends on the evaluative issues at stake. For purposes of this book's claims that advertising undermines a democratic press, I implicitly assume only that democracy involves the possibility of broad-based cultural and political participation of people with diverse inclinations. Therefore, I use "democratic" (or "free and democratic") to modify press in order to emphasize two dimensions of media output: (1) availability—a press is more democratic the more its products are widely available; and (2) content—the content of a democratic press should serve the diverse *desires* or, somewhat more controversially, the diverse *needs* of the various elements of the democratic society. Thus, the "democratic" aspect of the press relates both to circulation and to provision of "uncensored" information and opinion that readers desire or need. A democratic press should be both responsive and pluralistic in its communications.[17]

Advertising: Financial Support and Structural Subversion of a Democratic Press

ADVERTISING AS A SUBSIDY

ADVERTISING in the media confers obvious benefits. First, but mostly beyond the scope of this book, are benefits to the enterprises that advertise, to the buying public that relies on advertising for information about transaction opportunities, and to the economy as a whole because of advertising's stimulus to economic activity. Often, readers and viewers are as interested in the ads as in the media's nonadvertising or "editorial" content. (Throughout, I will refer generically to all of the media's nonadvertising content, including hard news, news analysis, features, and opinion, as "editorial content.") For example, three out of four women in a 1974 survey agreed that they were "about equally interested in [a newspaper's] advertising and news stories"; a 1979 study found that "58% of all adults consulted newspaper classified ads at least once" during the week; and in 1977 44% of the public said that "they look forward to newspaper advertising" (as compared to 9% who held similar positive views of television ads).[1] Of course, rather than providing these benefits, advertising sometimes imparts misinformation that is injurious to both the public and the economy. Moreover, normative assessments of our consumer society and of advertising's role in creating and maintaining it are contested. I put these issues aside.

Second, advertising provides financial support for the mass media. Virtually all of commercial radio and television broadcasters' revenue comes from advertising. The newspaper industry, which is the focus of this chapter, obtains approximately 75% of its revenues from advertising.[2] Of course, advertising also imposes costs—for ink, newsprint, solicitation of ads, composing, distribution (because of added bulk and weight), and the like. Conceivably, most advertising revenue could be expended on providing the ads, leaving little to subsidize other aspects of the newspaper's operations.[3] Since not only do advertisers value readers but often readers also value ads (as well as editorial content) and the paper sells to both, the direction of subsidy might be expected to reflect which party, reader or advertiser, values the other more. The relationship is likely to be histori-cally and contextually variable—for example, in the eighteenth century the availability of goods for sale might have been especially valuable news to the reader, while today mass marketers and competitive sellers most likely value the reader more than the reader does them.[4]

Virtually all observers and economic studies appear to agree that throughout the twentieth century advertising has paid a large portion of the costs of supplying the public with newspapers. One economic study estimates that without advertisements newspapers would cost as much as five times their current price and concludes that "a full cost-to-the-reader general newspaper free of advertisements would not be commercially via-ble."[5] Another study concluded that today's $.30 paper would sell for $1.15 if it could maintain present circulation, but since it could not main-tain circulation at that price, the absence of ad revenue would "result in the extinction of the press as it has functioned historically."[6] Thus, for a demo-cratic press the advertising "subsidy" may be crucial. Without advertising, the resources available for expenditures on the "news" would presumably decline, predictably leading to an erosion of quality and quantity. The cost of the "news" to the public would increase, thereby restricting its "demo-cratic" availability.

This assessment of advertising may seem uncontroversial—the applica-tion of simple economic logic. Both advertisers and readers willingly pay for and both benefit from getting the same product, a newspaper combin-ing editorial content with advertising, into the hands of the reader. The reader, who may be either relatively indifferent to or desirous of advertis-ing, is willing to pay some amount for the newspaper. The advertiser's goal of getting the reader to look at the advertising content requires that the reader pick up the paper. Therefore, in addition to paying the costs of advertising content, the advertiser is willing to pay part of the cost for editorial content in order to obtain readers for the medium containing the ads. This willingness to pay for nonadvertising content is in principle the same in newspapers as in over-the-air broadcasting where advertisers pay for (virtually) all the nonadvertising content. The newspapers' advertisers will even pay extra for more expensive, "high quality" editorial content if it attracts a particularly desirable readership.[7] Given that both purchasers—advertisers and readers—are willing to pay for editorial content, surely not collecting from one of two potential "joint" purchasers of a product would cause the seller to receive less for the product. Any blockage of newspapers' transactions with advertisers would produce an inefficient contraction of the supply of editorial content. Without advertising (or with reduced advertising) there would be less revenue to pay for the media; hence, less media production.

If advertising revenues were eliminated, a publisher might attempt to recoup part of the lost revenue by charging a higher price, but this higher price will cause a loss of marginal readers[8] and result in a smaller amount of total revenue than was previously received from readers combined with advertisers.[9] Eliminating (or, more plausibly, reducing) advertising apparently must result in some combination of an increase in price with a corresponding decrease in readership, and a decrease in the amount spent on news production, which is also likely to reduce readership—in sum, the reduction of advertising revenue will predictably lead to a net deterioration of the democratic press.

Despite its disarming simplicity, I will argue that the above analysis is wrong—primarily because it relies on too static a notion of the newspaper and of newspaper demand. To begin developing this critique, I present a hypothetical scenario in which the above simple economic logic does not pan out. I then show that the assumptions on which this scenario is constructed have considerable historical basis. This presentation substantially weakens the affirmative case for advertising's contribution to the media. Chapter 2's discussion of other negative effects of advertising further supports a pragmatic reconsideration of advertising's contribution to a democratic, free press—a press that is widely available and responsive to the needs of a diverse society.

Hypothetical: Advertising as a Destructive Force

Imagine two periods, one before and one after advertising is introduced into the newspaper world. During "Time 1," there are two principal types of relevant costs: variable costs, like those for paper, ink, printing, and distribution; and first-copy costs, which are primarily editorial or "news" expenses for gathering, writing, editing, and composing copy. ("Fixed" or long-term variable costs that exist irrespective of circulation size should be depreciated and added to first-copy costs; those that vary with circulation should be depreciated and added to variable costs. Precise categorization can be ignored here.) For a paper to be financially sound, revenue must cover both costs and presumably provide some profits. The break-even point would be where revenue equals costs, that is:

1. Circ × CP = (Circ × AVC) + FCC

where Circ = circulation; CP = cover price; AVC = average variable costs per copy; and FCC = first-copy costs.

This can be solved for FCC—the money available for editorial expenses. The revenue available to cover first-copy costs equals circulation times the amount cover price exceeds average variable costs per copy:

2. FCC = (Circ × CP) − (Circ × AVC) = Circ(CP − AVC)

Assume that at Time 1 three papers compete, each with its devoted readers. Also assume that the average variable costs, such as paper, ink, and distribution, vary from \$.17 to \$.20 per copy, being somewhat higher for the smaller-circulation, upscale papers. Thus, a possible situation at Time 1 is:

Paper	Circ	CP	Circ(CP − AVC)	=	avail. ed. resources
X	1,500	\$.50	1,500(.50 − .20)	=	\$450 for news
Y	2,000	\$.40	2,000(.40 − .18)	=	\$440 for news
Z	4,500	\$.25	4,000(.25 − .17)	=	\$320 for news

At "Time 2," advertisers enter. Consider each of two possibilities. First, assume that, beyond the paper's actual costs of securing and including the ads (the ink, paper, and composing costs devoted to the ads), advertisers as a group pay \$.12 per copy per reader of Paper Y but, for some reason, they advertise only in Paper Y. This exclusiveness could reflect a principled choice by Papers X and Z not to take advertising; or perhaps advertisers had no interest in using advertising to reach these papers' readers; or, possibly, advertisers refused to place ads in these papers for ideological reasons. Although as a practical matter, a complete absence of advertising in these papers is unlikely, reduced advertising in particular papers does sometimes occur for each reason mentioned above.[10] In any event, assuming advertisers do focus on Paper Y, what would be the consequences?

No certain answer can be given. Still, Paper Y will predictably be able to use its advertising revenue both to increase its editorial expenditures, producing a better paper, and to reduce its price. This change in Paper Y should attract readers from Papers X and Z, thereby further enriching Paper Y and allowing it to augment the changes described. The consequence for Papers X and Z could be severe. If they lose perhaps half their readers, this would reduce by at least half the revenue to cover their "first-copy costs." In response, they are likely either to reduce drastically the quality of their content or to increase their cover price, with either reaction's leading to a spiral of further loss of readers and new declines in content. The virtually inevitable result is closure, either before or after bankruptcy. This abstract scenario illustrates the historical observation of Noam Chomsky and Ed Herman that "an advertising-based system will tend to drive out of existence or into marginality the media companies and types that depend on revenue from sales alone."[11]

Alternatively, assume that advertisers willingly purchase advertising in all three papers—valuing readers on average at \$.12 each (beyond the paper, ink, and labor costs associated with the ad itself)—although distinctly more for elite readers of Paper X and less for the poorer readers of Paper Z. What would be the result? The competition could lead to a new equilibrium between the papers,[12] but not necessarily. The added advantage of gaining advertising revenue increases the gains for each from predation on the other papers' circulation—hence increasing the instability of any equilibrium. If one paper is best able to use new advertising income to change its combination of format and selling price in a manner that draws readers from other papers, those other papers are likely to enter a declining-circulation/declining-quality spiral which ends like the first scenario. This outcome corresponds to the local-monopoly daily newspapers that apparently constitute the equilibrium position in the United States today. Thus, it seems quite plausible that after advertising is introduced, a single paper would prevail. In both this and the first scenario, a paper able to use advertising revenue to make its product sufficiently desirable to enough former readers of the other papers undermines the other papers' financial viability. Without this advertising revenue, including the added revenue that advertisers pay for the newly secured readers, the prevailing paper could not have gained enough from trying to attract the other papers' readers to make the effort profitable.

Does the above scenario show that advertising subsidizes expenditures on news and makes the press democratically available? This question too cannot be answered abstractly. Consider a possible context that provides one possible answer. Assume that the single prevailing paper, Paper P (which may reflect a merger of Papers X and Y, with Paper Z failing) is able to sell for a cover price of \$.20 and still spend more for editorial content than did any of the previously existing papers. Suppose, however, that 20% of the original papers' readers valued distinctive qualities of "their" papers so much that they will not bother to purchase Paper P, even though it is the only paper available and sells at a low price. Still, not enough of these dissatisfied readers exist to keep their preferred paper alive. Meanwhile, Paper P picks up most of the former papers' readers plus some new readers who previously purchased no paper. Thus, Paper P reaches four-fifths of the 7,500 readers from Time 1 plus 1,000 new readers, for a total of 7,000.

In order to include the ads, Paper P becomes larger, thereby increasing its variable costs, but assume that advertisers pay those additional variable costs related to the advertising plus a further $.12 per reader. (Below I will ignore both the increase in average variable costs due to ads and the equivalent portion of ad revenue that pays for this increased cost.) Paper P also gets larger because of new editorial items, resulting in some additional variable costs over those at Time 1. Thus, at Time 2 the new hypothetical situation is:

Paper	Circ	CP	Circ(CP + ads − V.C.)	=	avail. ed. resources
P	7,000	$.20	7,000(.20 + .12 − .23)	=	$630 for news

Note that this scenario assumes that *some* readers value a particular type of paper sufficiently to be dissatisfied by a different, larger paper even at a lower cost. It also assumes that, although many readers will consider comparative price in deciding which of several papers to purchase, demand is sufficiently inelastic that a drop in price produces only a limited number of new purchasers. Both assumptions are realistic.

The significance of this possible scenario should not be underestimated. Free market advocates often admit the troublesomeness of obvious inequalities of income, but they usually claim that in a market system, if people value a product enough to pay for it, the market will produce it.*
This scenario illustrates that a news journal's survival depends in part on the preferences of other purchasers (advertisers) for other products (the readers of another newspaper). Readers could sufficiently value a particular journal that it would flourish even without advertising when readers provided all the revenue for all journals. The journal could fail, however, if advertisers in effect "purchased" some of the journal's less committed or poorer readers.

Consider, as a real-life example that closely resembles the case of Paper X in the above hypothetical, the failure in the 1960s of the *Daily Herald*, "the lone consistent voice of social democracy in the national [British] daily press." James Curran quoted the conventional analysis given by a free

---

* I put aside the possibility of invidious or exploitive reasons why this assumption may not be true, such as the likelihood that powerful social groups will restrict (or impose additional costs on) production of goods which could undermine their position of power—see generally Richard Edwards, *Contested Terrain* (1979) (showing that the details of work relations often reflect owners' concerns for control as much as their concerns for efficiency)—or that monopolists will restrict production in order to increase profits.

market advocate, Sir Denis Hamilton (the chairman of Times Newspaper Ltd.), who asserted that the *Herald* failed because it "was beset by the problem which has dogged nearly every newspaper vowed to a political idea: not enough people wanted to read it."[13] But Hamilton's explanation represents the victory of typical conservative ideology over facts. Curran notes that the *Daily Herald*, "on its death-bed, was read by 4.7 million people—nearly twice as many as the readership of *The Times, Financial Times* and *Guardian* added together." Surveys showed that its readers "constituted the most committed and the most intensive readers, with the most favorable image of their paper, of any national paper audience in the country."[14] The problem was not a lack of readers but that the *Daily Herald*'s readers "were disproportionately poor working class and consequently did not constitute a valuable advertising market to reach."[15] It failed because of a competitive environment in which other papers received advertising subsidies that it could not obtain.

Other features of the hypothetical merit attention. Although the introduction of advertising results in the surviving paper's being both bigger and cheaper than any of the initial papers, the total number of newspaper readers declined. The "consumer surplus"—the amount consumers value receiving the product beyond what they pay for it—cannot be abstractly calculated since it depends on actual demand, that is, actual preferences. Nevertheless, it is plausible that the readers' consumer surplus was greater when there were three papers than when most readers switched to the new, cheaper paper and others stopped purchasing a newspaper altogether. For example, readers of the *Daily Herald* apparently valued their paper more than others valued theirs—suggesting a higher average consumer surplus for the more diversified, non-advertiser supported press.

Thus, this hypothetical illustrates that advertising, or the move from a world without advertising to a world with advertising, *could* have some or all of the following consequences:

1. a single surviving, usually "centrist," paper that costs consumers less and has more resources available for expenditures on editorial content than any paper had before the introduction of advertising;[16]

2. the elimination of competitive newspapers and a reduction in diversity of newspapers;

3. (implicit in 2), the failure of papers that would exist, and that people would pay for, in the absence of advertising;

4. a decline in total newspaper readership;

5. a decline in consumer surplus produced by newspapers; and

13

6. a reduction in total resources spent on editorial content (although, of course, some expenditures by the different papers are surely duplicative, thus arguably wasteful).

If the hypothetical scenario described the real world, it would not be clear whether Time 1 or Time 2 was preferable from a policy perspective. Such a judgment would require both additional information and controversial value judgments. Still, from the perspective of democratic theory, each of the consequences described in points 2 through 6 should count as a real loss.

HISTORICAL CHANGE AND RELATED OBSERVATIONS

Many historical observations conform to the broad outline of the hypothetical scenario. First, daily newspaper competition in this country began to decline around 1890, shortly after the role and extent of advertising in the print media began a long-term expansion. Sometimes commentators indicate that advertising became a major economic ingredient of newspapers only around the beginning of the twentieth century, with the introduction of "mass advertising"—primarily by regional chains, often department stores, and by marketers of national products.[17] It is suggested that "before mass advertising, . . . papers succeeded solely because they pleased their readers."[18]

However, advertising has long been with us. Even the names of typical early nineteenth-century papers, like the *Boston Daily Advertiser*, illustrate its importance. In the first quarter of the nineteenth century, newspapers were usually at least half advertising, with some mercantile papers devoting more than four-fifths and political papers as much as three-quarters of their space to ads.[19] As early as 1803 Alexander Hamilton could claim that "it is the advertiser who provides the paper for the subscriber."[20] The typical paper in 1826 was four pages long, with the first and fourth filled almost exclusively with advertising.[21] The mass-circulation penny press, which Michael Schudson argues "invented" the category "news," was introduced in the 1830s in competition with the established six-penny papers.[22] According to Schudson, this penny press relied even more on advertising, particularly of patent medicines, which fortunately cured virtually every malady medical science had identified.[23]

Despite the pervasive presence of advertising since at least the middle of the eighteenth century, for purposes of understanding the economics of newspapers, the more relevant concern is advertising's contribution to newspaper revenues. A congressional opponent of a tax on advertising, adopted to help pay the expenses of the Civil War, asserted that "every member is aware that it is the advertisements and not the circulation of a paper that is profitable."[24] But this is not so obviously right. Much of the early advertising may have barely paid for itself. From both the readers' and the newspapers' perspective this could make sense. If most advertising merely provided specific information desired by readers, much as classified advertising does today, a newspaper could consider the advertising to be part of its news and be happy that the advertiser paid anything for its inclusion.

The meager data available roughly fit this description. First, early in the nineteenth century, advertising rates were reportedly quite low, with space for advertisements sometimes even given away.[25] Although without citing specific evidence, Leo Bogart plausibly asserts: "American newspapers of colonial times treated advertising as a form of news and interspersed it with other items on the front page, presumably because it was considered interesting to readers. But the readers were the paper's main source of revenues."[26] Not until the 1870s did display advertising become common.[27] Schudson suggests that most newspapers were somewhat hostile to advertising until the 1880s. Then department stores and marketers of brand name or trademarked national products began seeking large quantities of advertising space, and "the ratio of editorial matter to advertising . . . changed from about 70–30 to 50–50 or lower."[28] According to Dan Schiller, "in the mid-nineteenth century relatively unorganized advertising by relatively small companies did not exert decisive control over newspaper content, [but] by the turn of the twentieth century both the size and the increased expenditures of advertisers changed this."[29] Thus, it is no surprise that the proportion of newspaper revenue derived from advertising rose steadily for the fifty years after 1879. One early study, relying on census data, reports that the percentage of newspaper and periodical revenue from advertising increased at a rate of about 5% per decade over a fifty-year period:[30]

1879	44.0%	
1889	49.6	
1899	54.5	
1909	60.0	63.8*
1919	65.5	66.0*
1929	70.9	74.3*

* % revenue from advertising solely in newspapers rather than newspapers and periodicals combined.

15

After this steady rise over fifty years, the percentage of advertising revenue has since held at roughly this level, although dipping somewhat during the depression and war years and then rising slowly from 70% in 1950 to 79% in 1987, and possibly slipping some during the recession of the early 1990s.[31] Certainly these data suggest that the contribution of advertising expanded during the late nineteenth and early twentieth centuries. This increase corresponds to the hypothetical scenario, where advertising was introduced during the second time period.

Second, with only a slight lag (during which any competitive implications of the increase in advertising would presumably develop), the long and dramatic decline in local newspaper competition followed newspapers' increased reliance on advertising revenue. Despite the country's increasing population, the total number of daily newspapers has declined from 2,202 in 1910 to 1,586 in 1992, although remaining relatively constant since 1943.[32] Much more dramatic has been the decline in competition. This drop has been continuous, with competition among dailies reportedly declining since 1890 and the decline being clear at least since 1910—even as the number of cities and the portion of the country's total population living in cities increased.[33] Defining as competitive only those towns with separately owned and operated papers, the number of cities with competitive dailies were:[34]

1910—689	1960—61
1920—552	1978—35
1930—288	1986—28
1940—181	1989—26

The decline in the *percentage* of newspapers competing against another daily in the same city began even earlier; although the number of competitive dailies proliferated between 1880 and 1910, noncompetitive dailies increased even more quickly. Thus, the percentage of cities with a daily in which the daily faced competition was:[35]

1880—61.4%	1940—12.7%
1910—57.1%	1954—6%
1920—42.6%	1960—4.2%
1930—20.6%	1986—1.9%

Moreover, the percentage of newspaper circulation sold under competitive conditions, that is, in multipaper cities, has decreased at a relatively constant rate of roughly 10% per decade, shrinking from 88.8% of newspaper circulation in 1923 to 28.3% in 1978.[36]

The hypothetical scenario suggested that the effect of an advertiser-stimulated reduction in competition is that the single surviving paper would fail to fulfill the desires of some readers, thus tending to decrease circulation even as prices go down because of the advertising "subsidy." In contrast, the normal economic expectation would be that if advertising caused the "cost" to the reader to go down, circulation would go up. If advertising subsidies or economies of scale enable one firm to prevail competitively, selling the "same" product at a lower price (or a better product at the same price), everything else being equal, there should be an increase in circulation.*

Historical data are too crude to provide persuasive support for either hypothesis. For example, the sketchy, readily available data on the newspaper's price to consumer would need to be adjusted for general increases in consumer prices—that is, price in constant dollars. More troublesomely, a methodological decision must be made whether the relevant price is cents per page (or per page of editorial content), as is often suggested in economic studies, or cents per newspaper. Certainly, if the first standard is used, given the constant growth in newspapers' page count, the price per editorial page has steadily declined over the century—but this conclusion is less clear if the focus is on cost per paper.[37]

The underlying question of the cause of changes in circulation, however, would require sorting out effects of various historical changes—and this is even more difficult. A host of factors could explain circulation changes. A change in price is one explanation. But a circulation increase could also partly reflect increases in disposable income, changes in literacy, or reduced multiple readers of the same paper. A circulation decline could reflect new ways to spend leisure time or reduced reading on mass transit on the part of homeward-bound workers—a factor purportedly contributing to the reduction in evening dailies in contrast to morning papers. The most common explanation for any circulation decline emphasizes

---

* Alternatively, once becoming a monopolist, a paper may raise prices to obtain monopoly profits, thereby causing a reduction in circulation. This possibility is unlikely to be the dominant effect if there are: (1) comparatively low barriers to entry; or (2) monopolistic competition with other news/entertainment sources. Although the relatively high profitability of monopoly papers suggests that to some extent these papers increase prices, the increased profitability could reflect increases in cover price, increases in advertising rates, or reduced expenditures on first copy—that is, reduced editorial expenditures. There is at least some reason to expect that it will be primarily a result of the last two. See, e.g., W. M. Corden, "The Maximization of Profit by a Newspaper," *Review of Economic Studies* 20 (1953): 181, 188 (showing that at profit-maximizing point, circulation revenue will predictably amount to a loss covered by profits on advertising).

new competition from other media, especially broadcasting, an explanation also often given for the decline in competitive daily newspapers. But the second claim need not follow from the first. There is no particular reason to expect that increased audience attention given to broadcasting, even if it results in a decline in newspaper circulation, would be a cause of the historical decline in the number of papers competing for the remaining circulation. Moreover, advocates of these suggestions seldom provide evidence showing any effect on circulation.[38] In contrast, in arguing that "intermedia competition should not be considered an acceptable alternative to newspaper competition," Stephen Lacy cites recent studies that indicate that although "there is intermedia competition for advertising, . . . research also indicates little impact of such competition on circulation."[39]

In any event, during this period normal economic predictions would be that economies of scale which presumably follow consolidation and increasing advertising "subsidies" would together cause some reduction of cover price and some increase in circulation. Thus, any decline or even stability in circulation would provide some historical support for the notion that the resulting noncompetitive papers did not satisfy needs previously satisfied by the competitive press. Data arguably conform. Circulation per 100 persons slowly rose from 27 per 100 in 1921 to 34 per 100 in 1953 and has since slowly declined, to 29 per 100 in 1973 and 25.1 per 100 in 1991.[40] The probably more relevant figure, circulation per household, after being roughly constant at about 125 per 100 households between 1923 and 1953, has since declined more dramatically, to 97 per 100 in 1973, 84 per 100 in 1977, and 68 per 100 in 1990—only a little more than half what it was 40 years earlier.[41] Still, given multiple possible explanations of circulation change, too much should not be made of this datum for purposes of the current argument. What does seem clear is that the daily newspaper increasingly fails to generate reader interest.* The thesis that this reflects the absence of the differentiated products—which in the

---

* Although concerned with different issues, a recent study comments that newspapers' use of more antiseptic frames than are used by the public reflects a "shift away from the partisan press . . . to an advertiser-supported media [in which] economic pressures to maintain the largest possible audience by alienating the fewest consumers yields a neutral, 'least objectionable' style of news coverage" (W. Russell Neuman, Marion R. Just, and Ann N. Crigler, *Common Knowledge: News and the Construction of Political Meaning* [1992], 76). Among the study's most important conclusions was that "the structure and style of newspaper journalism make it hard[ ] for people with just average cognitive skills to learn information about political issues" (106). The authors' "inescapable" conclusion is that "the current structure of newspaper" news does not well serve people with average skills (115).

hypothetical scenario were eliminated by advertising-induced decline in competition—cannot be conclusively accepted or rejected.

This claim that there exists a potential reader interest that the existing press structure does not satisfy is somewhat supported by comparisons with other countries, which suggest that the American daily newspaper market may not be saturated. In the late 1980s, newspaper purchase rates per thousand population were: Japan, 566; Finland, 551; Sweden, 526; Switzerland, 504; United Kingdom, 421; West Germany, 347; United States, 259; France, 193.[42] Competitive papers with noticeably different content that appealed to differing portions of the population might stimulate greater demand in the United States. One study, which had predicted that competition would have no effect on circulation, found the hypothesis to be "only marginally tenable at this time."[43] According to the author, "historically, the loss of a daily has meant a net loss in market circulation— the survivors do not acquire all the subscribers of the deceased. Thus at one time, total market circulation was sensitive to the number of dailies in it, though that may not be the case now."[44]

The story of change could be told in the opposite direction. What would happen if the reverse occurred, if the role of advertising were reduced? On both the traditional account, in which advertising beneficially subsidizes the media, and the scenario offered here, in which advertising also causes a reduction in the media's orientation toward satisfying reader preferences, reducing advertiser support should force the media to increase prices to readers. However, on the traditional account, this price increase should result in a significant decline in circulation, while on the account offered here, the decline in advertising support should lead to an increased emphasis on satisfying the reader, a media focus that would limit the decline in circulation and might even lead to increased total circulation from an expanded, diversified number of titles offered.

In their study of American magazines, John Tebbel and Mary Ellen Zuckerman report that although advertising had previously accounted for approximately two-thirds of consumer magazines' revenue, during the 1980s this percentage steadily declined until it was only 48% in 1987, with the decline apparently continuing since.[45] Predictably, cover and subscription prices have increased constantly since the early seventies;[46] according to one report average cover prices rose from $2.50 in 1985 to $3.60 in 1989.[47] Most surprisingly from the perspective of standard economic theory but consistent with the hypothetical model presented above, despite the steadily rising price, paid circulation also increased 35% between 1979 and 1989.[48] Moreover, the number of competitors increased—going from about 2,500 consumer magazines in 1980 to about 3,300 by the end of 1991.[49] Explaining the continued increase in titles during the advertising "recession" of the late 1980s, Deirdre Carmody noted that the magazines whose revenues "come mainly from circulation, like most smaller niche publications, are far better off [when advertising drops as it has this year]. . . . When a circulation-driven magazine falls on hard times, it can raise its cover price."[50]

Is Advertising "a" Cause of the Decline in Competition?

The historical data summarized above suggest that advertising may have been a major factor in the decline of daily newspaper competition, but a deeper understanding requires consideration of alternative explanations and a more specific account of how advertising could have produced this hypothesized effect.

Several explanations of the decline in competition can be easily ruled out. It cannot be explained by economic or technological changes that require profitable modern papers to have a large circulation base. In 1989, 52% of our country's daily newspapers were located in cities of under 25,000.[51] In 1985, 39% of all daily papers in this country had circulations of less than 10,000.[52] Small towns and small circulations routinely support daily newspapers. Today, however, much larger populations typically do not support *competing* papers.

The explanation that the profitability of newspapers has declined so that they are no longer a very viable business is also unavailing. All studies suggest the opposite. In terms of percentage return on sales, newspapers are possibly twice as profitable as the median Fortune 500 company.[53] Leo Bogart reports a 27% return on assets in 1986.[54] A composite large city newspaper for 1978 had a (pretax) operating profit of 20.7% of revenue, while an average medium-sized daily had an operating profit of 31.4%.[55] Even in 1990, when publicly owned newspaper companies had their worst year in the twenty years tracked, their operating margin averaged 14.7%.[56]

So why the decline in competition? According to media critic Ben Bagdikian, the cause is "mass advertising."[57] He argues that "the process by which mass advertising has produced monopoly and monopoly like media is not a mystery except in the silence with which the subject is treated in the media."[58] Bagdikian's explanation is that as a newspaper gains market share of circulation, it gains greater revenue than its competitors from both sales and advertising; with this greater revenue, it can "spend more on sales-people, on editorial vigor, and on circulation promotion," while the competing papers have progressively less to spend on these items, which increases their competitive disadvantage and assures their continual shrinkage.[59] The publisher of the *Honolulu Advertiser* made virtually the same argument:

> A newspaper's economic strength depends largely on its advertising reve-
> nues, which in turn depend on readership. Since readership depends on
> content, which includes advertising as well as news matter, the process is
> almost a vicious cycle: a drop in advertising dollars means a drop in money
> that can be spent for promotion and editorial content, which leads in turn
> to a drop in circulation, which leads to a further drop in advertising, and
> so forth.[60]

Agreeing with the publisher's argument, one scholarly commentator con-
cluded, as did Bagdikian, that advertising is the problem and that only legislation which "mitigate[s] reliance upon advertising" can stop the trend toward monopoly.[61]

The problem with this explanation is that the same dynamic should occur even if the papers obtained all their revenue merely from circulation—a circulation increase for one paper would increase its revenues and allow greater expenditures on product quality, enabling it to win circula-
tion away from its competitors, who then would have even less to spend. That is, advantage for one newspaper would push others into a downward revenue/circulation spiral. More generally, the version of Bagdikian's explanation noted here merely illustrates that a firm with declining marginal costs tends to be a natural monopoly. Reliance on advertising might accel-
erate a downward spiral. Economists have argued that dependence on two revenue channels, advertising and sales, might "amplif[y] the effect of changes in output upon profits," thus making predation and ruinous com-
petition more likely.[62] But advertising could be removed from the circle, and the cycle would still be vicious. Any profitable increase in circulation will allow the paper to spend more on editorial content, which should further increase its circulation, and so on until it eventually drives out its competitor.

For newspapers, this declining-marginal-cost dynamic occurs because a significant portion of their costs are "first-copy costs"—the costs of reporting, editing, and composition.[63] According to another study, in 1978, editorial expenses for a composite large-city newspaper were 11% of all

21

costs and 17% of direct (variable) costs. For a medium-sized daily, the corresponding percentages were 18.4% and 29.4%.[64] The dynamic leading to monopoly is that as a paper's circulation grows, the first-copy costs are spread over a larger number of papers. Hence, it is not surprising that the percentage expense of newsprint and ink would increase as a paper's circulation increases—going in 1976 from 18.6% of operating costs for a "typical" 34,000-circulation paper to 36.7% of total expenses for a 250,000-circulation paper.[65] Additional economies of scale may reduce other expensive aspects of newspaper production[66] (see paragraph below). Thus, even if all of a newspaper's revenues came from circulation, the paper with the larger circulation would have the advantages Bagdikian described and, at least on that argument, should become a monopoly. Neither his example nor his discussion shows why advertising—even "mass advertising"—is a unique part of the problem.

Therefore, the decline of local newspaper competition could be the natural result of tremendous economies of scale. Declining marginal costs of increased local circulation could make a local newspaper a natural monopoly. Effectively presenting this view, James Rosse shows that "economic competition between two similar newspapers seeking to attract the same audience cannot survive in the long run," and argues that such competition has led to the prevalence of one-newspaper towns.[67] The newspaper's first copy is essentially a "public good"—unlimited numbers of copies can be made available without any additional costs for news gathering, editing, and composing. Rosse explains, in a now widely accepted analysis,[68] that competition is doomed because of this "public good" quality of newspapers, combined with other scale economies.[69] These additional scale economies include a continuous decline in the average reproduction costs as the number of copies increases, and predictably smaller distribution costs for one newspaper serving a given group of readers than for two papers attempting to serve the same group.[70] These scale economies mean that it is always cheaper for the dominant firm to increase the supply than for any other firm, such as a competing newspaper, to supply a similar good. Thus, economies of scale have been "pivotal" in the growth of single-newspaper towns. Each firm faces declining marginal costs, the key condition for natural monopoly.

This account, however, does not explain why, historically, newspaper competition was the norm in this country. Presumably, economies of scale and the consequent declining marginal costs would have been present then as now. Thus, the change, the historical decline in competition, still must be explained. Rosse does recognize that there are circumstances in which competition would be possible. Specifically, a newspaper would have "to isolate a market segment and differentiate the newspaper product"; despite this possibility, according to Rosse, "the historical record demonstrates" that in this country effective segmentation of local audiences has not been successful.[71] More precise might be another economist's observation "that historical accounts of US newspaper markets . . . stress the *decreasing* differentiation of newspapers in terms of alignment with particular political parties, social classes, or ethnic groups."[72]

Given a declining-cost industry, segmentation or product differentiation is a prerequisite for successful competition.[73] If papers serviced sufficiently different consumer demands, competing local papers might survive. An understanding of the end of local newspaper competition may follow from an explanation of the decline of economically relevant market segmentation and the corresponding product differentiation. On this issue Rosse must be expanded upon, and within this expansion the role of advertising becomes relevant.

Rosse offers several possibilities. Market segmentation would decline: (1) if advertising clients became more homogeneous, possibly because some were bled off by other media; (2) if advertisers' preference for differentiated audiences weakened; (3) if subscriber demand shifted downward; or (4) if reader preference for a tailor-made newspaper product (a Republican or Democratic paper, for instance) weakened.[74] This list is fine as far as it goes. The first and second points recognize that one purchaser who could want, or not want, a differentiated product is the advertiser. That point is important. Bagdikian also argued that the nature of the advertiser affects the nature of the newspaper industry. Rosse's description ignores, however, how advertising can also reduce the economic influence of readers' preferences. I will argue that, in several identifiable ways, advertising undermines not readers' desire (Rosse's third point) but rather the economic influence of readers' desire for differentiated, that is, diverse, newspaper perspectives.

Survival of competing newspapers can occur only where there is product differentiation that responds to a demand for the differentiated product—responds, in other words, to market segmentation. But what is the product? The obvious answer is newspaper content—that is, of course, the product readers buy. But when the analysis includes the additional purchaser, the advertiser, it is clear that a reader's purchase of a paper involves the newspaper's delivery of two products, newspaper content sold to the reader and a "reader" sold to the advertiser. Although readers will pay some amount for a differentiated paper, for the moment assume that advertisers treat all readers, within the geographical range of the paper, as interchangeable, as undifferentiated. (To the extent that advertisers are local, they strongly reward geographical segmentation, such that there are "local" daily papers and, more recently, zoned editions. Much of the present structure of the industry reflects this point.) Introducing the second purchaser, the advertiser, for whom segmentation is irrelevant reduces the *proportionate* contribution to total newspaper revenue of the amount that the reader will pay for a differentiated product. Thus, the advertiser's involvement reduces the economic significance to the seller of the reader's willingness to pay for differentiation. Increasing the proportionate contribution of advertising to operating profits should increase the paper's willingness to give up "differentiation" revenue in order to increase circulation. This is the point repeatedly made, but never fully explained, by Bagdikian: "Before mass advertising . . . papers succeeded solely because they pleased their readers," and, at that time, "readers were clustered in terms of their serious political and social ideas."[75] A simple example can make the point more starkly.

Assume there exist two competing papers, each with a circulation of 100 relatively loyal readers and each selling for 10 cents a copy. A typical reader would switch to the alternative paper only if it undersold her preferred paper by slightly more than a nickel; in simple terms, the typical reader will pay $.05 for diversity. Neither paper would reduce its price to $.04, thereby driving the competing paper out of business and obtaining its 100 readers. Even if doubling circulation imposed no costs on the expansionist paper, a fanciful assumption, this strategy for competitive success in circulation would hurt the prevailing paper. Rather than obtaining $.10 times 100 or $10.00, the paper would now receive $.04 times 100 from the old customers plus $.04 times 100 from the new customers, a total of $8.00. The move is clearly absurd. It is even more absurd given that the expanded circulation would create additional costs for items like more newsprint.

Now assume readers' preferences and willingness to pay for diverse products have not changed, but advertisers arrive who are willing to pay newspapers $.07 for every reader, in addition to paying the direct costs of added newsprint, ink, and costs related to the additional bulk necessary for the newspaper to include their ads. Now that the newspaper also sells to advertisers, lowering the price to the reader causes a smaller proportionate loss of the revenue it obtains from the old customers; that is, it does not reduce the amount the paper receives *from the advertiser* for the old readers. In addition, lowering the cover price potentially produces a larger proportionate gain from the new readers. A paper obtaining 100($.10 + .07) or $17.00 from its old circulation* could reduce its cover price to $.04, drive its competitor out of business, and increase profits, now receiving 200($.04 + .07) or $22.00.† Introducing this joint purchaser of the newspaper, advertisers who are not concerned with diversity, significantly reduces the potential proportion of revenue that could result from the paper's fulfilling the readers' desire for a differentiated product. Thus, advertising can reduce the economic value of product differentiation, thereby creating the condition necessary for natural monopoly.

Of course, the process of one paper's gaining the other's readers would be contested. Both papers would compete for advertisers—predictably reducing the advertising's value to the paper. Only when one paper gains a circulation lead on which it can capitalize is it able to drive out the competition and obtain the economic rewards described above. This reflects the observation that today, in most two-newspaper towns, circulation is quite evenly divided; only a relatively even division allows an (unstable) equilibrium.[76]

The discussion above underdescribes advertising's effect in undermining the influence of readers' willingness to pay for differentiated products. First, the simplifying assumption, that advertisers are indifferent to the readers' identity, must be dropped. Advertisers want the readers most likely to buy their products. Depending on the medium's advertisers, a variety of types of media differentiation might result. For example, particular advertisers' preferences for particular audiences help explain profitable special-interest magazines.[77] Therefore, the nature of advertisers who do (or the potential advertisers who might) advertise in geographically local daily newspapers merits examination. Without arguing the point, I suggest

---

* In the example, the ten cents and seven cents are not strictly comparable since the ten cents is total revenue from readers and the seven cents from advertising is assumed to be after deducting the expenses for obtaining and including advertising. Therefore, the totals, $17 (and $22 in the next part of the hypothetical scenario) are neither revenues nor profits but instead revenues after advertising expenses are deducted.

Still, this seven cents from advertisers after deducting advertising expenses compared to ten cents from subscribers is plausible, at least under some circumstances. In William Reddaway's classic study, London's "quality" national dailies made fivepence per copy from advertising (after advertising expenses) compared to revenue of fourpence per copy from sales to readers (although the advertising "profit" per copy was much less for the "popular" dailies) ("The Economics of Newspapers," *Economic Journal* 73 [1963]: 201, 206–7).

† This example continues the text's choice to ignore newsprint and related per-copy costs. If they are higher than $.05 per copy, the competitive change described in the example would not be profitable—but it would become so as the amount readers pay for diversity, and hence the amount the prevailing paper would need to reduce cover price, declines.

that daily newspapers depend primarily on commercial advertising biased toward a very broad, relatively undifferentiated, middle to upper-middle market of people with comparably large disposable incomes. As Michael Schudson puts it, "marketers keep their eyes on the main prize—pocketbooks, not persons."[78] This can be a strong preference. The study of English dailies referred to earlier reports that the advertising rate per copy sold was 3.9 times higher in the "quality" national dailies than in the "popular" national dailies.[79] After paying the expenses of publishing the ads, the popular daily received a halfpenny "subsidy" per copy from advertising, which could go to profits or to pay for costs such as editorial expenses. In contrast, the "quality" paper received a fivepence-per-copy "subsidy" from advertising.[80] Advertisers paid much more for these readers or, in effect, for the newspaper content that would attract these readers.

If different income groups prefer different newspaper content, either of two results is possible. Market segmentation could occur and support competing newspapers;[81] or if one newspaper is read by a large enough portion of the readers targeted by advertisers, it may gain sufficient strength, using advertising revenue to reduce cover price or to add features, that it drives out the competition.

The first alternative is most likely to occur if the audience least valued by advertisers is the wealthy, for whom a higher cover price would matter little; the second is most likely if the audience least supported by advertisers is the relatively poor. Of course, usually advertisers favor relatively affluent readers. In any event, the second possibility, eliminating competition, has generally prevailed among daily newspapers in the United States. This result, monopoly, is the worse outcome for democracy. Note, however, that even if the paper preferred by the poor survived, the advertiser-oriented segmentation is still troublesome. As noted, advertisers generally favor the paper with relatively more affluent readers, subsidizing these readers' preferred content. Thus, the advertising "subsidy" magnifies the normal inequality whereby the poor have less money to pay for media products than the wealthy. An advertising subsidy for papers preferred by the more affluent dramatically biases our information environment—in a direction opposite what a democratic equality or "one-person-one-vote" principle would require. The poor must pay almost the full cost of the media product they prefer if it is available; or, if it is not available, they must either do without or purchase media content that they would not choose if both their favored and the other paper were sold at full cost. In contrast, advertising works to the benefit of the more affluent: their preferred media product is available and is sold considerably below cost.

When readers pay the costs, newspapers can gain by responding to desires for product differentiation. Under these circumstances, a paper faces competing pressures—toward product differentiation in order to be able to sell at a higher price to readers willing to pay for the differentiated product, and toward a more common-denominator product in order to gain circulation. Response to either pressure obviously affects content. For example, a response to the first pressure, which is strongest when there is no advertising, could lead to lampooning or exposing the evils or the political wrongheadedness of its nonreaders, thereby contributing to a valued product differentiation. Strong partisanship could be profitable.

When advertisers pay for readers, incentives change. The relative influence of the second pressure, to gain readers, increases. The newspaper can pursue readers by lowering prices. While the paper's original readers had been willing to pay more than the new lowered price, the new readers now buy only because of the lowered price. But at the lower price, the paper gives its original readers a boon, an unnecessary consumer surplus. The paper, however, might find a more cost-effective strategy. It could make content changes favored by potential new readers even if these changes were marginally disliked by the original readers, thereby dissipating, in a sense "spending," what otherwise would have been consumer surplus for the original readers. This content-change strategy (which presumably flattens the demand curve) permits the paper to adopt a smaller price reduction than would be necessary by itself to gain the new readers. A limited content change may eliminate some of the "consumer surplus" that the original readers receive from the price reduction, while enticing new readers to pay a higher price than they would pay if the content were kept the same. The key point here, however, is that it is the advertising regime which provides the incentive to the newspaper to reduce product differentiation.

What content changes might appeal to potential new readers but not be too costly in terms of the original readers? At a very general level, the paper might gain by dropping material that is offensive or otherwise unappealing to the new reader—the lampooning and partisan exposés that the original reader valued. Bagdikian reports that "newspapers neutralized information for fear that strong news and views pleasing to one part of the audience might offend another part and thus reduce the circulation on which advertising rates depend."[82] Dropping this "offensive" material may also be affirmatively desired by advertisers who fear offending, and thereby losing, any potential customers. Then the question becomes: can this exclusion of offensive material be routinized? Possibly. The ideal method to avoid offense is to appear to be more "objective," taking less of an (overt) position in the presentation of the news.*

This account of possible consequences of introducing advertising corresponds to actual changes that occurred during the late nineteenth and early twentieth centuries. During this period, the economic contributions of advertising and the role of advertising agencies, which gave advertisers more self-conscious muscle, increased. At roughly the same time, the most significant content change in newspapers was the move away from political partisanship and toward objectivity. According to one commentator, "early in the 19th Century, American editors demonstrated a remarkable dedication to party service, working as party organizers and using their newspaper columns to promote parties and candidates."[83] In 1850, census data showed that 95% of all U.S. newspapers had a political affiliation.[84] Even when journalistic independence became popular, it often meant only that the newspaper avoided formal subservience to party and maintained sufficient distance to criticize its party for failing to live up to the party's ideals.[85] Party allegiance often continued during the middle of the century even as the paper proclaimed independence. Many papers basically followed the example of Horace Greeley who, in the 1840s, while disavowing formal partisanship, still thought his paper merited Whig party patronage.[86]

But this partisanship declined late in the century, roughly at the time objectivity was becoming the dominant norm. A study of all English-language papers, including weeklies, found that 42% of the 813 New York papers and 44.7% of the 392 California papers were "independent" by 1899.[87] As the analysis here would predict, this independence correlated with monopoly status—in cities with a newspaper monopoly, 65% of the papers were independent.[88] In fact, independent papers dominated numerically everywhere except in medium-sized cities (with two or more papers), where papers were roughly 70% partisan, and over 80% partisan in county seats.[89] County seats offered partisan papers greater opportunities to obtain economically beneficial patronage, including government advertising that state law required to be in two papers of different political orientation. This government "subsidy" in county seats predictably reduced the

---

* This refers to objectivity as it has come to be seen in American journalism. Critiquing the role of objectivity in preventing the media's exposure of the Reagan presidency's incredible inadequacies, Mark Hertsgaard quotes I. F. Stone: "Objectivity is fine if it's real. . . . Every society has its dogmas, and a genuinely objective approach can break through them. But most of the time objectivity is just the rationale for regurgitating the conventional wisdom of the day" (*On Bended Knee: The Press and the Reagan Presidency* [1989], 65–66).

effectiveness of an advertiser-induced orientation toward "objectivity" or independence.[90] Unsurprisingly, competition correlated positively with partisanship—whether because competition required product differentiation or because forces inclining toward partisanship, like county politics and patronage, also stimulated competition.

The decline of partisanship could have reflected changes in political parties or in internal development of journalistic norms. However, both historical evidence and contemporaneous commentary point to a significant role for advertising. Gerald Baldasty quotes late nineteenth-century newspaper trade journals for the proposition that "advertisers wanted newspapers to de-emphasize politics and present 'more of the bright side of life.' "[91] These "trade journals warned editors that advertisers wanted less criticism of public officials and reminded publishers that partisanship hurt circulation and, consequently, advertising revenues. The *New York Evening Post* in 1898 noted that strongly partisan newspapers simply could not sell advertising space."[92] Newspaper trade journals also explained that political affiliation was suicidal in small towns because it encouraged the opposing party to establish a paper. With only limited advertising support, the trade journals predicted, both papers would die.[93] Although journalistic ethics sometimes proclaims that monopoly papers have a special responsibility to be balanced and objective, this may be a post-hoc rationalization—these papers may have gained their monopolies precisely by becoming balanced and "objective."

Today, objective news reporting is unquestionably the "most pervasive ethic of American journalism. . . . Objectivity forms the core of the Code of Ethics of the Society of Professional Journalists."[94] Like the reduction of political partisanship, the rise of objectivity as the press's dominant norm is a complex development. Scholars dispute its causes (and timing). Although "Walter Lippmann introduced the term 'objective reporting' in . . . 1919 . . . and seems to have been the first to discuss objective journalism . . . [and] Nelson Crawford's widely used 1924 journalistic ethics text propagated the ideal,"[95] this self-conscious emphasis on objectivity merely ratified a protracted evolution of practice. Defining objectivity as a "reportorial form" that "contains only verifiable assertions, does not make claims to significance, and avoids statements of . . . value . . . without clear attribution to source," a study of news reports from three periods found objective reporting to constitute 41% of the sample in 1865–1874, 66% in 1905–1914, and 80% in the 1925–1934 period.[96] Contrary to a popular theory attributing objectivity to technological developments, the study found that whether the news report's source was a wire report had "no

29

statistical effect on whether the news is objective . . . in any of the three time periods."[97]

Whatever the causes of the partisan press's demise, advertisers could benefit from and be a significant influence on the development of the norm of objectivity.[98] One commentator observed that the balance in reporting that was absent in the first decade of the nineteenth century became dominant in the last, as newspapers "increasingly seemed to avoid controversy—most likely because it might alienate readers."[99] William Greider, assistant managing editor of the *Washington Post* in the early 1980s, explained: " 'If you're going to be a mass circulation journal, that means you're going to be talking simultaneously to lots of groups that have opposing views. So you've got to modulate your voice and pretend to be talking to all of them' "—that is, " 'become what we think of as quote objective.' "[100] Another commentator suggested that "structural change made newspapers rely heavily on advertising lineage, and the widest possible circulation increased the pressure to avoid offending readers. Sticking to a 'neutral rendition of the facts' was the answer. So, the ethical principle of objectivity was 'at least equally motivated by commercial considerations.' "[101]

In sum, there are economic reasons to expect, historical evidence to suggest, and contemporary consciousness to indicate that both the decline of political partisanship and the rise of objectivity were at least partly caused by the increasing availability of advertising revenue and the consequent increased value of the circulation on which advertising revenue depends. These content changes also correspond to a decline in an important element of the product differentiation on which competition depends. Thus, advertising's role in creating an incentive to be objective and to reduce partisanship provides an additional, major explanation for how the increased financial significance of advertising leads to a decline of competition and to increased local monopoly of the daily newspapers.

The Significance of Newspaper Competition

Does Competition Matter?

The discussion thus far has implicitly assumed that competition among local daily newspapers is a meaningful, valuable phenomenon. This assumption is widely shared. Many commentators have explained its value,[102] while its decline has been constantly studied and bemoaned. Considerable policy in this and other Western democracies has been based on the desirability of maintaining newspaper competition. Important government commissions appointed in various Western democracies considered responses to what is uniformly considered a problem; many countries implemented policies, often including governmental subsidies, designed to respond to the decline.[103] The United States adopted the Newspaper Preservation Act, which allows exemption from the antitrust laws for "Joint Operating Agreements" between a comparatively strong and a failing newspaper to prevent the failing paper's demise, saving a presumably independent editorial voice. Mostly, I will merely accept the dominant view that the decline in competition is to be regretted or, if possible, reversed. Nevertheless, some brief comment on three popular challenges to this view is appropriate.

The United States Is Media Rich. Some commentators suggest that we are media "rich." The lack of competition among daily newspapers should not blind us to the fact that the daily newspaper faces plenty of competition and that people have many alternative sources of news—television often being cited. By 1986, 66% of the public report that they got most of their news "about what is going on in the world today" from television; and 55% said that if they got conflicting reports from television and newspapers, they would believe television, as compared with 22% who would trust the newspaper.[104] Thus, it should not be surprising that 80% of the public identify TV as the most influential news medium, compared with 9% naming newspapers.[105]

These survey reports, however, are questionable bases to assess either the current role or the potential importance of newspapers. Leo Bogart suggests that these reports "tap the feelings of strong dependence that most Americans now have toward the medium that is their most common leisure-time diversion," but observes that when asked about where they would turn to get specific information, people most often named newspapers.[106] And in a 1991 survey, when asked where they get their news about local government, which for many people is the more salient concern, people named the newspaper roughly 2 to 1 over television.[107] Even if their first instinct is to name TV, people may in fact get most of their news either from newspapers or from interpersonal discussion with people who got their information primarily from newspapers. The central finding of a thorough review of studies examining the source of people's news-type information was that "television should not be considered the public's main source of news."[108] Apparently, even for stories covered by both media, reading newspapers leaves a much greater collective mental residue

31

than does television news.* Thus, as compared to television, newspapers may provide more of the data that get into people's consciousness and become available for discussion. Given repeated documentation of the finding that "interpersonal discussion of news may be at least as powerful a predictor of news comprehension as exposure to mass media,"[109] newspapers may consequently be even more important than studies looking at individual usage would recognize. (This would be even more true if opinion leaders, people who are most consistently involved in discussions about current affairs, read newspapers to a degree greater than the norm.) Thus, however media-rich our culture is, newspapers may presently play a unique and central role. Moreover, even these observations may be too "positivist." Both the accessibility and the importance of the news and vision presented by newspapers might be greater in a world where more partisan, competitive newspapers encouraged more diversity and more psychic involvement with the news.

Weekly Papers Provide Competitive Alternatives. A critic could observe that virtually all scholarly studies of newspapers look at the decline of competition among *daily* newspapers. What about other papers—for example, what about weeklies? Once weeklies are considered, the observations about decline of competition and circulation arguably need revision. Thus, the question arises whether weeklies provide relevant competition and relevant diversity. Certainly, weeklies have been the major, seldom reported, story of the last thirty years in the field of newspaper journalism. Telling the story, however, is not easy. Despite abundant ad hoc information, generalizable data are hard to come by.[110] Even statistical summaries appar-

---

* A contrasting conclusion could be given about the capacity of the different media, as currently structured, to impart information to the average audience member. One finding of an important recent study is that the "entire relationship between television news preference and lower knowledge . . . was entirely accounted for by the cognitive skill differential between those who prefer [the different mediums]" (W. Russell Neuman, Marion R. Just, and Ann N. Crigler, *Common Knowledge: News and the Construction of Political Meaning* [1992], 113). It is not that newspapers impart more information but that those most likely to learn are also most likely to be newspaper readers. In fact, when interest levels are held constant (generally, newspaper readers have greater interest and are thus more prone to learn), television did better at imparting information to the public at large (82). The authors found evidence that people with strong cognitive skills would not learn more from newspapers than from television but those with lower skills learned less from newspapers, a result the authors were able to attribute not to the visual aspects of TV but to the objective or distancing journalistic conventions used by newspapers (83, 106). This finding could support the claim here that a less objective form of newspaper presentation could stimulate political interest as well as stimulate newspaper competition.

ently use, without specifying, different definitions, producing notably different numbers. Still, a few observations are possible.

Although there were roughly 16,000 weeklies during the first decades of the century, weeklies declined to about 8,900 in 1960. After an apparent further decline in the mid-1980s, by 1991 the number was back to about 8,500.[111] However, the main development has been in circulation. From 1960 to 1991, a period during which daily circulation increased a mere 5% to 62 million, weeklies' circulation soared 260%, from 21 million to about 55 million.[112] With weeklies approaching the circulation level of dailies, 80% of the public were "exposed" to a free weekly in 1988, 62% saying one was delivered to their home, and, reportedly, "39% read a paid weekly and 55% look at a free one" during a sample week.[113] However, in a study of four large urban/suburban markets with strong "free" weeklies and where home delivery of these free papers exceeded paid dailies 66% to 59%, 90% of adults reported reading some edition of the daily/Sunday paper while only 57% reported reading a free paper during the week.[114] That is, free circulation guarantees neither readership nor impact.

For policy purposes, the issue is substance more than numbers: What are these weeklies? Do they provide a competitive alternative to the daily as a source of news and opinion, or do they play an entirely different social role? Answering is hazardous because the category includes radically different types of papers—but I suggest that, even at their best, twentieth-century weeklies have not provided the alternative sought by those who bemoan the decline in daily newspaper competition.[115] They usually differ from dailies in the scope of reporting, in their role in people's lives, and in the information they develop and transmit. Most weeklies are on a continuum ranging from free "pennysavers" or "shoppers" with no or minimal editorial content to real community papers, often with a paid circulation and a significant amount of news, but with news generally restricted in range to local events and without the editorial resources available to a daily.

Although weeklies are becoming increasingly hard to categorize, most of the increase in circulation since 1960 apparently has been in free weeklies,[116] and—despite a reported trend toward free papers' having more editorial content and more serious journalism[117]—most of these free papers appear to offer readers quite minimal gains in serious editorial content.

Even if in some respects outdated, Morris Janowitz's classic 1952 study of weekly newspapers in Chicago, *The Community Press in an Urban Setting*, supports these conclusions about weekly papers. Janowitz shows that, for its readers, urban community weeklies are not competitive with the daily newspaper. These weeklies apparently serve entirely different functions, for example, providing very "local" news and, most importantly according to Janowitz, integrating people into their local community.[118]

The papers in Janowitz's study may be comparable to many of today's weeklies. As now, a common view then—held, for example, by major advertising agencies and daily newspapers—was that these local weeklies consisted almost entirely of advertising. Actually these weeklies devoted roughly the same proportionate space to editorial content as did Chicago's daily papers.[119] Moreover, their editorial space was much more "news"-oriented than the dailies', 87% versus 46%, while the dailies had more "feature" material, 47.6% versus 7.5% for the weeklies.[120] Interestingly, these community papers had prevailed in their competition with earlier free "shoppers," which in 1952 were extinct in Chicago.[121] Janowitz also reported that the weeklies, although often begun as free papers, were tending away from free or optional circulation toward paid circulation. ("Optional circulation" was a common practice in which recipients would be asked to pay but would still receive the paper if they did not.) Moreover, the book's second edition reported that this trend toward paid circulation was continuing as of 1966.[122]

Unlike the present study, Janowitz professed concern about advertising only in relation to the desirability of these weeklies' receiving a fair share.[123] His complacency should not be surprising. His thesis was that the community newspapers served the socially and politically prodemocratic function of integrating the individual into urban social structure. The papers did this, he argued, by presenting content that avoided controversy and emphasized consensus, as well as by democratizing prestige and providing helpful information about the local community.[124] Janowitz recognized that advertising created pressures for content of precisely the sort that he saw and praised. He describes many forces that cause the publisher to play an integrative community role and avoid a vigorous (controversial) editorial policy, but notes that "the threats of reduced advertising and reduced circulation are basic and cannot be separated from the publisher's role in the local community."[125] He casually refers to the community weeklies as "instruments of local merchants" and explains that for the weekly, "as a communications medium oriented around the interests of the local business and residential community, fear of alienating any wide sector of the business or readership clientele is a major factor in limiting political orientation."[126]

The press that results from these economic forces may fortuitously be as socially beneficial as Janowitz suggests. Maybe it is best, for example, that community papers even in working-class communities almost completely avoid mentioning labor unions.[127] Modern political and social theory is divided about when or whether working through or suppressing controversy and conflict better serves progressive community needs. I will not speculate about that debate. Still, as a minimum, media oriented toward consensus and avoidance of controversy do not obviously or necessarily constitute the ideal. Arguably a more desirable community might be produced by partisanship and editorial leadership that takes on controversial matters.

For example, this consensus orientation observed by Janowitz, which corresponded to requirements of commercial pressures, led the Chicago community papers to support maintaining the community "through racial segregation," which in turn explained the community papers' opposition to federally supported public housing.[128] Imagine, however, a community press that responded to different pressures or interests—for example, the editors' own values, those of a church or political organization, or the intense interests of differing subgroups of readers. The resulting papers might well be more diverse, more evaluative, more partisan. Such papers might stimulate a greater integration of local community-level political culture into people's lives—which starkly contrasts to the politically quietistic social life encouraged by the advertising-influenced press, as illustrated by the view of the publisher who reported partisanship to be "old fashioned."[129] Some, although surely not all, of the papers responsive to these nonadvertising pressures would predictably adopt affirmative stands on public housing. The implications for Chicago's future would have contrasted sharply with what resulted from the influence of the consensus-oriented, advertising-dominated weeklies. In a different context, James Rosse speculated whether "the ghetto and anti-war disturbances of the 1960's would have occurred (or would have been given different journalistic treatment) if blacks and nineteen year olds were better advertiser audiences"[130]—or, I would add, if advertisers did not determine the structure of the newspaper industry or the nature of journalism.

In the imagined, non-advertising-dominated press, even "shopping" information would presumably exist but would take a different form. Janowitz found that information provided by display advertising was quite important to the readership, read regularly by 72% and ranking as the second most read category following community news, read regularly by 80%.[131] Any press oriented toward satisfying reader wants would presumably need to supply commercial information—news of sales, for example. But the non-advertising-dominated press would be likely to provide the shopping "news" in a more evaluative and informative form. Suddenly, people would think of papers as serving a consumer protection function!

Thus, Janowitz's study provides little basis for reassurance that the decline in competition among dailies is alleviated by continuing competition from weeklies, particularly given their apparently different roles in people's lives.[132] Moreover, his study reinforces the broader point that advertising support influences the nature of media content, and that these influences are appropriate subjects for critical evaluation.

Possibly these comments about weeklies have been too hasty. Although often only marginally distinguishable from other weeklies—it is as if there is a continuum of closely related types—another increasingly important category consists of self-proclaimed "alternative papers," sometimes viewed as the descendants of the underground press of the 1960s. Although often denying membership to applicants that do not meet its by-laws' requirement that members "merit designation as a positive editorial alternative to mainstream journalism," by 1992, the Association of Alternative Newsweeklies had 80 member papers in 32 states (16 in California alone) and 3 Canadian provinces and a reported combined press run of 4,865,928.[133] These papers—some winning journalism awards, engaging in investigative reporting, challenging the mainstream from both the Right and the Left, and producing longer and more partisan reports than the dailies—are an important addition to the media environment. Still, even these "alternative" weeklies should probably not be considered equivalent to a competing daily. These papers typically lack the resources, editorial scope, or circulation reach of the dailies. Moreover, their generally younger, better-educated, higher-income readership,[134] reflected in both their advertising and their tendency to devote a large part of their journalism to dining and entertainment, means that they seldom serve the egalitarian need of supplying news and opinion to the poorer part of the community not valued by advertisers.

More investigation is required, but if the alternative weeklies do not serve the same (democratic or personal) functions as does the daily press or if their prevalence is distinctly limited, the occasional existence of these "alternatives" should not suffice to alleviate concern about the decline of competition among dailies or about the effect of advertising on the structure of the press. Still, these self-proclaimed "alternative papers" could themselves be a very valuable development. Moreover, they could serve to remind us that various dissident presses have been an important, reoccurring, but often underrecognized part of the American journalistic scene.

Illustrative of this diversity are the more than 2,700 African-American newspapers, magazines, and other periodicals that have been started since the *Freedom's Journal* was published in 1827, growing to have a paid weekly circulation of more than 2 million at the end of World War II and reportedly 4.3 million readers during the mid-1970s;[135] a foreign-language press that, for instance, in 1920 consisted of 1,500 entities, printing in 33 languages and garnering a circulation of 8 million;[136] the 1,000 Populist papers united by the National Reform Press Association in the 1890s;[137] the more than 400 "underground" papers of the late 1960s and early 1970s, which claimed a 20-million-person readership;[138] the 60 anti-war GI papers during the Vietnam War led by the *Bond*, which claimed a circulation of 100,000 in 1971;[139] the anarchist *Catholic Worker* with 100,000 readers during the 1930s and again a 100,000 circulation during the Vietnam War;[140] or the more than 500 feminist newsletters, newspapers, and periodicals produced during the late 1960s.[141] Add to this the press of utopian communities, labor, socialists, and other groups, and the press begins to look quite diverse, quite significant in reach, and, on closer examination, quite important for politics, for culture, and especially for the process of democratic or popular change.

For purposes of this book, a number of questions should be raised about these dissident or alternative presses. First, do they provide the relevant competitive alternative to local dailies? The answer merits more extended treatment, but I expect it is no—if for no other reason than the much more restricted resources available to these papers. Moreover, although they vary among themselves, often these papers play a somewhat different role in the community and in their readers' lives than the local daily. For example, a 1920 survey of New York readers of Yiddish dailies found that 66% also read English-language papers but most said these did not provide adequate news of Jewry.[142]

Second, given the large circulation of many of these alternative papers, cannot the media market as a whole be said to be receptive to diverse voices? Again, the answer is probably no or, at least, not very. These papers, mostly sustained by major personal commitments of those involved in their publication, struggled financially and were seriously restricted by inadequate resources. All the problems attributed to advertising discussed generally in this book work against these papers. Most of the radical publications received virtually no support from advertisers and had to depend on circulation sales and outside support—for example, from benefactors or a political party.[143] The potential for these papers, like the failing paper in my earlier hypothetical scenario, was limited both by their inability to obtain advertising and by their competition with advertising-subsidized media. Moreover, like the suggestion that the daily press changed from partisanship to objectivity in part because of the influence of advertising, these alternative presses' editorial agendas were often bent by their need for advertising. Laureen Kessler describes the change over time in "many foreign-language newspapers in the twentieth century [in terms of their becoming] less ideological, less idealistic, and less educational," publishing "more news and less opinion," shying "away from weighty political discussions," and coming "to see themselves as forums for advertising."[144]

Although precise financial data on these dissident presses is not readily available, most accounts of the African-American press suggest both of the difficulties described above. Apparently this press has always had trouble obtaining advertising: the average life span of nine years per paper has been attributed to a "poor advertising base."[145] A 1990 survey of African-American publishers and editors found that by far the most commonly accepted reason for the failure of their publications was lack of advertising support (with insufficient starting capital listed second).[146] Then there is the parallel problem of pressure on editorial content created by the need for advertising. As a result of Roscoe Dunjee's militant civil rights views and aggressive editorial support for peaceful change, according to his nephew and successor as editor, Dunjee's crusading African-American newspaper was unable to gain much advertising and the paper was forced to depend on circulation for its economic base.[147] Bending is the other alternative, and sometimes it is the only alternative consistent with survival. Although noting that the two highest-circulation African-American papers in the 1970s were *Muhammed Speaks* and the *Black Panther*, Kessler suggests that in the second half of the twentieth century most "Black newspapers and magazines abandoned political controversy in their quest for advertising dollars."[148] Detroit mayor Coleman Young argued in 1974 that "there has been a tendency on the part of Black papers to look to the advertising too much"—and he asserted that these papers were "forget[ting] that power rests with the people."[149]

Thus, although the alternative and dissident press is too varied for rigid generalizations, its general history suggests that these publications are an often ignored form of communication which could contribute significantly to the media realm. But it also suggests that, although many but not all of the current "alternative weeklies" are fully advertiser-supported free weeklies, often the problems of advertising dependence discussed in this book apply even more acutely to this press. This press would likely have had an even greater role—or new titles would be even more likely in the future—if there were policies in place that enhanced the role or amount of subscription revenue or that reduced publications' dependence on advertising revenue.

They Are All the Same.   A few commentators, frequently empirically oriented communications scholars, have suggested that, like the three virtually identical network news programs, two competitive papers often are essentially duplicative. This duplication arguably wastes resources, while a lack of competition does not systematically lead to a decline either in consumer satisfaction or in the quality of the remaining paper. Competition may correlate negatively with the revenues on which a newspaper depends to deliver a desired product. Competition will split a fixed pool of potential advertising dollars and potential readers between the competitors. In contrast, a monopoly paper's presumably larger circulation and advertising base could provide the financial resources to produce a better newspaper than is possible under competitive conditions,[150] while the *potential* entry of a new paper or present competition from other media, such as broadcasting, could induce the monopoly paper to make this investment in quality.

In an interesting study, Barry Litman and Janet Bridges evaluated two purportedly competing hypotheses: (1) competition between newspapers stimulates consumer-oriented performance, while monopoly denies consumer freedom and misallocates resources; and (2) increased monopoly helps newspapers achieve efficiencies (allowing for cheaper provision of a better product) and stimulates technological progress.[151] This study grew out of a debate that arose because many researchers had trouble finding actual evidence of benefits deriving from (the occasional) competition among daily newspapers today.[152] In order to find benefits to support the procompetitive thesis, Litman and Bridges looked for evidence that competitive papers were more committed to quality, which they thought would be measured by financial commitment to quality.[153] Their regression analysis of various criteria of financial support showed "moderate support" for the procompetition view.[154] Surprisingly, despite their splitting the revenue base, competitive papers apparently spent more on editorial quality. A similar study found that competition affected papers' budget allocations, inducing them to subscribe to more wire services and use more reporters to fill a given amount of space. As the author put it, "intense competition means a newspaper must spend more money to differentiate itself and to remain a substitute for its competitor."[155]

Although this procompetitive conclusion is important, these studies are curious in their implicit assumption that the merit of competition would lie primarily in financial commitment rather than diversity of content—that is, product differentiation. This assumption may reflect the dominance of the ideology of objectivity in modern thought about newspapers—if all good papers merely report the facts, value would lie not in taking different perspectives but primarily in doing a better job of gathering and presenting facts, which requires investment in quality job performance. In addition, this focus on financial commitment arguably should be accepted as a fallback measure because, as the authors noted, other recent studies had already failed to find differences in objective measures of *content* among competing papers.[156]

Nevertheless, a combination of methodological restraints and implicit ideological frames may cause serious inadequacies and generate misleading results. These studies typically either compare existing competitive newspapers to newspapers in otherwise comparable cities without competing dailies or compare versions of the same newspaper before and shortly after competition ends.[157] Such studies are prisoners of the investigator's need to find hard, quantitative measures of comparability. They examine such things as the proportion of space allocated to different categories of news and find few differences. With such a methodology, a radical and a mainstream paper with dramatically different perspectives could appear identical as long as they allocated similar space to similar categories. More important, the studies' observational methodology that requires analysis of actual newspapers prevents consideration of what competitive newspapers would be like under those conditions required to make competition viable. Today, the presence of competitive alternatives may appear (relatively) unimportant precisely because of structural conditions that prevent them from being different in ways that matter much. Considered in the context of the argument made here about advertising's effects, the studies are ill-equipped to describe the form competitive papers would take where advertising exercised less influence. For either critical or policy purposes, it is misleading to consider the value of competition only under conditions that have made competition (virtually) impossible. Real knowledge requires consideration of competition's value under conditions in which it could flourish. The "truth" may be not that competition lacks value but that advertising has destroyed, for now, the conditions of successful and valuable competition.

Consequences for Politics

Nondifferentiated newspapers and the related, modern, "objective" style of journalism may have had profound consequences for American democracy. At election time, "good-government, get-out-the-vote" rhetoric implies a commitment to widespread political participation or, at least, to high voter turnout as an essential element of a living democracy. Commentators continually lament that voting in this country has been in steady decline[*] and is much lower than in most other Western democracies.[158] Current high turnouts in European democracies, as well as widespread voting in nineteenth-century America, belie the explanation that the poor and uneducated inherently do not vote.[†159] Like explanations for the decline in partisanship and rise of objectivity in the press, accounts of the "vanishing voter" are complex. Still, the two could be related.

Until late in the nineteenth century the press was strongly partisan[160]— as well as often competitive within a single town. The plausible and intended result was that the partisan press reinforced partisan loyalty, partisan conflict, and general political excitement: "Traditional party journalism . . . eased readers' participation in politics by creating an accessible political world. Party papers made politics seem important, simplified issues . . . and urged voters to display their political beliefs."[161] If this characterization of the press is correct, high voting rates or other forms of political participation should be no surprise.

---

[*] Our first five presidents were elected with participation of only 4% to 6% of the (small) *eligible* electorate. During the Jacksonian era, turnout increased dramatically, rising to 57% in 1828 and 80% by 1840. Participation remained high throughout the rest of the century; the lowest rate recorded was 69.4% in 1852. Scholars suggest that this high participation rate is "rooted in the highly partisan nature of political campaigns" (Ruy A. Teixeira, *Why Americans Don't Vote* [1987], 8–10). A downturn in voting occurred between 1896 and 1912, giving rise to a scholarly debate between proponents of two main views: those who attribute the decline largely to a weakening in the partisan character of parties and those who focus on increased legal obstacles in voting (10–11); Frances Fox Piven and Richard A. Cloward, *Why Americans Don't Vote: Turnout Decline in the United States, 1960–1984* (1989), 17 (emphasizing the latter view). As new legal restrictions "took effect between 1888 and 1924, voting rates fell: from 64% to 19% in the South; [and] from 86% to 55% in the North and West" (viii).

[†] Walter Dean Burnham observes that the people who do not vote in the United States, the "party of nonvoters," demographically occupy the place occupied by Left parties in European countries (*The Current Crisis in American Politics* [1982], 188). Comparing two landslide elections in the United States, Burnham notes that the Republican party candidate secured virtually the same degree of support from the potential electorate in each: Wendell Wilkie received 28.3% of the potential electorate in 1940 and Ronald Reagan gained his historic "mandate" from 28.0% of the potential electorate in 1980 (188–89).

The early independent papers were still routinely committed to parties but claimed that independence permitted them to criticize the party on the basis of the party's principles.[162] However, the nature of newspaper independence and even of partisanship changed in the last decades of the nineteenth century. According to Michael McGerr, "the independent press gave broader expression to an essentially elitist political style. . . . [It] offered a less exciting political world than the one created by the old party sheets. . . . Independent journalism was, as Whitelaw Reid lovingly described it in 1872, a 'passionless ether.' "[163] McGerr explains that "with the rise of the independent press . . . politics became less simple and accessible and the partisanship that sustained high voter turnouts lost its cultural hegemony."[164]

Of course, the changed nature of the press needs explanation. I have argued that, largely as a consequence of advertising, papers became increasingly homogenous. Given an advertising-oriented press, it is not even clear that much would be gained from the addition of more (nonpartisan) competition. This may explain recent empirical studies' difficulty in finding any significance in competition. But product differentiation that fosters a revival of partisanship, while ideally avoiding the excesses of nineteenth-century journalism, could contribute to a renewal of politics and political participation. In any event, as a historical matter, in addition to reducing product differentiation and destroying local competitive dailies, advertising may have transformed the press in a manner that contributed significantly to the decline of a partisan political culture and the corresponding political participation.

The above point about the decline of partisanship only begins to indicate the significance of the rise of objectivity as journalism's fundamental principle. Because the subject of "objectivity" has received frequent comment, I will only touch on the issue here.

Ben Bagdikian correctly describes journalism as an "essentially subjective," constantly "value-laden" process; he argues that, under the rubric of objectivity, it has become "superficial," "official and establishmentarian."[165] More flamboyantly, commentator Jack Newfield asserts: "Objectivity . . . is believing people with power and printing their press releases."[166] Bagdikian and others' criticisms most often elaborate one or more of three points.[167] First, critics emphasize that the media's "gatekeeper" role, their selection of what to report and their decisions about how to treat the material, is heavily, inevitably, and *properly* value-laden. These critics sometimes note that objectivity has taken a form which requires attributable sources, and for various reasons the press relies primarily on governmental figures, thereby becoming " 'more conduit than critic of government.' "[168]

Second, the "objective" style may be especially subject to manipulation by political actors outside the press. Keen observers argue that the press's version of objectivity, particularly the tendency merely to report statements of political elites no matter how stupid or demonstrably false, helped sustain the Reagan presidency,[169] while the McCarthy era "showed how vulnerable journalistic objectivity was to manipulation by the demagogue."[170]

Third, the objective style has ideological content. Among other effects, it reinforces an image of the world that splits fact and value, reason and emotion; and it proclaims the special value of facts. Christopher Lasch forcefully argues that democracy depends on public debate—argument and discussion, not information (except as it is made relevant by, and is the by-product of, the debate). He concludes "that the job of the press is to encourage debate, not to supply the public with information."[171] From this perspective, objectivity may be fundamentally at odds with democracy as a type of government and an approach to life. Lasch suggests that both debate and political participation began to decline around the turn of the century when newspapers became more "responsible," more objective, and less opinionated.[172]

The critique of objectivity as itself ideological has been taken further by some scholars. Robert Hackett argues that the impartial, objective form of television news situates the "viewer" as a "passive observer, a mere consumer of news."[173] He contrasts this with commercials, which ask us to "become active, . . . to do something, to change, indeed to improve something. But what we're asked to improve is not the world but our own private situations or selves. And this improvement . . . simply requires the purchase of commodities."[174] According to this analysis, news (objectivity) and commercials (partisanship) act together to "position viewers as depoliticized consumers."[175] Still, after critiquing the unreflective category of objectivity as serving the state as well as dominant economic forces, Hackett asserts that "we would presumably prefer orthodox objectivity to the deliberate propagandizing of nineteenth-century journalism."[176] This does not rule out, however, a journalism more conscious of its constructed nature, more reflective about the ideological quality of objectivity, and more committed to its value-based role.[177] Democratic politics may require a mobilizing press, not just a watchdog. The corresponding journalism would encourage competition—and would not maximally serve advertisers.

☆ CHAPTER II ☆

Advertising and the Content
of a Democratic Press

Don't like news that connects the product you sell or your company to death or murder? Demand silence. Want an appealing, upbeat media environment for your ads? Pay to get it. Concerned that your advertising expenditures are wasted on media consumers, like the poor, who are unlikely customers? Just tell the media producers to stop providing material of interest to that audience.

Chapter 1 described structural effects of advertising on the newspaper industry. Structural effects pervasively, even if only indirectly, control media content. Advertising causes a decline in content diversity among newspapers and helps establish a particular, ideologically laden style of journalism—roughly, objectivity. This chapter considers four systematic ways in which advertising more directly affects the media's nonadvertising content.

These direct effects can be characterized either as the corruption of the media due to advertisers' use of their (economic) power to "censor" and control content, or as normal economic exchanges in which advertisers "purchase" content favorable to their interests. Either way, it can be shown that the incentive of advertising revenue encourages the media to tailor message content: (1) to treat advertisers' products and their broader interests charitably in both news reports and editorials; (2) to create a buying mood that will incline readers or viewers to react favorably to advertisements; (3) to reduce partisanship and often to reduce controversial elements in order to avoid offending advertisers' potential customers and to increase the media's potential reach; and (4) to favor the middle- to higher-income audiences whose greater purchasing power advertisers value most.

Economic rationales for each of these four effects are obvious. This chapter will offer illustrations and will speculate about their prevalence and significance. The later discussion can be contextualized by preliminary comments on three of its shortcomings: (1) this chapter's concern with only one way in which advertising relates to *total* media content; (2) the chapter's merging of discussion of different media—a format intended to emphasize the similarities of influence among all the media but which ignores some important differences; and (3) its inability to clearly demonstrate the pervasiveness or the seriousness of the problem given its reliance on ad hoc illustrations and anecdotal evidence.

Advertisements Themselves. The effects of advertising on nonadvertising content is the subject of this book. This is only a slice of advertising's influence on media content since advertising itself constitutes an incredibly large portion of that media content—roughly 65% of newspaper space and 22% of television time.[1] I do not attempt to evaluate obvious merits and demerits of advertising itself. A full assessment of the impact of advertising, however, would have to consider the ads themselves. Advertising, which Michael Schudson calls "capitalist realism," is a major element of social life, shaping the nature of our culture of consumption.[2] As a "central *symbolic* structure," Schudson argues, "advertising may shape our sense of values even under conditions where it does not greatly corrupt our buying habits." Moreover, advertising constitutes a large portion of the media's explicitly ideological messages. Michael Parenti cites a 1980 study for the claim that "today, one-third of all corporate advertising is directed at influencing the public on political and ideological issues as opposed to pushing consumer goods."[3] For example, Erik Barnouw describes ITT's effective use of a heavy corporate-image advertising campaign in 1974–1975 to reverse the negative public opinion generated by exposés of ITT's connection with corruption in the Nixon White House and its role in the overthrow of the democratically elected Allende presidency in Chile.*[4] Despite the importance of advertisements themselves, this chapter is limited to advertisers' influence on the media's purportedly nonadvertising content. That is, it examines violations of the press's proclaimed wall of separation between church and state—its editorial office and its business side.

Differences between Media. The media all vary somewhat in their susceptibility to each of the four forms of influence discussed in this chapter. Nevertheless, I will mix examples from various media, primarily newspapers and broadcasting but sometimes magazines, adding occasional comments about whether a particular medium is more or less vulnerable to a

---

* ITT's advertising expenditures may also have influenced direct news treatment of ITT, which is an effect this chapter does examine. In 1973 and 1974, network newscasts continuously featured negative material about ITT. Then, during the first half of 1975, while ITT's "good-deed commercials" were being constantly shown on evening newscasts, the news programs did not mention ITT.

particular form of influence. Although a fuller analysis might more carefully distinguish between different media, this chapter's approach emphasizes similarities and the pervasiveness of the phenomenon. Still, it might be useful to note several factors that could affect the extent of advertising's influence within a given medium or over a given media firm.

First, the greater the proportionate contribution to the media enterprise's revenue from an individual advertiser or organized group of advertisers, the greater the likely influence. Classified advertising by the public, although very profitable to newspapers, is generally thought to exercise little influence because of its dispersed nature. (Classified ads of auto dealers are, however, an entirely different story.)

Second, influence over any element of a conglomerate can often be transformed into influence over other elements. If a conglomerate owns different media enterprises of different types, advertisers may leverage influence over one enterprise into influence over another. After the *New York Times*, which seldom carries medical advertising, ran a newspaper series on medical malpractice that antagonized pharmaceutical firms, these firms threatened to withdraw 260 pages of ads from a medical magazine owned by the *Times*. Rather than buckle, the *Times* sold the magazine.[5] This response, however, is not likely to be the norm. In a 1968 incident, many people in the advertising field became upset after their trade journals received advance copies of a book critical of the advertising industry. An editorial in *Advertising Age* called the author an "ungrateful dog." Although the book contained no advertising and thus had none to lose, the publisher was a subsidiary of *Reader's Digest*. Confronted with the advertising industry's reaction just one month before the scheduled publication, *Reader's Digest* ordered the publisher to cancel the book as contrary to the best interests of *Reader's Digest*.[6] Similarly, "in 1974, Time's Fortune Book Club . . . broke its contract and dropped . . . [its plan to distribute Gerard Zilg's *Dupont: Behind the Nylon Curtain*] after Dupont threatened to withdraw its ads from Time publications."[7]

Third, the specific media format or type of enterprise involved may affect the amount of influence that media producers and consumers will find acceptable—and hence the "cost" to the medium of allowing the influence or, at least, the cost of allowing public knowledge of it. Many people may be less disturbed that a company pays to have a character in an entertainment program drink a Coke or smoke a Marlboro than if the company pays for favorable "news" about the company's products.

Fourth, professionalism sometimes leads media producers to resist advertisers' intrusions. When the publisher of *Look* decided against publishing Gloria Steinem's interview with Cesar Chavez because of fear about its effect on Sunkist's advertising, the managing editor, Patricia Carbine, threatened to resign. Her threat was effective—the story ran.[8] Context and tradition can affect the strength and power of this sense of professionalism, and these traditions are likely to vary both between types of media and within the individual medium.

Fifth, and related to the above point, accepted industry practices and prejudices can affect the degree of influence that advertisers demand and that the medium permits—although this merely pushes back the question of why these practices and prejudices developed as they did. In the first issue of the new, advertising-free *Ms.*, Steinem reports that the original *Ms.* faced an accepted industrywide view that advertisers had a special right to dominate, and had a tradition of dominating, the content of "women's" magazines—a tradition that they did not enjoy to an equal degree in other magazines.[9]

Sixth, if media consumers identify advertisers more with the content surrounding their ads in some contexts than in others, this would increase the advertisers' incentive to control that surrounding content. Stephen Seabolt, advertising sales director at *Time*, reported having been told by a client "that TV [advertising] spots often are perceived as program sponsorships, but magazine ads aren't since a consumer pays for a magazine."[10]

Probably the most important factor affecting the degree of influence is, however, the portion of the media firm's revenue provided by advertising. The officers of the Australian company that purchased *Ms.* in 1987 were reportedly " 'shocked' " at the extent of advertiser control in the United States but then noted that " '[Australian] readers pay two times more for their magazines . . . so advertisers have less power to threaten a magazine's viability.' "[11] Advertisers presumably have much less influence on the content of books, where they provide virtually none of the revenue, than on broadcasting, where they provide virtually all. Newspapers should be somewhere in between, in both the portion of revenue advertisers provide and the extent of advertisers' influence.

Lapses or Pervasive Self-Censorship?   The very newsworthiness of advertisers' influence on media content—for example, the newsworthiness of the examples discussed in this chapter—may indicate the rarity of the influence. Nevertheless, another interpretation is more plausible. Newsworthiness may reflect the importance of the norm that is violated combined with the relative infrequency of discovery of violations. Given that exposure of advertiser influence typically does damage, including economic damage, to the influenced media firm and is hardly helpful to any but the most brazen advertisers, both parties to the transaction will strive to avoid public exposure. It is likely that many more cases of overt influence occur than are disclosed.* More important, *even if* active advertiser intervention is relatively rare, most experienced observers conclude that advertisers' concerns result in extensive media "self-censorship," sometimes even unconscious censorship reflecting ingrained knowledge of the boundaries of what is permissible.[12] Knowledge of occasional advertiser retaliations for violations of their interests, even if the media sturdily resisted the influence in the particular publicized example, creates a pervasive awareness that deviation can be costly.

For example, Les Brown reports that NBC stood up to Coca-Cola in 1970 when Coke forcefully pressured NBC to change a documentary, "Migrant," which showed Coke as one of the perpetrators of offensive treatment of laborers in the Florida citrus industry. After NBC broadcast the show uncensored, the president of Coca-Cola, Inc., J. Paul Austin, admitted before a congressional committee that the broadcast had accurately depicted housing and working conditions and that Coke would act promptly to change the situation—quick results of good journalism. A second result, however, was that NBC lost all its network billings from Coke, amounting to several million dollars.[13] When Brown's story was reprinted eight years later, the introduction observed a third result: "NBC ha[d] not . . . produced a documentary on a controversial domestic issue involving an important advertiser since."[14]

Discussing network documentaries, Erik Barnouw made an observation that applies to the media more broadly: "The most formidable impediment is not censorship, but self-censorship. Its monuments are proposals

---

* In a survey of top editors of popular consumer magazines, 49% of the editors reported that they had complete independence from the business office (Vicki Hesterman, "Consumer Magazines and Ethical Guidelines," *Journal of Mass Media Ethics* 2 [1978]: 93, 96). That only 49% personally felt unconstrained (and they are likely to know of others who do not) should give some support to the claim of Chris Welles, a former journalist and instructor at Columbia School of Journalism, that " 'anyone who has been in the business for more than a few months can cite plenty of examples of editorial compromises due to pressure, real or imagined, from publishers, owners and advertisers' " (Martin A. Lee and Norman Solomon, *Unreliable Sources* [1990], 98). Equally interesting is another finding of the survey. Before buying a "well-written story detailing the dangers of a product advertised in the magazine," 55% of these editors reported they would first consult their business office and an additional 24% reported that they would buy the story but warn the business office. In other words, many of the 49% of editors who feel that they have complete independence still consciously work with the business office in relation to their editorial choices.

not budgeted, ideas never proposed."[15] Actual intervention by advertisers may be common even if difficult to demonstrate unequivocally. But if self-censorship is the more pervasive problem, as I think it is, the anecdotal accounts of advertiser interventions are best read as illustrative of much more deeply entrenched problems. Actual interventions by advertisers may be like the government's punishment for crime—occurring only when the generally accepted constraints are violated, the intervention deters further violations.

Mechanisms of advertisers' control of media content may work best if they operate in a manner that discourages consciousness of what otherwise would be seen as improper censorship. One mechanism involves the steering implicit in subtle hiring and advancement decisions within the media organization. Concern with one's career can operate powerfully at all levels of the psyche, teaching the bounds of the acceptable and unacceptable. Those employees who require too much overt direction, if not fired, are at least not likely to be advanced. Although referring to censorship by owners rather than by advertisers, Parenti argues that "*anticipation* that superiors might disapprove of this or that story is usually enough to discourage a reporter from writing it, or an editor from assigning it."[16] Eventually, this system of predicted disapproval dissuades reporters or producers from even thinking about a problematic story. Having learned "not [to] cross any forbidden lines, [journalists] are not reined in. So they are likely to have no awareness they are on an ideological leash."[17] As C. Terence Clyne, the vice president of a large advertising agency, noted in 1959 testimony before the FCC: "There have been very few cases where it has been necessary to exercise a veto, because the producers involved and the writers involved are normally pretty well aware of what might not be acceptable."[18]

The hidden control system is not perfect. Sometimes awareness of the leashes still exists. In 1972, David Rintels, chairman of the Committee on Censorship of the Writers Guild of America, West, stated that of those members of the Writers Guild who responded to a poll, 86% reported from personal experience that censorship exists on TV, and 81% believed that "television is presenting a distorted picture of what is happening in this country"; only 8% believed that "current television programming is 'in the public interest.' "[19] As Frank Stanton, a leader in American journalism, explained in 1960, "since we are advertiser-supported we must take into account the general objectives and desires of advertisers as a whole."[20]

AVOIDING OFFENSE TO ADVERTISERS: A KEPT-PRESS

Advertisers would prefer that the media avoid, bury, or downplay media content that casts their products, firm, or industry in a negative light; better would be media that present content supportive of their interests and their products.

The most direct route to content favorable to advertisers is to pay the media to have apparently nonadvertising content conform to advertisers' desires. Newspapers all over the country commonly accepted this practice during the late nineteenth and early twentieth centuries.[21] Advertisers paid for insertions, generally referred to as "reading notices," that were printed as news stories or editorials with no markings or placements identifying them as advertising. Since technically "reading notices" could be viewed as merely a form of advertising, they illustrate the blurriness of the line separating advertisements from advertiser-influenced news. I consider them here, however, since from the perspective of the public, which receives these messages as if they were editorial content, reading notices epitomize advertisers' control over nonadvertising content.

Publication of reading notices blatantly undermined the integrity of journalism. Nevertheless, in New York City alone, they were published at one time or another in William Randolph Hearst's *Journal*, the *New York Tribune*, the *New York Post*, the *New York World*, and the *New York Times*.[22] Advertisers continually wrote reading notices to promote their products or interests, often disguising the advertisement by focusing on prominent people and other unrelated information, and then mixing in plugs and "news" about the advertiser's patent medicine, railroad, real estate, or other products and services.

Reading notices were also used to manipulate public policy. Beginning just after 1900, both large and small companies, including Standard Oil, Armour & Company, and Prudential Insurance, paid newspapers to include apparent news items and editorials designed to influence legislation and to advance their political agendas. These corporate "advertisers" required that the insertions be indistinguishable from the newspaper's normal news and editorial content.[23]

Some in the industry defended the practice. In an 1890 issue of *Printers' Ink*, the *St. Paul Globe* "asserted that reading notices were perfectly legitimate—and successful."[24] But over time the practice received increasing criticism. Its ethical bankruptcy seems obvious. However, the eventual opposition to the practice within the newspaper industry was often couched in commercial as well as ethical terms. Since readers do not have personal access to the events of the world or to a full range of views about their society, they may value newspapers, as they value the disinterested judgments of physicians and lawyers, for providing content that represents editors' and journalists' professional assessments of what information and opinion should be presented to the reader. To the extent that reading notices undermined the basis of this value, newspapers could be shortsighted in publishing this "tainted" news. Thus, E. W. Scripps concluded that it made "good business sense" to avoid publication of unlabeled reading notices.[25] Similarly, the editor of the *Boston Post* publicized its refusal to print a street railway's reading notice, implicitly concluding that public knowledge of its refusal would improve its reputation and, thereby, increase the paper's value.*[26]

Widely disparaged, publication of reading notices declined during the Progressive Era—although some advertising handbooks still promoted their use as late as 1911.[27] Finally, in 1912, "all editorial or other reading matter . . . [for] which money or other valuable consideration is paid" were prohibited by the Post Office Appropriation Act in any publication using the second-class postal privilege unless plainly marked as an "advertisement."[28]

Given publications' heavy reliance on the mails and second-class rates, the 1912 act effectively outlawed routine *direct* payments for control of the news. However, that legislation hardly eliminated advertisers' control over mass media content. Arguably, the most deadly case of advertiser influence has been mass media's virtual silence about the dangers of cigarette smoking long after these effects were well known among medical researchers.[29] Clear scientific evidence concerning health dangers of smoking has been available at least since the mid-1930s, but fifty years later the public is still woefully ignorant—surveys show that "half the general and two-thirds the smoking population [do] not think smoking makes 'a great deal of difference' in life expectancy."[30] And media silence contributes to ignorance that in turn affects behavior. Smoking rapidly declined during the

---

* These arguments are equally current today. Some in the industry, believing that weak, distorted real estate coverage loses readers and hence advertisers, conclude that the common practice of assigning responsibility for the paper's real estate section to the newspaper's advertising department is economically shortsighted, "especially in more sophisticated markets." When the *Miami Herald* gave the real estate section to the news department after twenty years of publishing the section as an advertorial, ad linage from real estate firms jumped 46% as the better coverage produced better readers, which "translated into more business for the local real estate industry" (Elizabeth Lesly, "Demand Happy News . . . and Often Get It," *Washington Journalism Review*, Nov. 1991, 21, 23).

two periods when the government either required or sponsored antismoking ads or information campaigns.[31] Of course, some silence may reflect what we have learned counts as "news"—a much deeper problem. Imagine the comparative chances of two stories for becoming a front-page headline: "Plane Crash in Arizona Kills 78 Today" or "Reports from Hospitals around the Country Show 822 People Died Today from Cigarettes." One problem is that the second headline could run every day. Still, the media's silence stands out when contrasted to their extensive coverage of many suspected causes of cancer and other health problems.

Despite 300,000 deaths a year now attributable to smoking and earlier evidence of harmful effects that finally led the American Medical Association to ban tobacco advertising in its journals in 1953, reports on the dangers of smoking have been virtually absent in those media in which tobacco companies advertise.[32] The reason is not hard to fathom: "The tobacco industry spends $4 a year for every American man, woman, or child" on advertising, or over $1,000 since 1954 per smoking-related death, making tobacco the most heavily advertised product in the country. A recent article in the *New England Journal of Medicine* showed statistically that the likelihood of a magazine's publishing an article about smoking's ill effects decreased as the proportion of its revenue that came from cigarette advertising increased.[33] An editor of the *New Republic*, which deleted a commissioned article criticizing tobacco companies after the article was already typeset, defended the magazine on the ground that the deletion was unusual and occurred only "because of the relative size of the [advertising] account."[34] In 1983 *Newsweek* published a health supplement written by the American Medical Association, and in 1984 *Time* published one basically written by the American Academy of Family Physicians. To the outrage or embarrassment of the authors, each magazine either deleted or resisted any mention of smoking's adverse effects, except to warn against smoking in bed.[35]

Clearly, the tobacco industry does not like criticism of its product. *Cosmopolitan* and *Psychology Today* explained their refusal to take advertising for a stop-smoking clinic on the ground that it would offend their tobacco advertisers.[36] When *Reader's Digest*, one of the few magazines that refuses cigarette ads, ran an article on the medical dangers of smoking, its advertising agency deserted it.[37] The agency's action may have been rational. When Saatchi and Saatchi, a major advertising firm, prepared ads touting Northwest Airlines' no-smoking policy, RJR/Nabisco, a food and cigarette conglomerate, canceled its $80 million contract for advertising food products.[38] This conglomerate's response helps explain why even magazines that do not take cigarette ads, if they carry ads for the cigarette conglomerates' other products, may feel constrained not to report too much about the dangers of smoking.[39] In 1980, when *Mother Jones* ran an article linking tobacco to health dangers, the tobacco companies canceled their ads.[40] Unfortunately, such cancellations are usually unnecessary—the media know what behavior is expected and have complied.

The tobacco industry's "purchase" of media silence is merely a slightly more subtle version of the turn-of-the-century practices of the patent medicine industry.[41] At that time, patent medicine manufacturers were one of the country's largest advertisers. The medicines, which contained as much as 80% alcohol and often included cocaine and morphine, were medically mostly worthless. Often the "medicines destroyed health, and made drunkards and dope addicts out of their users."[42] The medicine dealers, however, had uniform content in advertising contracts with thousands of newspapers throughout the country. These contracts provided that the advertiser could cancel its advertising from the date of enactment of any law harmful to its interests. When legislatures considered bills harmful to the patent medicine industry, newspaper editors, after receiving letters from the patent medicine producers that merely referred to the contract language, printed articles or editorials favoring the industry. Thus, an association of patent medicine producers gratefully attributed its consistent legislative successes to aid from the American Newspaper Association and from individual papers.[43] Controlling newspapers' editorial policies even more directly, the advertising contracts also provided for cancellation if any detrimental matter "is permitted to appear in the reading columns or elsewhere in the paper."[44] The result was either silence or praise of "proprietary" medicines.[45]

Although overt contractual obligations requiring that media content promote advertisers' interests may no longer be deemed acceptable (admittedly, I say this without much confidence), the media do not forget that favorable treatment of advertisers is good business. According to Michael Parenti, *New York Times* publisher Arthur Ochs Sulzberger openly admitted that he urged his editors to present the automobile industry's position in coverage of safety and auto pollution because, he said, it "would affect the advertising." The auto industry was a major newspaper advertiser.[46] This proadvertiser orientation is by no means new. Along with more recent examples, Parenti describes an Ohio mill town early in the century where reporter Art Shields was cautioned by his paper's editor/

advertising manager "to report nothing the merchants and brewers didn't like. . . . 'Be especially careful when you write about the brewery. . . . It's our best advertiser.' " And in regard to the steel plant, Shields was told " 'Better check with management before you write what workers tell you.' "[47] Similarly, the *New York World* reportedly rejected O. Henry's "An Unfinished Story" out of fear that it would offend department store owners.[48]

Advertisers' power lies largely in their willingness and ability to withdraw ads. After "60 Minutes" discussed health hazards of Alar, a chemical used on apples, the Washington State Fruit Commission, a trade association, withdrew $71,300 worth of advertising for cherries from three CBS affiliates in protest.[49] Real estate advertisers should have little reason to fear negative coverage—44% of newspaper real estate editors in a national survey reported that "publishers or senior editors prohibit[ed] [balanced coverage out of] fear of offending advertisers."[50] Nevertheless, these advertisers can still take offense. "More than 80% [of the surveyed real estate editors] said advertisers had threatened to pull ads because of negative coverage."[51] Farm publications report similar problems. Of the 190 members of the American Agricultural Editors Association responding to a survey, 62% reported threats of advertising withdrawal because of editorial copy, 48% had had advertising withdrawn, and a quarter reported "direct demands for editorial copy as tradeoff for advertising."[52] *Ms.* won awards for its 1980 story on an underground feminist movement in the Soviet Union, but Gloria Steinem reports that its "years of efforts to get an ad schedule from Revlon" were undone "because the Soviet women on [the] cover [were] not wearing makeup."[53]

Proctor & Gamble publicly announced that it would withdraw all advertising from any TV station that broadcast a "highly offensive" anti-Folgers commercial.[54] A political advocacy group, Neighbor-to-Neighbor, sponsored the ad, which was supported by groups such as the National Council of Churches and narrated by actor Ed Asner. The ad said: "The murderous civil war in El Salvador has been supported by billions of American tax dollars and by the sale of Salvadoran coffee. . . . Boycott Folgers. What it brews is misery and death."[55] Most television stations refused the ad.[56] After WHDH in Boston broadcast the ad, Proctor & Gamble withdrew all its advertising from the station, which had been running about $1 million a year.[57] WHDH apparently has trouble avoiding advertisers' wrath. It also lost about $4.5 million annually in automobile dealers' advertising as a result of a series of investigative reports broadcast in May 1990 concerning questionable practices by car salesmen.[58]

Advertisers' concerns go far beyond their own products. Television's largest advertiser, Proctor & Gamble, stated in a 1965 memorandum on broadcast policies: "There will be no material that may give offense, either directly or by inference, to any commercial organization of any sort."[59] Proctor & Gamble's requirements were quite detailed: "Characters . . . should reflect recognition and acceptance of the world situation," and "writers should minimize the 'horror' aspects [of war]. . . . Men in uniform shall not be cast as heavy villains or portrayed as engaging in any criminal activity."[60] Its policies specified what would be inappropriate treatment of businessmen as well as "ministers, priests and similar representatives of positive social forces" and required convincing rejoinders to any attack on a "basic conception of the American way of life."[61] Moreover, "no material on any of our programs . . . [should] in any way further the concept of business as cold, ruthless, and lacking all sentiment or spiritual motivation."[62] According to Proctor & Gamble's advertising manager, these policies applied both to entertainment programs and to news and public affairs documentaries.[63] And these broad concerns extend to print media. Many advertisers in *Ms.* have very specific directives controlling the editorial content permitted adjacent to their ads. Proctor & Gamble, however, barred its products from *any issue* of the magazine "that included *any* material on gun control, abortion, the occult, cults, or the disparagement of religion."[64]

Advertisers also consider the overall editorial orientation of the publication. According to Gloria Steinem, after she reported survey evidence to Leonard Lauder, president of Estée Lauder, to show that readers of *Ms.* are more likely than those of *Cosmopolitan* or *Vogue* to use his products, Lauder responded that "*Ms.* isn't appropriate for his ads" because "Estée Lauder is selling 'a kept-woman mentality.'"[65]

The examples described above and, even more, the routine proadvertiser practices that such interventions encourage among publishers, suggest that advertisers buy a "kept" mentality in relation to the press. Of course, this observation does not deny that the free press as experienced in this country is valuable—it often develops and usually publishes important information. Reports of the dangers of smoking are not outlawed and throughout the century have been available in published materials. But advertising has prevented this information from being *readily* available to most people until long after it was widely accepted among medical researchers. Anything preventing the press from effectively providing information and commentary that the public would want, or that an "independent" press would conclude the public needs, is a serious threat to sound social policy and a properly functioning democracy. Advertising operates as a social control mechanism that is often more effective than government censorship in limiting press freedom.

The Need to Avoid Offending Anyone

Advertisers often wish to avoid association with controversial content or, more specifically, with content that offends or takes a position on a controversial issue on which its customers are likely to be divided. There are mutually reinforcing explanations for this avoidance.

First, controversial material may provoke critical thought believed to be inconsistent with a "buying mood."[66] Second, because advertisers' economic interests are usually advanced by dominant values and since controversy normally exists when these values are challenged, controversial content often will be contrary to advertisers' larger interests.[67] Third, partisan material may lose a portion of the audience desired by the advertiser; thus it may interfere with the media enterprise's attempt to capture a larger audience to "sell" to the advertiser. Fourth, and differing from the objective of attracting the largest possible audience, is the advertiser's desire not to offend any potential customer. This fourth point may be the most important. Given the weak, speculative evidence concerning advertising's effectiveness in attracting customers,[68] the last thing advertisers want is for their advertising to drive customers away. Even a tasteful treatment of an emotionally charged subject or a balanced treatment of a truly controversial subject is risky. Thus, network insistence led Norman Lear to modify a "Maude" episode portraying a character's decision to have an abortion. Lear added a character supporting an antichoice position. No commercials appeared in the summer rerun of this episode even though when it first aired it gained a hefty 41% share of the prime-time audience and commercial slots on the other rerun episodes were sold out.[69]

Still, the problem for the broadcaster is not controversy per se. Maybe the better formulation is that advertisers avoid programs which can be predicted to give offense to even a relatively small portion of the targeted audience and that controversial programming often but not always runs counter to this dictate. But controversial programming itself can draw attention and attract large audiences. If carefully designed according to criteria dictated by its advertising-supportive function, controversial content should be capable of being commercially successful. Possibly to rise above the commercial clutter, a few advertisers contradict the norm by seeking carefully crafted controversy.

For example, leaving its products entirely out of its ads, Benetton presents ads featuring startling photos—a black person and a white person handcuffed together; colorful, unfolded condoms; a nun and a priest kissing; a car firebombed by terrorists; a Christlike image of a young man dying of AIDS. Peter Fressola, Benetton's North American director of communications, suggests that rather than using Benetton's $80 million ad budget to "show pretty girls in sweaters," the company's admirable objective is "to create dialogue"—and that the ads try to draw attention to important social issues.[70] The company's president, Luciano Benetton, asserts that the company is "looking for new ways to communicate."[71] In contrast, critics suggest that Benetton is not encouraging social discourse but rather corrupting it to make a buck.[72] Whether or not this criticism is right, these ads show the need to narrow the general claim that advertisers avoid controversy. Instead, what Benetton's ads do is avoid taking a partisan position likely to offend any significant number of its targeted customers. Fressola claims that "we're not telling people what to think about them. We're saying, 'Here they are, draw your own conclusions.' "[73] Moreover, he observes that the ads promote "brand awareness, name recognition, that sort of thing," and says the ad campaign "creates a certain energy and identity for the company that will appeal to a youthful consumer that is our target audience."[74]

Advertisers' desire to avoid offending anyone may also affect the media's construction of news as well as entertainment. Chapter 1 argued that the concern to maximize advertising revenue arguably contributed to the development of objectivity as the ruling ideology in journalism. Bagdikian explains:

> As mass advertising grew, the liberal and radical ideas—in editorials, in selection of news, and in investigative initiatives—became a problem. If a paper wished to attract maximum advertising, its explicit politics might create a disadvantage. To obtain more advertising it needed readers of all political persuasions. . . . The answer in the news was a technique called "objectivity." . . . The doctrine of objectivity . . . has given American standard news a profoundly establishmentarian cast.[75]

This leads directly to the question of what impact "objectivity" in journalism has on our understanding of the world and on the nature of the political order—questions, briefly touched on in chapter 1, that I put aside here.

The advertisers' fear of offending potential customers leaves the media disproportionately subject to actual and threatened consumer boycotts of a particular sort—those directed at getting advertisers to avoid and thereby to suppress material offensive to some organized group.[76] After a careful study of these boycotts, Kathryn Montgomery concluded that as in the past, so in the future, "variations in program offerings will be based on the needs of advertisers, [which] is very different from the political and cultural diversity essential to a healthy democracy."[77]

These boycotts have a long history. Threatened boycotts of advertisers during the McCarthy period helped keep programs with "politically suspect" performers off the air.[78] Alcoa is legendary for standing behind Edward R. Murrow during his programs on the "See It Now" series that dealt with McCarthy and McCarthyism. Alcoa president Irving Wilson presumably wished to comfort Murrow when he said: "I wouldn't ask you not to do such programs, but I would hope you wouldn't do them every week."[79]

This tactic has recently been used by groups such as the Moral Majority and Donald Wildmon's Coalition of Christian Leaders for Responsible Television. After Wildmon's organization initiated boycotts of Pepsi, the company canceled its Madonna ad campaign as demanded.[80] After a boycott, Clorox stopped advertising on the "objectionable" programs and agreed to avoid future advertising on shows with gratuitous sex and violence.[81] Wildmon explained to his followers that they must " 'forget writing to the networks. . . . The real clout that churches have is [with] the advertisers, the sponsors.' "[82]

Of course, the technique is not the exclusive province of reactionary groups. A CIO boycott of Philco products led the company to drop sponsorship of a right-wing news commentator in 1938.[83] Between 1975 and 1977, the liberal National Citizens Committee for Broadcasting, headed in 1974 by former FCC commissioner Nicholas Johnson, along with the National Congress of Parents and Teachers, the American Medical Association, and the United Church of Christ, tried to make individual advertisers accountable for program content and applied pressure to discourage them from sponsoring violent programming.[84]

AN ASIDE: THE PROPRIETY OF BOYCOTTS

Consumer boycotts constitute democratic, expressive activity that should be fully protected by the First Amendment. I do not suggest otherwise. Although the power-generating aspect of boycotts fits only tenuously into the notion of debate implicit in traditional marketplace-of-ideas theories of the First Amendment, it is easily encompassed within a conception of the First Amendment that protects individual expressive liberties.[85] Nevertheless, three structural features of boycotts directed at advertisers as a means of influencing media content make them peculiarly disturbing from the perspective of a free and democratic press.

First, in other contexts, most boycotts try to induce their targets to adopt behavior that the government could have itself mandated. The boycott protected in *NAACP v. Claiborne Hardware Co.*[86] was designed to end racially discriminatory treatment that the government could and should have prohibited. A boycott against Nestlé was designed to pressure the company to stop distributing products (infant formula in the third world) that the government presumably could have forbidden it to distribute.[87] Likewise, the government could have required recognition of the farm workers' union and made the United Farmworkers' original boycott against grapes unnecessary,[88] just as it could regulate pesticides to obviate their more recent boycott.[89]

Of course, government action cannot substitute for boycotts. The politically creative activity of boycotting is itself both educational and self-defining expression—an appropriate response to Brandeis's warning "that the greatest menace to freedom is an inert people."[90] The persistent danger that the government will not act properly also requires that the public retain this power. Nevertheless, most boycotts aim at goals that the government could have mandated. These boycotts are less troublesome than those attempting to force people to do (or not do) that which fundamental principle prohibits the government from requiring—for example, boycotts designed to control or prevent expression. Picketing in front of a movie theater that is showing offensive, possibly "adult," films is often an attempt to stop communications (although sometimes the picketing is equally an attempt to initiate communication by raising awareness, raising the salience, of some issue purportedly distorted, stereotyped, or exploited by the film presentation). Exhibition of these movies is protected (from government interference) by the First Amendment. It is arguably anomalous to then withdraw protection and allow private groups, such as the boycotters, to stop their exhibition. Although I disagree with their reasoning, some judicial decisions support the proposition that the government can outlaw boycotts—or picketing—designed to induce illegal behavior.[91] And if the government can outlaw boycotts that are objectionable because they are designed to achieve statutorily prohibited results, it would seem analogous to permit it to outlaw boycotts that are objectionable because they are designed to limit constitutionally protected freedoms.[92] In more jurisprudential terms, if the constitutional "public/private" line were erased, it would be unconstitutional to permit any boycott aimed at the media that attempts to bring about a result which the government cannot mandate.[93]

Second, most boycotts are democratic in that their power is roughly proportional to the number of people who join them—or, at least, is related to the summation of the boycotters' buying power.[94] The target balances the injury its offending behavior causes some people, roughly measured by the damage imposed on the target by the boycott participants, against the benefit of continuing the offensive behavior, often measured by nonboycotting people's willingness to pay for the target's offending behavior. The movie house compares the gain from ticket sales with the costs imposed by those who picket or boycott. Of course, the target also has long-range strategic concerns, such as demonstrating a willingness to stand up to pressure. Still, most boycotts encourage targets to take a rough account of the activity's costs and benefits from the perspective of the public. The boycott both stimulates normative public debate and forces the target to "internalize" into its decision making some of the offensiveness of its activity. It is a form, if a rather crude form, of democratic politics.

In contrast, a consumer boycott aimed at pressuring *advertisers* to avoid being associated with certain media content magnifies the boycotters' power, arguably reducing its democratic character. First, costs and benefits are calculated only from the perspective of the advertiser, who receives only a portion of the benefit or value to the consumer of the media product. Given the small chance that an advertisement will achieve the advertiser's goals in relation to influencing any particular viewer, each alienated viewer costs the advertiser more than is gained from each viewer pleased by the programming. Each boycotter, and each nonboycotting but offended potential customer for whom the boycotter is a stand-in, is as significant to the advertiser as a large number of pleased viewers. Second, as long as most of the advertiser's gain from offensive "show X" can be obtained at a similar cost from benign "show Y," even if the controversial content of "show X" is particularly valued by its viewers, the economically rational advertiser, unable to capture this consumer surplus,* has no reason to sponsor "show X." A small number of boycotters are thus able to impose a cost on an advertiser that is greater than the small gain it could obtain by providing the "offensive" material even if the material is highly valued by a large

---

* Interestingly, advertisers' virtually reflexive tendency to avoid potentially offensive material may apply less to sellers of more sophisticated products, which have fewer, more selective buyers. For example, Xerox's television policy stated that its programs "will not only entertain [but] will tend to stretch the mind, to inspire, to stir the conscience and require thought. Our programs should try to advance TV over what it has been" (Erik Barnouw, *The Sponsor* [1978], 112). This strategy may capitalize on the "consumer surplus" of this programming, and because of its audience, these advertisers may have less to fear from boycotting activity.

audience. This dynamic systematically denies effective "voice" to audience members who desire the media product.

Thus, even if the vast majority of television viewers would like to see a program that took a controversial position, a realistically threatened boycott by a relatively small number of viewers often leads a "rational" sponsor to withdraw. After the National Rifle Association organized a letter-writing campaign directed in part at sponsors of the CBS documentary "Guns of Autumn," the only advertiser that did not withdraw sponsorship was Block Drug Company.[95] During the McCarthy era, Block Drug complied with the demands of Laurence Johnson, who threatened organized consumer pressure because of Block's sponsorship of television programs that included "politically suspect" performers. Wisdom may take longer to learn than economics. Leonard Block, now regretting having "knuckled under" in 1950,[96] boldly said " 'It doesn't pay to give in to those fellows.' "[97]

Boycotts work effectively only to restrict programming. Media solicitousness of advertisers increases the difficulty of organizing opposition to advertisers who *withdraw* sponsorship. Although furious when advertisers pull sponsorships at the last moment because some controversial program element has slipped past the network's censors, television networks recognize their dependence on advertising revenue. They have adopted the practice of not identifying sponsors who withdraw, thereby reducing the potential embarrassment to these sponsors[98] and helping them avoid the ire of those whose programming wishes are thwarted. But if this does not work, advertisers would likely become even more restrictive in their original sponsorship decisions. Conceivably, desirous viewers could boycott advertisers that fail to advertise on controversial programming or that only sponsor mindless mediocrity. Problems of organizing such a boycott would be formidable. In part because it is harder to pinpoint responsibility for nonaction (for example, for not sponsoring a program), boycotts aimed at forcing advertisers to sponsor broader coverage are hard to imagine.

From a democratic perspective that values both responsiveness and pluralism in communications, these boycotts should be troublesome in at least two ways. First, as a result of advertisers' vulnerability to pressure, the views of a comparatively small number of viewers become disproportionately influential in decisions concerning the content offered in advertiser-supported media. This process causes those who control programming content to fail to internalize the benefits of the programming. In advertising-supported media, boycotters occupy a more powerful structural position than do readers or viewers favoring particular contents.[99]

Second, the boycotts' net effect is systematically to reduce offerings, not to expand them. Kathryn Montgomery's portrayal of the wide variety of activist groups trying to affect prime-time programming suggests a pattern to their politics.[100] Sometimes, through lobbying or developing working relationships with network executives or program producers, a group effectively secures more as well as better portrayals of itself or its cause. Gays and Gray Panthers, she reports, have been particularly adroit at this politics.[101] Pressure on advertisers and use of boycotts, however, have been effective only in keeping material out. These boycotts restrict the diversity and pluralism of our informational and entertainment environment.* In addition, the boycotts are objectionable from a perspective that values individual liberty and autonomy. Social choices about the options made available to a person should not reflect others' preferences that she not have those options. Respect for liberty and autonomy in a society requires that the collective not count such preferences as a reason to restrict the person's options.[102] But counting such preferences is precisely the effect of these boycotts.

A Buying Mood: The Proper Surroundings for Ads

Advertisers want more than editorial content supportive of their products. At least in broadcasting, they also want the surrounding content to promote a frame of mind that leaves readers or viewers most open to advertising messages.[103] Thus, Du Pont "told the FCC that the corporation finds its commercials more effective on 'lighter, happier' programs."[104] Bob Shanks, an ABC-TV vice president for programming, indicated that shows should "attract mass audiences without unduly offending these audiences or too deeply moving them emotionally [because, it is thought,

---

* Sometimes this might not seem so bad. Television's exploitation of violence and sex (at least implied sex) is criticized for its mindlessness and, more importantly, its possible corrupting influence. Many who would be offended if the government censored this possibly harmful programming would be happy if popular action, such as consumer boycotts, pressured networks to restrict these presentations. Often the argument focuses on children, for whom paternalism is recognized to be legitimate. I have no clear answer to whether this concern justifies leaving broadcasters vulnerable to these boycotts. Still, even majoritarian private pressure to restrict offerings, and often this pressure is not majoritarian, should be problematic whether or not we paternalistically like the results. In a later article, I plan to recommend changes in media structure that would increase the journalistic, creative, and artistic professionals' role in controlling media content, a change that I predict would result in a net enrichment of offerings along with a potential reduction of emphasis on sex and violence.

this would] . . . interfere with their ability to receive, recall, and respond to the commercial messages."[105] Shanks continues, noting, "This programming reality is the unwritten, unspoken *gemeinschaft* among all professional members of the television fraternity." And although many react with indignation to this reality, Shanks argues that any complaints should be directed not at the advertisers but at the "complex system"; that only structural changes, some of which he recommends, would modify this situation.[106]

Examples abound. For instance, "advertising agencies were reluctant to recommend to their clients the 1980 CBS movie *Fania Fenelon*, about an Auschwitz survivor, because of the movie's 'utterly depressing nature.' "[107] Chrysler explained that it withdrew advertising from ABC's miniseries *Amerika* because "our upbeat product commercials would be both inappropriate and of diminished effectiveness in that environment."[108] This can be compared with the statement of a vice president of Coca-Cola: "It's a Coca-Cola corporate policy not to advertise on TV news because there's going to be some bad news in there and Coke is an upbeat, fun product."[109]

To the extent that the media respond to advertisers' concern with program packaging, they are guided by neither what the viewers want nor what media professionals think the public needs. Instead, advertisers pay the media to provide content the advertiser believes will leave that audience emotionally and intellectually most vulnerable to commercial messages. Erik Barnouw describes how critically acclaimed anthology television series, despite large audiences, "virtually passed out of existence" beginning in 1955 because sponsors were resistive. These programs had social implications, and their complexity made the simplicity of product commercial solutions seem frivolous or fraudulent. Moreover, characters were often too lower-class. The "commercials looked out of place in Bronx settings."[110] In contrast the newer episodic series rely on formula scripts, with the formula providing a control mechanism, taking much of the initiative away from writers who previously could produce "policy crises," and allowing the advertiser to maintain confidence that programs consistently provide the right buying mood.[111]

A "buying mood" is what the advertiser-dominated media create for grown-up "children." For the real child, the "buying mood" is created by the program star—in "program-length commercials" for children, the sponsor's toys star during the entire show. In response to pressure by groups such as Action for Children's Television, the FTC proposed to prohibit, as inherently "deceptive," all television advertising directed at very young children and to regulate a variety of other commercial practices such as program-length commercials aimed at somewhat older children. This reform was seriously deflated by fierce industry opposition.[112] Possibly even more objectionable from a policy perspective is not the direct evils of these programs but the loss of the programming they implicitly supplant. The economic advantages of these programs largely push "legitimate" children's programs off the air.[113] Thus, whatever the evils of pervasive advertising directed at children, there is an additional evil in the advertiser's effectively insisting that the ad be supported by the right surrounding material.

Although the "buying mood" phenomenon applies mainly to broadcasting, the rough equivalent is the print media's introduction of surrounding editorial content provided not so much because readers desire or would pay for it or because editors judge that it ought to be printed but because it focuses the attention of an advertiser-relevant group of readers and because its themes arguably increase these readers' interest in products the advertiser sells. If the newspaper is many people's major window on the world, it should be troublesome that the picture of that world, the newspaper's implicit statement about what subjects and concerns are important and worth considering on a daily basis, is determined by the need to provide advertisers with "an editorial ambience that enhances their advertisements' effectiveness."[114]

This structuring of the press's subject matter is arguably the most significant of all the ways that advertising controls the content of newspapers. James Curran suggests that both the size and form of English national newspapers' extensive financial sections, although read by only a small, but influential, portion of the readership, reflect newspapers' provision of an appropriate editorial environment for advertisers. Curran notes that although new ordinary share capital represented an almost de minimis portion of new capital raised in England during the 1971–1976 period, the two largest space allocations of economic news in the English national dailies were stock prices and investment news, with management news coming second, and national and international economic news trailing far behind.[115] This allocation reflects the tremendous advertising revenue from investment and job advertisers. The net result, however, is not merely a "misleading definition of the economic process," but a drastically distorted image of the economy and the public issues relating to it.[116]

More generally, even if advertisers would most like free, product-identified, affirmative support in the nonadvertising space, even "uncorrupt" publications are willing to promote the general themes or desires to which the advertisers' products allegedly respond. Newspapers create whole sections—focusing on fashions, food, travel, technology, and real estate—in a form that provides a suitable context for advertisements.[117] The vice president for sales and marketing of the *Houston Chronicle*, one of many newspapers in which the advertising department supplies all the "news" for large sections of the paper, explained: " 'We do nothing controversial. . . . Our only concern is giving editorial support to our ad projects.' "[118] Bagdikian notes that despite surveys indicating readers' desire for more hard news, the major trend among newspapers has been toward more "fluff," which is desired by advertisers to support interest in their products. He cites a prominent editor's warning that "newspapers would eventually sink under the weight of . . . 'Revenue Related Reading Matter.' "[119]

It would be comforting to assume that the need to support a buying mood, even if it influences entertainment, stays out of the newsroom. Of course, some incursions are obvious. News programs end with an ironic comment, accompanied by an endearing smile, from the newscaster, and the explanation is straightforward—create the right mood. Edward Epstein reported that CBS's decision generally to devote the last five minutes of its news program to "back-of-the-book" material reflected a compromise with network sales executives who sought a concluding "sports package" in order to satisfy an auto manufacturer's desire to advertise in a sports or soft news segment.[120] Moreover, advertising dollars, independent of either audience preferences or journalistic judgments, influence the initial decision of whether to present news or entertainment programming, as Fred Friendly dramatically underlined by resigning in response to CBS's decision to show reruns of "I Love Lucy" rather than a live telecast of the Senate's Vietnam War hearings.[121]

More disturbingly, America's attack on Iraq in 1991 produced unusually explicit indications of advertisers' impact on news content. Beginning with the intensive coverage of the aerial bombing of Iraq, many companies decided to avoid advertising during war programming.[122] One advertising executive explained about ads during war news: "I just think it's wasted money. . . . Commercials need to be seen in the right environment. A war is just not an upbeat environment."[123] This advertising pullout produced serious financial problems at each network.[124]

CBS executives admitted a willingness to allow advertisers' response to affect programming decisions. Even though its war specials all received higher ratings than other channels' entertainment shows, thereby indicating that viewers wanted this broadcasting, the low ad sales on war programming "[made] them economically unfeasible for the network."[125] As a result, fewer prime-time war specials were shown. The CBS executive explained that "in fairness to our shareholders" CBS could not afford the million-dollar-plus loss that resulted from each prime-time news special on the war.[126] Most troubling, however, is the possibility that pandering to advertisers' concerns will distort news content. Since advertisers demand upbeat surroundings for their ads, CBS offered to tailor war specials "to provide better lead-ins to commercials . . . [and] to insert the commercials after segments that were specially produced with upbeat images or messages about the war, like patriotic views from the home front."[127] A happy war brought to you by your sponsor!

CONTENT TAILORED FOR THE "RIGHT" AUDIENCE

Democracies always distribute some goods on a more egalitarian basis than the market system's criterion of willingness and ability to pay.[128] Most modern democracies at least "formally" distribute political authority on a one-person-one-vote basis rather than the market system's one-dollar-one-vote. Likewise, most democracies consider certain goods—education, food, medical care, and housing, for instance—too important to allow anyone to do without. The close relation of a free press, protected by the First Amendment, to democratic processes suggests that access to news and information,[129] like the right to vote, ought to be distributed on an egalitarian basis. Everyone should be able to receive the news, information, and other products of the mass media that they find helpful in their lives. Public free libraries represent a small attempt to move in an egalitarian direction.

The assumption that advertising results in lower prices and, hence, widespread availability of mass media designed for the population as a whole might imply that advertising serves this democratic goal. Nevertheless, advertising often has the exact opposite effect. Although advertising influences the distribution of media content in multiple, crosscutting ways, one tendency is to make that distribution even less egalitarian than it would otherwise be. Advertising also makes the media even less responsive to the needs of the poor and other marginalized groups than would a market system in which people paid the full costs of the product.

Advertisers "pay" the media to obtain the audience they desire, providing a strong incentive for the media to shape content to appeal to this "desired" audience. The right audiences are crucial for television. "Gunsmoke" is probably the most frequently cited show canceled while still high in the ratings. The same apparently happened to the "The Virginian."[130] The shows' viewers were simply too old and too rural to be worth much to advertisers.[131]

Similar pressures operate in the print media. Bagdikian describes how in 1967 the *New Yorker* suddenly began to lose advertisers and money.[132] Although there was no drop in circulation, readers' average age dropped from 48.7 to 34 years as young people responded to the *New Yorker's* critical coverage of the war in Vietnam.[133] These young people were simply the wrong readers. Bagdikian postulated that only unusual ownership conditions permitted this economically unwise reporting, with changes eventually leading the magazine to pursue the "right" audience again.[134]

Since newspapers and magazines generally sell for less than the cost of production, they lose money unless they can sell the reader to the advertiser. Thus, it should not be surprising that newspapers sometimes purposefully limit or reduce circulation in areas or among groups that advertisers do not value. The *Times* (London) "twice increased circulation only to find advertisers were uninterested in reaching the students and lower income intellectuals who made up the bulk of the new readers."[135] In order to stem this massive loss caused by having gained the wrong sort of readers (too poor, too working-class), the *Times's* (London) management in the early 1970s adopted a conscious policy of shedding part of the impressive 69% circulation gain it had obtained between 1965 and 1969.[136]

In the United States, a 1979 industry report commented: "One universal element of all our circulation marketing strategies is to increase penetration in target demographic areas, say households earning above $20,000 per year."[137] In 1991, the American Newspaper Publishers Association's Competitive Analysis Project Task Force reported that of four strategic options it considered for the newspaper industry, the 'Class Appeal' approach, which would involve raising circulation rates and improving demographics of its readers, would generate the highest profits and operating income.[138] It noted the *Toronto Globe and Mail*, which "abolished its city desk and refocused coverage on business, international and national news," with the result that circulation dropped but ad revenue increased 9% for the year.[139] The U.S. Commerce Department's 1991 annual industrial forecast suggested that "to meet the changing needs of advertisers, some [American newspaper] publishers may take the route of several prominent papers and cut their circulation base to get rid of circulation that is not considered valuable to advertisers."[140] And even if this restriction of circulation based on demographics is most evident in newspapers, a major study of American magazine publishing similarly predicts that a future result of advertiser-induced targeting by magazines is "that entire neighborhoods will be eliminated as publishers and advertisers zero in on the most affluent markets."[141]

Otis Chandler, head of Times Mirror, explained that "the target audience of the [*Los Angeles*] *Times* is . . . in the middle class and . . . the upper class"; elsewhere he said that the *L.A. Times* had "arbitrarily cut back some of [its] low-income circulation," because "American newspaper publishing is based on an advertising base, not a circulation base."[142] Chandler noted that giving more attention to minority issues "would not make sense financially . . . [because] that audience does not have the purchasing power and is not responsive to the kind of advertising we carry."[143] Until after the 1992 riots (when change purportedly occurred in response to civic consciousness, not profit-maximizing strategy), inner-city Los Angeles was "the only part of the *Times'* circulation area without its own special section."[144] In 1981, *Editor and Publisher* quoted a *New York Times* marketing executive's assertion: " 'We make no effort to sell to the mob.' "[145] In a 1987 interview, William Randolph Hearst III, publisher of the *San Francisco Examiner*, explained that his paper aimed " 'at people who are desired by advertisers, mainly in terms of purchasing power.' "[146] Given a newspaper world dominated by advertisers, pursuing a circulation increase without thought about its character is an economic mistake.

This tilt is hardly egalitarian. Newspaper and broadcasting advertisers are comparatively disinterested in media production designed to satisfy the needs or preferences of anyone without the disposable income that advertisers covet. In a 1960 study of national daily newspapers in Britain, the advertising rate (the rate per column inch per thousand copies sold) of "quality" papers was roughly four times the rate of the popular papers.[147] This study reported an advertising surplus (i.e., the amount of advertising revenue not spent on obtaining and publishing the advertisements and hence available to subsidize editorial content or to go to profits) per copy of a halfpenny for the popular papers and fivepence for the quality papers.[148] A 1973 British study showed similarly that the popular dailies received an advertising surplus per thousand copies of two pounds while the quality dailies received an advertising surplus of nineteen pounds per thousand.[149] This point was pressed home on the *New York Post* when, at a time in the early 1980s when its circulation exceeded that of the *New York Times*, it sought an advertising account from Bloomingdale's. In rejecting the request, Bloomingdale's reportedly explained: " '[The *Times*] readers are our customers; your readers are our shoplifters.' "[150] In other words, advertisers pay much more of the newspaper's cost when, as is the case with the "quality" papers, the paper's content appeals to the "right" audience.

The result is that advertising subsidizes newspapers designed for precisely the people most able to pay without a subsidy.[151] It subsidizes news designed for the affluent, not the poor.

Purported deregulatory, "Pollyannish" implications of economic theory should be viewed with suspicion; but here, economic theory clearly predicts that an "unregulated" market will produce social results that are widely and properly condemned. A subsidy normally promotes consumption of the subsidized good. Subsidizing products made for a particular group should result, generally, in benefiting that group and, more specifically, in making that group relatively greater users (purchasers) of that product. Thus, the advertising "subsidy" slants press content toward the interests of the more affluent and predictably leads to increased newspaper purchases by this group.

Not only does the search for the right consumer lead to a direct molding of content to appeal to that consumer; as William Blankenburg has argued, "circulation policy is a form of editorial policy, and withheld circulation is akin to suppressed information." He further explained, "The trouble with expelled subscribers, whether they meet marketing standards or not, is that they are citizens."[152] If, as studies report,[153] media usage promotes political involvement, particularly among those to whose political interests the media respond, and if, as economic analysis predicts, advertising leads the media to be oriented toward the more affluent, then the advertising-supported media should stimulate political participation primarily among the comparatively affluent. Thus, advertising's subsidy not only distributes news in an even less egalitarian manner than would a market system where readers pay the full costs of the paper, but it also quite likely depresses the comparative political participation of the poor.

.   .   .   .   .

Advertising is only one factor determining the content of mass media. Reader or viewer preferences, levels of competition and ownership concentration, preferences and interests of owners, press traditions and professional norms (which are presumably "partially" autonomous, that is, only partly reflective of the economic and legal structure), values and backgrounds of press professionals, government pressures and subsidies, technology and organizational dynamics are among the other determinants. Nevertheless, if for no other reason than that it pays much of the bill, advertising plays a major, systematic role that pushes the mass media in readily predictable and observable directions. First, advertising disfavors media accounts of inadequacies or dangers of advertisers' products, exposés of wrongdoing by advertisers, and serious critiques of those aspects of the social world on which advertisers depend. Advertisers generally favor a view of most societal problems as nonsystemic and resolvable by good-faith individual initiative just as they favor viewing individual concerns as solvable by appropriate product consumption. Second, since advertisers wish (with the caveat mentioned in my fourth point below) both to reach a maximum audience and to avoid offending any potential purchaser, advertising encourages the media to forgo taking partisan positions on controversial issues. Advertising is fully supportive of the objective stance—and of "balance." Third, since critical thought or attention focused on serious social problems is believed to undermine a buying mood, advertising often favors lighter material. Fourth, advertising systematically causes the media to adopt the perspectives and to serve the informational and entertainment needs of the comparatively affluent.

Each of these four systematic effects of advertising represents a profoundly troubling failure from a democratic perspective. Exposure of major wrongdoing and of dangerous conditions (and products), a willingness to lead partisan crusades for change, media content that educates about and inspires people to confront major issues, and content presented in a manner that responds equally to the needs and concerns of diverse readers/viewers are qualities that should characterize a democratic press. But these are precisely the qualities that advertising undermines. Any program aimed at a more effective, more egalitarian, more participatory political and social order must consider whether the media structure that produces these negative consequences can be usefully changed without inhibiting or stifling the positive effects of advertising in a free press.

Chapter 4 will propose and evaluate legal changes that respond to the negative effects of advertising. First, however, a detour will be helpful. Despite the specific criticisms of advertising, media output reflects the decisions of various "purchasers" who pay in a free market to obtain results they prefer. Free markets are often thought to lead to "efficient," socially desirable results. Therefore, chapter 3 will subject my criticisms of advertising's influence to an economic evaluation.

Economic Analysis of Advertising's Effect
on the Media

T HE INFLUENCE of advertising on the media's nonadvertising content described in chapters 1 and 2 should be very disturbing. Most readers either will rationalize the first two chapters as presenting only isolated problems with a larger institution that is fundamentally sound or will agree that something is terribly wrong with our press. However, a few doctrinaire free market advocates may be more defensive, arguing that advertisers' influence is actually not bad at all. Readers who find their claim absurd or who do not find economic analysis appealing (although technical language is largely avoided) may choose to skip this chapter. Nevertheless, this doctrinaire claim requires some response.

These free marketeers assert that an unregulated market, which encompasses purchases by advertisers, leads to optimal outcomes.[1] They admit that most consumers would prefer that advertisers had less influence on the mass media. But according to their analysis, the relevant question is what trade-off media consumers would willingly make to reduce this influence. If the relevant datum is current purchases, the analysis may seem circular. Still, this evidence shows that media consumers' are unwilling to pay enough to make an "independent" media prevalent. Apparently, media consumers prefer a world in which advertisers pay much of the cost of media products. Advertisers provide the media consumer with both advertisements, which the consumer can ignore but often desires as a source of information, and cheaper, somewhat advertiser-influenced media products, thereby making the media more widely accessible. The market combines preferences of readers, viewers, and advertisers to produce welfare-maximizing (or, at least, "efficient") results preferable to anything that would result from regulation.

The free marketeer's claim depends, however, on crucial empirical and normative assumptions. First, the claim requires that the market brings the positive and negative effects of media production fully to bear on media decision-makers. Second, it depends on the propriety of relying on preferences as expressed by willingness- and ability-to-pay to determine media production and distribution.* In economic terms, the free marketeer's claim assumes that the media market leads to "efficient" results and that "efficiency" is a proper goal of production and distribution. This chapter describes some reasons why, in relation to the effects of advertising,[2] neither assumption is correct.

Note, however, that this chapter considers only questions concerning the "efficiency" of advertising's effect on nonadvertising media content. Ubiquitous questions concern whether advertising itself is efficient and whether efficiency is the correct criterion with which to evaluate routine advertising. For example, does advertising benefit the economy by stimulating demand and improving allocation, or are resources wasted on an "unproductive" activity? Some argue that too much advertising results because tax laws treat advertising as a current business expense rather than a capital expense (i.e., as an investment that creates depreciable "good will"), with the consequence of a comparative overinvestment in advertising as compared to productivity-related investments (e.g., on plant and equipment). Does advertising provide consumers with useful information or stimulate misguided consumerist values? Since economic analyses' efficiency-premised defense of the market typically presumes to accept an existing set of preferences as the "given," some argue that efficiency analyses cannot provide a proper basis to evaluate advertising since advertising plays the more political role of creating preferences, which then provide the foundation for both actual markets and theoretical efficiency analyses. In any event, these issues concerning the merit or efficiency of advertising itself are not addressed here.

MARKET FAILURES

The Decline of Competition

Chapter 1 showed that the success of a largely advertiser-supported newspaper may put competitive differentiated, reader-supported papers out of business. (I use the terms "advertiser-supported" and "reader-supported" in a comparative sense, referring to papers that receive a comparatively high portion of support from that source.) As the advertising "subsidy"

---

* The free marketeers could also defend this claim on the ground not that these assumptions are true but that they are close enough, and that any alternative to the free market would be worse. This version of the claim can be assessed only empirically and comparatively. An analyst would have to evaluate each proposed deviation from the "free market" to determine whether it should or should not be expected to improve media performance. Within the limits of insufficient information, chapter 4 engages in that inquiry.

makes the advertising-supported paper cheaper to the reader, some readers desert their preferred, more narrowly focused, "differentiated" papers. In economic terms, the advertising-supported paper's entry into competition causes a leftward shift in the demand curve for the differentiated, reader-supported papers. This leftward shift could result in the downward-sloping average cost curve's being constantly above, no longer crossing, these papers' demand curves. When this occurs, the advertising-supported paper's entry would cause the failure of the competing, differentiated papers.[3] The question is whether this result can be criticized on economic grounds: whether the new competitive equilibrium is or is not "efficient."

The question cannot be answered abstractly, and there is insufficient empirical information for a clear-cut answer. The answer depends on the shape of the respective paper's demand (and cost) curves, or, more specifically, on the consumer surplus obtained by their readers.[4] If the differentiated, reader-supported papers had much more steeply declining demand curves than the surviving, advertiser-supported paper—that is, if the reader-supported papers produced much larger consumer surpluses—then the social value produced by the competitive winner, the advertiser-supported paper, will likely be less than the value produced by the failed, reader-supported papers.

This conclusion that the competitive winner may not be socially optimal can be seen in various ways. Consider the following argument:

1. Without price discrimination, a declining marginal cost industry (or firm) may not be viable even though it would be profitable (and efficient) with price discrimination. That is, its demand curve may be constantly below the average cost curve, with the result that there is no price at which sales would cover costs; still, the "consumer surplus" on sales at some prices will be greater than the firm's loss on sales at that price.

2. The introduction of new product B can cause a downward (leftward) shift in demand for product A because some previous purchasers of A now prefer B at the price at which B is offered.

3. The downward shift in demand for product A caused by the introduction of product B can cause the producer of A to change from being a viable natural monopoly—that is, a firm whose demand curve does cross the average cost curve—to a firm like the one described in (1) above that is not economically viable (without price discrimination).

4. Depending on the nature of the demand for products A and B—that is, depending on the extent of consumer surplus each produces—the introduction of A could cause a net decline in social welfare (efficiency).

The following table illustrates the above numerically.

	Paper A				Paper B	
	costs	d1	d2		costs	d2
copy 1	20	22	19	c1	16	14
copy 2	5	21	12	c2	11	15

where, for Paper A, d1 is the willingness to pay for Paper A at Time 1 (that is, if Paper B does not exist), and d2 is willingness to pay for Paper A at Time 2 (that is, after the introduction of Paper B at a selling price of 14 cents).

The example embodies the assumption that the readers of Paper A would pay more for it if there were not the alternative of buying Paper B for 14 cents. The example assumes much higher first-copy costs for Paper A, possibly suggesting lots of investigative reporting but relatively small size of final paper as compared to Paper B, which may use many inexpensive features requiring considerable space (ink and newsprint).

Stories can easily be constructed to explain each reader's demand under the alternative conditions. For example, the first reader highly values the news gathered by Paper A, but is slightly less willing to pay for it if a cheap alternative paper is offered. The second reader values newspapers somewhat less but much prefers the features in Paper B to the hard news in Paper A.

On the crucial assumption that price discrimination is impossible so that the paper can be sold only for a single price, Paper A is clearly viable if Paper B does not exist (with two readers, its average cost is 12.5 cents and the readers will pay up to 21 cents each), but is not viable once Paper B is introduced (the first reader would not pay the cost of 20 cents and the second reader would not even buy at the lower average cost of 12.5 cents). "Surplus" is the amount that value, measured by willingness to pay, exceeds the costs of producing and distributing the product. Without Paper B, Paper A sells to both readers (under demand condition d1) and produces a surplus of 18, that is, value minus costs, $(22 + 21) - (20 + 5) = 18$. With the introduction of Paper B only Paper B survives, and it produces a surplus of 2, that is, $(15 + 14) - (16 + 11) = 2$. Thus, as compared to Time 1 before Paper 2 was introduced and prevailed competitively, the equilibrium free market position uses more resources (27 compared to 25) to produce less value (29 compared to 43), thereby producing less surplus (2 compared to 18). The competitive equilibrium clearly is not "efficient" or "welfare-maximizing."

This example of how competition can result in inefficiency assumes that, in this monopolistic competition,[5] firms are not able to effectively price-discriminate. To a significant degree,* the assumption seems true for daily newspapers.[6] Of course, if each paper could perfectly price-discriminate, and if the demise of the reader-supported papers would have been inefficient,[7] then the reader-supported papers could survive even after the introduction of the advertising-supported paper.

Without more empirical information, the most efficient arrangement cannot be identified with certainty. Some factors, however, point in favor of the differentiated, reader-supported papers. Differentiated papers rely most heavily on fulfilling readers' special interests instead of being aimed at some lowest common denominator. Thus, each of the differentiated papers could be expected to be highly valued by the comparatively small, discrete group at which it aims—that is, a relatively steeply declining demand curve could be expected. In contrast, the advertiser-supported paper is less oriented toward fulfilling any focused desire for its content. Rather it tries to make a product acceptable to a wide range of readers and to obtain these readers by its comparative cheapness. Fewer people are likely to value this advertiser-supported paper much more than they pay for it— that is, it is likely to have a *comparatively* flat demand curve. These predictions concerning the nature of the demand for different newspapers support the claim that if the advertiser-supported paper prevails competitively over otherwise viable reader-supported papers, this competitive outcome will cause a net loss of social value as measured by people's willingness to pay—that is, a net loss of consumer surplus.†

* Newspapers engage in some, but relatively limited, price discrimination. For example, by devoting circulation promotions to affluent areas, papers price-discriminate by charging less interested affluent readers less than other readers.

† Except for the book cited in the next paragraph considering video media, which have somewhat different characteristics from the newspaper market, I have found no discussion in media economics of either the possibility that advertising could reduce competition or the notion that this could result in inefficiency, that is, a welfare decline. However, in a more general, very mathematical discussion, Clement G. Krouse demonstrates that in monopolistic competition, assuming no price discrimination (which was my assumption above), the equilibrium position could involve either an under-, over-, or appropriate supply of product diversity (*Theory of Industrial Economics* [1990], 190–218).

Krouse shows that whether there will be too little (or too much) diversity will depend on the specific nature of people's demand curves and producers' supply curves. In a summary passage, he concludes: "A firm offering a new product gives consideration to the net revenues that will be created, not the amount of consumer surplus. This tends to produce *too little product variety*" (214; emphasis added). For example, the reader-supported papers, which I argued would have the steepest demand curves and hence the greatest proportionate consumer surplus, would not consider this consumer surplus and, therefore, would be less likely to be introduced (or continue); this would lead to too little product variety.

Krouse continues: "Against this, the firm gives no consideration to the external effect that

Although this newspaper example suffices to make the relevant economic point, analogous conclusions could be reached through comparison of ad-supported and viewer-supported broadcasting. Using a somewhat different methodology, Bruce Owen and Steven Wildman reached conclusions very similar to those offered here. According to their analysis of program offering under different competitive conditions, the biases "against programs that cater to minority tastes, against expensive programs, and in favor of programs that produce large audiences . . . are less pronounced for pay television [than for advertiser-supported television], because the intensity of viewers' preferences is reflected in the prices they pay." Owen and Wildman observe, however, that "from a social welfare perspective, there is no unambiguous ranking of alternative ways to organize the television industry."[8] But they also showed that as preference for diversity increases, the welfare-preferred outcome is increasingly likely to be a viewer-supported industry.[9] However, since preferences are partly a product of the programming system that exists, and since the given industrial structure will produce one set of programming rather than another, Owen and Wildman's analysis has reached the point at which practical reasoning and policy choices must go beyond economics.

Advertiser Distortions of Content

Journalistic purists will object to *any* advertiser influence over nonadvertising content—to any violation of the media's wall of separation between church and state. Surely, many people object to the advertiser influence over the content of news and entertainment described in chapter 2, to advertiser-induced bias in favor of corporate products and values, to the design of programming to stimulate buying moods rather than critical thought, and to the middle-of-the-road avoidance of offense and partisan advocacy.

The free marketeer responds that both advertisers and media consumers engage in transactions with media producers. Both purchasers, the consumer and the advertiser, have an opportunity to pay for the content they

---

its entry has on the demand for substitute products offered by existing firms, an effect which tends to produce too much variety." Assuming that the advertising-supported firm has the largest effect on demand functions for other firms, the advertising-supported paper will tend to be the variety not justified by welfare criteria, even though market-supported. In other words, competition tends toward introduction of advertising-supported media that are not optimal and that tend to drive out of existence diverse, reader-supported varieties that are socially optimal.

prefer. (In the case of broadcasting, the consumer "pays," that is, indirectly brings her preferences to bear, by choosing whether to watch and what programs to watch.) Grant that most consumers prefer a product uninfluenced by advertiser interests. The question is whether they desire the "pure" product enough to pay for it or, alternatively, they prefer the "influenced" content at the lower price. The free marketeer emphasizes that this question cannot be answered abstractly, but argues that the market does provide an answer—the right answer, given people's preferences. If people purchase advertiser-influenced media content, as they do, their purchase says that that is what they want, given the products' cost and the cost of its alternatives.

This analysis does not hold up. First, as newspaper publishers know, most readers or viewers do want media content untainted by advertiser influence. Being known to slant news in favor of advertisers injures a newspaper's reputation and its ability to sell its product (at a given price). Chapter 2 described how many of the more successful media owners at the turn of the century reached precisely this conclusion. Increasingly, these owners publicly opposed the practice of accepting "reading notices"—advertisements disguised as news. Most media enterprises attempt to maintain the public's belief that they live up to the fundamental professional norm of separating the enterprise's business side (advertising) from its journalistic or creative side. Apparently these firms conclude that the public would pay more for purity than advertisers would pay for influence. Media enterprises typically try to cover up or minimize any advertiser influence that does occur. At least since the muckrakers' revelations of journalistic integrity's being for sale,[10] exposés of advertisers' influence on the media have been news items—to be publicized in *Columbia Journalism Review*, books of media criticism, and sometimes other newspapers or magazines. The damage an exposé can cause an offending enterprise illustrates the high value placed by the public (and the profession) on media purity.

Even if a media enterprise concludes that it is better off being "pure" than being *known* to be influenced, it will be tempted to try to sell both influence and (false) purity—to sell influence to advertisers without letting the reader know. Since no reader can know all the judgments figuring into the decisions about what news or entertainment to offer, constant opportunities arise for the media enterprise to secretly allow advertiser influence. Advertiser influence can become so embedded in journalistic routine that even media personnel are unaware of it—although advertisers continue to reward the media enterprise for their compromises. The public's demands for objectivity, even if misplaced, may illustrate the public's concern for a product untainted by hidden considerations. Many in the public would be offended by journalists who were influenced, even unconsciously influenced, by advertisers and, if they could, would pay some amount to avoid such bias. (This result is what, for example, subscribers to the ad-less *Ms.* pay for. However, arguably this solution requires them to pay "too much" in the sense that they are charged both the price of doing without advertiser influence, which is presumably what they want to purchase, and the price of doing without the ads themselves.)

There is even a word for consciously selling influence to the advertiser and simultaneously selling purity to the consumer. Fraud. The media purport to give the reader an untainted product under circumstances in which it is difficult for the reader to identify the deception. All the standard economic reasons why fraud should be prohibited apply here.[11] The media enterprise "externalizes" harm onto readers who, because of lack of knowledge, cannot "efficiently" bring the economic "injury" to bear on the media enterprise's decision making. The reader's only recourse is to gather information about advertiser influence and then engage in joint action with all the other injured parties against the offending media enterprise.* Cultural practices—for example, the development and spread of reputation—can partially serve the policing function. Still, effective information gathering and collective action are usually just too expensive to be an effective deterrent.

There is a second aspect of this market failure. Advertisers' influence on media content affects third parties beyond the immediate readers. In a world where we are all interdependent—which is a fairly good general description of the human condition but is virtually the definition of the political sphere—what others think affects us all. One person can benefit if other people's views about war, welfare, nuclear power, the economy, honesty, land use, consumerism, ethnicity, tobacco, politeness, and the like are influenced by journalists' and writers' honest attempts to make sense of the world rather than being manipulated by advertisers. Even the person who does not use a particular medium might be willing to pay to

---

* Another way a paper externalizes the harm of advertisers' influence, thereby avoiding taking into account the full consequences of its action and avoiding pressures to act "efficiently," is to externalize the harm onto a "commons"—the public's general perception of the media. Public perceptions of the media's integrity are partially generic. If it is exposed that advertisers influenced a particular paper, some of the public will remember the fact of advertisers' influence on the media without recalling which paper acted improperly. Even those who connect the right paper with the "impropriety" will often assume (probably properly assume) that the impropriety illustrates a more pervasive problem that does, or could, involve other papers.

have it untainted by advertising. However, no market efficiently brings these third-party "preferences" to bear on media enterprises' decisions. In the absence of such a market mechanism (or an alternative, effective cultural mechanism), the enterprise will fail to take into account a real cost of advertiser influence, thereby "externalizing" this cost and producing an injurious "inefficiency."

INAPPROPRIATENESS OF THE EFFICIENCY STANDARD

The efficiency criterion, as generally defined in economic models, must take as given some distribution of wealth and some set of preferences. In fact, this is the central theoretical reason economic analysis is inherently indeterminate in its "law and economics" applications. "Law and economics" analyses attempt to identify the legal rule or legal outcome that is most efficient or most efficiency-promoting. In this analysis, the efficient outcome depends on a given distribution of wealth. The choice of law, however, partly determines the distribution of wealth—hence there is no "given" distribution on which to rely in deciding which law to favor.[12] Similarly, the choice of law can often be expected systematically to affect preferences, leading to a second cause of indeterminacy. The preferences favored by one choice of law would make that choice efficient, but the preferences encouraged by an alternative choice would make the corresponding, alternative law preferable. Economic theory has no internal basis for concluding whether preferences existing at the time of the choice of the law or those preferences influenced by the law provide the appropriate evaluative standpoint.[13]

Usually the efficiency analyses, and certainly the "free market" analyses, take existing distributions of wealth and existing preferences as "given." Thus, these analyses are inappropriate anytime these existing distributions and preferences are not properly accepted as the given. Most obviously, these analyses are inappropriate when the relative desirability of different distributions and various preferences (or values) is at issue. These contexts require other evaluative standards. The most defensible candidate for at least part of the evaluative work may be a one-person-one-vote dialogic politics.[14]

Evaluations of advertising's effect on media content and media distribution should turn on answers to questions that are logically prior to, and that strive to be independent of, the existing distributions of preferences and wealth. An appropriate evaluation asks, first, how egalitarian should the distribution of news, information, and culture be? Second, it asks, under what circumstances will the content of media properly serve people in their development of values and preferences?

Media usage is a form of entertainment—a form of consumption. But it is often something more. The mass media can serve as an important educational force. The press is probably the primary source of current political knowledge and a locus of political debate. Unsurprisingly, a "free" press, not just an entertaining press, is widely seen as an essential element of democracy. These uncontroversial observations suggest that the distribution of the vote and of education provide the most obvious analogies for the assessment of the proper distribution of media content. Further considerations reinforce this conclusion.

An ideal democracy depends, among other things, on citizens' being adequately informed. Therefore, a commitment to democracy strongly supports treating media content as a "merit good" to which all citizens should have access, at least access to some reasonable amount. Arguments for "cultural democracy" support the same conclusion. As is true of the right to vote, and arguably of such goods as food, shelter, medical care, and especially free public education, people have a rightful claim to access to the media whether or not they have the resources necessary to pay for access in the market. Thus, liberal democratic theory suggests that even a properly functioning market, as long as that market coexists with a very inegalitarian distribution of wealth, is deficient here. Democratic theory calls instead for a comparatively more equal distribution of media content.

Even if a market is inadequately egalitarian, to the extent that advertising reduces the cost of media content to the consumer, advertising serves this democratic goal. But as was shown in the last section of chapter 2, advertising primarily subsidizes media content most desired by the relatively more affluent. To the extent that there is no divergence between the media content desired and needed by the rich and the poor, the poor can "free ride" on the subsidy. But to the extent that there is a divergence, the poor are comparatively disadvantaged. As illustrated in chapter 1, advertising can even cause the cost of media desired by poorer people to go up or its availability to go down. These distributive effects of the "free market" are perverse. From the perspective of democracy, which is the proper perspective from which to evaluate most distributional questions, the market fails.

Second, markets aim at satisfying people's, including advertisers', existing preferences. This objective is inappropriate for determining the media content that people need in order to properly develop values and preferences. Education, much of religious inquiry, and authentic politics involve people engaged in value formation. People transform the information and perspectives they receive into values and preferences. Media content plays a major role in this process, and people value media to a significant degree because of that role. In performing this role properly, the media should give people not merely what they knowingly want to hear or see, or what advertiser-dominated, market-oriented media find most profitable to give them. What people "want," or ought to want, in journalists and editors is what they want, or ought to want, in educators, priests, and politicians: practitioners who exhibit, first, integrity and, second, wisdom and judgment in their communications. People's immediate "preference" may be to kill the messenger who brings bad news. Too often the market defers to such preferences.* Still, frequently people also expect, and in some sense want, journalistic professionals to provide even the bad news. Politics and preference formation are corrupted if the utility companies pay to control news about nuclear power or if General Electric controls our information on weapons programs and defense needs.[15] Given the media's role in value or preference formation, they should not merely reflect market-expressed preferences or, even worse, market-dictated enterprise interests. Rather, like education and politics, the media should be structured to embody and encourage processes of value or preference formation that are congruent with our images of what it means to be a wise person and a democratic society. This conclusion, however, lives in tension with our practice of leaving the media mostly subject to the market—and even more so with the view that being so subject is what freedom of the press means. Albert Camus gave a much better, even if somewhat utopian, interpretation of freedom of the press when he wrote: "The press is not an instrument of commercial profit; it is an instrument of culture. Its purpose is to give accurate information, to defend ideas, to serve the cause of human pro-

---

* In explaining "CBS Evening News"'s recasting of its coverage of Reagan and Reaganomics in 1982–1983, Mark Hertsgaard describes a changed management more focused on the bottom line. According to "Evening News" producer Richard Cohen, the new management "had a view of what kind of news made for good ratings: more features, make it light and bright, soften it up. Don't be negative about the President, people don't want to hear that." (Certainly it does not induce a "buying mood.") One reason for the shift in the coverage of the president was "a belief that upbeat, positive, 'patriotic' reporting about the President would make people feel good and thus produce higher ratings." CBS's coverage demonstrated that it did not want to be the bearer of the bad news about our president (Hertsgaard, *On Bended Knee*, 163, 170).

gress. . . . The press is free when it does not depend on either the power of government or the power of money, but only upon the conscience of its journalists and readers."[16]

．　．　．　．　．

However viewed, advertising's influence on media content is objectionable. First, such influence predictably leads to market failures, frustrating the "efficient" creation and distribution of media content. Even a doctrinaire free marketeer cannot defend this result. Second, the norms underlying our democracy suggest that market considerations should not determine either media content or distribution. Advertising's influence on media content exacerbates the distributive and preference-formation problems associated with the market. Of course, this criticism of a (partially) unregulated market does not imply the existence of better alternatives. But it does suggest the wisdom of looking.

Policy Proposals

Convinced that advertising results in censorship, skews content, contributes to inequality, and impairs media competition, one might propose banning advertising in the media. Such a move would be as undesirable as it is untenable. The proposal ignores the significant positive contributions of advertising in the media, the two most important being advertising's financial support of media communications and advertising's provision of useful information that media consumers desire. Nevertheless, targeted policies that reduce specific objectionable effects of advertising may provide net social benefits even if these policies also marginally reduce its positive contributions.

Governmental responses to the problem can take one of several tacks. Structural proposals can attempt to reduce advertising's leverage over the press. Alternatively, the policy could be to increase the comparative influence of forces other than advertising. Or regulations could attempt to reinforce appropriate barriers between the media enterprise's commercial and editorial sides. But before discussing specific regulatory and tax proposals relating to advertising, I should note several difficult-to-evaluate, but troublesome, potential effects of any regulation or tax of advertising.

First, any tax or other regulation of advertising will raise its price. This will predictably lead to some decline in advertising and cause some shift of advertising expenditures to advertising media not subject to the new tax or regulation. Policy evaluation of these changes (from the perspective of promoting a democratic press) will be equivocal.[1] For the goal of reducing advertising's influence on the media, the change is a plus; but for the goal of financing media production, it is a minus. The more any proposal reduces advertising's influence without reducing its subsidy, the better. Other considerations can also affect the preferred design of a tax or regulation. For example, there would be less shift of advertising to other media, such as direct mail, billboards, and point-of-purchase promotion,[2] if the tax or regulation of advertising applied to advertising in these media too. For most policy proposals described in this chapter, which recognizes value in "subsidy" of the media, a broader tax on all advertising would be preferable to a tax on newspaper advertising alone.

Second, local advertising revenues provide a major incentive for a newspaper or broadcaster to be local rather than national—although increased ease of producing zoned or even individualized editions of national or regional media may reduce this incentive. (The variation in the zoned editions may consist entirely in different advertising or may also provide extensive zoned editorial content.) Since 1939, when national advertising was 19.2% of newspaper ad revenue, national advertising has never constituted more than 25% of total newspaper advertising; in the 1970s and 1980s, newspapers received about 85% of their advertising revenues from local advertising, 88% in 1988.[3] Thus, a tax on advertising could reduce support of localism. Alternatively, under some conditions, reducing advertising's influence encourages a more politically oriented localism. Bagdikian suggests that the sixfold decline from about 1.2 daily newspapers for each urban area in 1900 to 0.2 papers for each urban area in 1980 reflects in part newspapers' following the new regional advertisers of the shopping centers, creating regional papers, rather than ones that conformed to political boundaries.[4] A reduction of advertising's influence and the corresponding increase in readers' influence could create incentives for either new papers or editorially zoned editions that respond to, or generate, public interest in local news and politics.[5] In any event, in a country where important elements of politics are local and where newspapers provide the primary source of local news, information, and investigation, any decline in local papers is troublesome.

Exempting classified ads placed by individuals (in contrast to those of commercial enterprises—for example, auto dealerships) from a tax scheme might alleviate this reduced support of localism.[6] Classified ads are apparently very profitable to papers and account for a sizable portion of daily newspapers' advertising revenues—29% in 1980 and 37% in 1988.[7] Their typically local orientation encourages papers' localism. Moreover, the large number and diversity of classified advertisers reduces the likelihood that they will often have the power and organization necessary to apply pressure on a paper's content or editorial choices.[8] Finally, the classified ad is probably the best example of an advertisement that provides not only information, but information sought by the readers who make use of the ad—during a week in 1979, "58% of all adults consulted newspaper classified ads at least once."[9]

Third, restriction on advertising might encourage a move toward replacing newspapers and "free" broadcasting with media that are less useful for advertising, that receive smaller proportionate advertising "subsidies," and that are, therefore, currently at a competitive disadvantage because of broadcasters' and newspapers' advertising "subsidy." For example, a tax on advertising might change the economics of using computer video display forms of "news" publishing as a means of delivering editorial content (although it is hard to predict the role of advertising in such a medium). I will not attempt to assess the policy implications of such a development.

Tax-Advertising/Subsidize-Readers (TA-SR) Proposal

The goal of the TA-SR proposal is to reduce the influence of advertising on editorial content and to increase the newspapers' responsiveness to readers. This change should reduce advertisers' power to censor and could also stimulate greater competition as content diversity becomes increasingly valuable as a response to readers' preferences.

A medium's attempt to obtain advertising revenue leads it to tilt media content toward what advertisers, not readers or viewers, want—assuming that their content preferences diverge. This tilt increases as advertising provides a larger and larger share of a media enterprise's revenue (or, more precisely, as advertising revenue provides an increasing surplus in excess of the expenses directly attributable to advertising). Thus, any arrangement that reduces the economic incentive for a newspaper to obtain advertising or that increases the economic incentive to have readers pay more of the costs of publishing the paper would shift the paper's editorial orientation away from advertiser control. A reform that either taxed advertising revenue or that multiplied circulation revenue would increase the newspaper's incentive to focus on readers' content preferences.

Government could employ both methods by *taxing advertising* (TA) and using the tax revenues to *subsidize reader-generated circulation revenue* (SR). I will refer to this combination as the TA-SR proposal. For example, the government could impose a 10% sales tax on newspapers' advertising revenue and redistribute this money back as a subsidy based on the paper's circulation revenue. If, as is roughly true, the industry as a whole received three-quarters of its revenue from advertising and one-quarter from circulation, and assuming only a negligible change in advertisers' newspaper-advertising expenditures as a result of the tax, from the perspective of a media enterprise, the TA-SR proposal would reduce the revenue the newspaper obtains from advertisers by 10% and increase its revenue from circulation by 30%.[10]

The immediate result of TA-SR would be, first, to reduce papers' incentive to respond to advertisers' wishes concerning editorial content and,

85

second, to encourage papers to provide a product for which readers are willing to pay. A tax on an economic activity amounts to a discouragement. The tax means that the paper will receive less advertising revenue. Either the price of the ad to the advertiser will go up, reducing the number of ads purchased; or, if the paper absorbs the tax, the price to the advertiser will stay the same, but the tax will reduce the paper's receipts; or, predictably, both effects will occur to some extent. In any case, the tax will lessen papers' incentive to respond to advertisers' concerns, and thus increase their incentive to respond to the other purchaser, the reader.

A subsidy generally creates an incentive to have more of whatever is subsidized. A direct subsidy of *circulation*, that is, a payment for each reader obtained, provides an incentive to increase readership—for example, by lowering the copy price. Whether the circulation subsidy also causes an increase in expenditures on quality in order to attract more readers or a decrease in quality-oriented expenditures in order to help "pay for" the reduction in copy price is uncertain—it will depend on the specific nature of reader demand. In contrast, the TA-SR proposal would subsidize *circulation revenue* rather than circulation itself. Rewarding circulation revenue focuses responsiveness on reader demand; that is, it encourages the media to provide content that readers value rather than merely to increase nominal circulation.

The specific consequences of the TA-SR proposal on price and circulation are difficult to predict. First, since the paper gains more than before from people's expenditures on purchasing the paper, it will have an incentive to increase the investment in paper quality. This illustrates the increased responsiveness to readers discussed above.

Second, the paper might either raise or lower its cover price to readers, depending on which move would increase revenue after the changes' effect on costs is accounted for. (I assume that circulation is somewhat elastic, generally going up if prices go down and vice versa;[11] and that advertising revenue is a direct function of circulation; thus, lowering cover price must increase advertising revenue, as well as increasing total costs of producing papers—that is, costs of paper, ink, production, and delivery). Assuming adoption of a profit-maximizing cover price before (and after) the introduction of TA-SR, the effect on cover price turns out to depend largely on the proportion of the newspaper's revenue it receives from advertising as compared to circulation.

The tax-on-advertising portion of the TA-SR proposal reduces the incentive to gain circulation (and, therefore, to lower cover price) since the advertising tax reduces the advertising revenue from the increased circulation. (The incentive to increase circulation in order to obtain more ad revenue causes cover prices to be lower than they would be to maximize profits from circulation revenue alone.) This incentive created by the advertising tax to increase the cover price should be stronger the higher the proportion of operating income that previously came from advertising.

The subsidy portion of the TA-SR proposal has more ambiguous effects. I assume that a lowering of cover price results in greater circulation. At the profit-maximizing or equilibrium price before the subsidy's introduction, an increased circulation (that is, a lower cover price) means ad revenue should go up; total production costs (which reflect, for example, increased paper, ink, and distribution due to the higher circulation) should also go up; and circulation revenue, depending on the elasticity of demand, could go either up or down. *If ad revenue per copy was high* (or more precisely ad revenue surplus per copy after the ads' production costs are covered), this suggests that there would be a comparatively high gain of ad revenue from the increased circulation, which further suggests that the reason the paper did not further decrease the cover price was that this advertising revenue gain would be outweighed by a loss of circulation revenue; this lost revenue, combined with the increased operating costs (paper, ink, distribution, and so forth), represents the cost to the paper of the cover price decline. On the other hand, *if ad revenue per copy was low*, then comparatively little gain in ad revenue would result from increasing circulation, which suggests that a cover-price decline may increase circulation revenue but not enough, even when combined with the small increase in advertising revenue (which in the extreme could be a zero increase), to compensate for the increased operating costs. That is, *if advertising revenue is sufficiently high*, it is likely to mean that a lower cover price would correspond to lower circulation revenue (and a higher price would increase this revenue), *but if advertising revenue is sufficiently low*, a lower cover price would correspond to some increase in circulation revenue. Since a subsidy intensifies the effect of the change on circulation revenue, introduction of a subsidy should cause some shift in cover price in the direction of higher circulation revenue. Thus, the subsidy should lead to a higher cover price when per-copy ad revenue was high, and cause a decrease in cover price when per-copy ad revenue was low.

Combining these considerations, the net result of the TA-SR proposal is that the tax tends toward increased cover price, the more so the more the paper's revenue came from ads; likewise, the subsidy is also likely to encourage higher cover prices the higher the proportion of the paper's revenue coming from ads. The subsidy, however, creates the opposite incen-

tive—toward lower cover prices—when the proportion of the paper's revenue that comes from circulation is sufficiently high (which is also the condition in which the advertising tax's pressure for higher cover prices is
weakest). Hence, TA-SR will lead to an increase in the cover price of some
papers and a decrease for others, with a decrease in cover price more likely
the higher the portion of the paper's revenue that comes from circulation.
In the pure case of a paper without ads, the tax would have no effect and
the subsidy would encourage some combination of increased investment
in quality and lower cover price. (This argument is presented mathematically in the Appendix.)

The TA-SR program can be evaluated as follows. It should lead to increased investment in quality and responsiveness to readers. This is a clear
gain. The program should also lead to a reduction in the cover price (and
expansion of circulation) of papers that are comparatively less dependent
on advertising, and should cause an increase in cover price of papers that
are more dependent on advertising. The lower price (and consequent circulation gain) of the more reader-oriented papers (that is, circulation-reve-
nue-dependent papers) is also a clear gain. The tendency to make advertising-supported papers more expensive is presumably a social cost, but this
loss is persuasively outweighed by the other gains.

Compared to a subsidy on mere circulation size, a subsidy based on
circulation revenue more strongly favors increased expenditures on product quality. The subsidy on circulation revenue provides a gain to a paper
from both high price and high circulation; this form of subsidy reduces
(but does not eliminate) the incentive to increase circulation merely by
reducing price, making quality enhancement an increasingly favored strategy. If society benefits (or if the press better fills its constitutionally protected function) when the press is (1) more responsive to readers' rather
than advertisers' concerns, and (2) financially rewarded for providing people with content for which they will pay (such that papers will invest more
in product quality), the preferred form of TA-SR would be to provide a
premium for circulation revenue.

An initial objection might be that TA-SR appears elitist. Upscale papers
aimed at the affluent often sell for a higher cover price than presumably
more working-class tabloids and would therefore receive a higher subsidy
per copy. Moreover, the proposal does nothing to reduce the purchasing
advantages the affluent have because of their wealth. Appearances mislead.
These objections ignore the underlying economics. A major problem with
advertising is that it values affluent readers more highly and, thus, from an

egalitarian perspective, creates a perverse allocation of subsidies. The TA-SR reduces the subsidy advantage that upscale papers normally receive from advertising and, thereby, favors more popular papers. In Reddaway's 1960 study of British national newspapers, a typical "popular" daily received about 52% of its revenue from circulation while the "quality" daily received only 27% from circulation, even though the "quality" sold for 4*d*. compared to 2 ½*d*. for the "popular"—an advertising advantage for quality dailies that has since grown even greater.[12] Thus, the TA-SR proposal would benefit the popular daily rather than the elite paper. Of course, commentators can always argue about which particular papers merit subsidy, but the abstract principle embodied in the TA-SR proposal is hard to reject. That principle, supporting reader rather than advertiser preferences in the production of media content, conforms to the best democratic visions of press freedom.[13] Moreover, given the distributional perversity of advertiser preferences, increasing the economic salience of people's willingness to pay for the paper typically operates in a distributionally egalitarian manner.

The TA-SR proposal has additional desirable qualities. It would help a publication survive without advertising support; it would help publications that serve small groups of readers unwanted by advertisers.[14] The proposal would reduce the cost to the paper of exposing advertiser misconduct. It would reduce the "cost" of being controversial in a manner that alienates some people who, if the paper were advertising-supported, could use an advertiser boycott to put pressure on the paper to change. More generally, the proposal would promote greater pluralism and diversity in media content by systematically favoring content desired by readers.

Questions remain about the design of TA-SR. Giving it greater precision presents further policy issues. For example, should the proposal apply to "shoppers" or "free papers" that are presently solely advertiser-supported and usually most available in more affluent neighborhoods? The question deserves considerable attention but, tentatively, my answer is yes.[15] If it did not apply, the tax/subsidy proposal would encourage advertisers to move to this medium, thereby hurting the daily newspaper and all the paid-circulation press. Currently, competition with free weeklies takes revenue from the paid-circulation press—apparently even causing the demise of some major dailies, such as the *St. Louis Globe-Democrat*.[16] This shift to "free" papers seems undesirable from the perspective of a desideratum that advertising support reader-preferred and valued editorial content, with value indicated by readers' payments. Of course, some free papers provide relatively good coverage of local or community affairs and even engage in effective investigative journalism (see the discussion of weeklies in chapter 1). Some "alternative papers," which are sometimes but not always operated as free papers oriented usually toward a comparatively affluent, youthful audience, provide useful, partisan alternatives to the daily press. Nevertheless, probably the overwhelming bulk of free papers are essentially advertising vehicles with minimal provision of news. And those entities within this group that are most valuable from the perspective of a diverse, democratic press are also probably the ones that could most successfully convert to paid circulation—or that could survive as free papers under the TA-SR proposal. If the proposal did apply, it would, of course, disadvantage the free-circulation papers—some would go out of business, others would reduce editorial expenditures, while some that contain reader-desired editorial content would convert to paid-circulation papers. Given that most serious, reader-oriented journalism occurs in papers sold to readers, broader coverage that includes free papers best supports the values represented by the commitment to a free press.

Whether this proposal should apply only to newspapers or also to magazines, or even more broadly to other media such as broadcasting, cable, and computer services, must also be considered. The general argument for favoring the media valued by readers (and by listeners and viewers) and for limiting the influence of advertisers over content is surely applicable more broadly. For example, applying the proposal to magazines makes sense; and it eliminates the incentive for advertisers to move from newspapers to magazines. Given the desire to provide economic support to reader-desired media content, the best version of the TA-SR proposal would probably tax all advertising and promotional expenses, including direct mail, billboards, point-of-purchase promotions, and corporate public relations expenditure, thereby both reducing advertisers' incentive to leave mass media and raising tax funds from these other sources to support the mass media.[17]

If the proposal applies to both newspapers and magazines, should the tax revenue from each category be combined into a single subsidy pool or segregated in order to subsidize only other members of that category? The issue is complicated because a single pool would produce some degree of cross-subsidy between quite different types of media that serve somewhat different social functions. A unified program might add simplicity, always a desirable trait in any regulatory or tax scheme; it could reduce or eliminate incentives for publishers to change their format to fit the most profitable category given their publication's own mix of advertising and circulation revenue. Likewise, a unified program could reduce the danger that state officials might commit censorial abuses in placing publications in one category or the other. This issue requires more consideration.

ALTERNATIVE TAX AND SUBSIDY PROPOSALS

Various aspects of the TA-SR proposal can be highlighted through comparison with other possible tax or subsidy schemes.

The Kaldor Proposal

In 1961 in a recommendation to the British Royal Commission on the Press, the economist Nicholas Kaldor advocated a tax-and-subsidy arrangement much like the TA-SR proposal.[18] Kaldor proposed to tax newspapers' advertising revenue and redistribute the proceeds to the newspapers. The tax *rate* would rise with circulation. The redistribution would rise proportionately with circulation up to a certain "optimum" circulation level, after which no additional circulation subsidy would be provided. Kaldor's scheme, formulated with the circumstances of the British national dailies in mind, was designed to promote competition by encouraging circulation gains up to a certain point but to prevent single-paper dominance by discouraging increases in circulation beyond that point.

Three main differences distinguish Kaldor's proposal from the TA-SR plan offered here. First, the subsidy in the TA-SR proposal enhances circulation revenue (i.e., per dollar of sales) rather than, as in Kaldor's proposal, rewarding mere circulation (i.e., per copy distributed). At the extreme, Kaldor's goal of merely achieving a higher circulation would justify subsidizing an advertising "free sheet" that has virtually no serious reporting—a result that hardly seems useful. In contrast, the TA-SR subsidy reflects the goal of increasing editorial expenditures and enhancing reader/consumer influence over content, not merely increasing circulation. The more advantages TA-SR gives papers that use their resources to provide editorial content, the better. Second, the TA-SR proposal taxes advertising at a constant rate. Progressivity is not needed because there is no attempt to limit circulation but rather only to reduce the economic influence of advertising and to reward all circulation chosen by readers/consumers. Third, the proposals differ in the manner in which they promote competition. Kaldor's scheme merely places economic obstacles in the way of papers' getting *too* big, combined with incentives for smaller papers to increase their audiences. In contrast, the TA-SR proposal hopes to increase both competition and diversity by rewarding papers for gaining circulation valued by readers. It encourages editorial expenditures on the product differentiation* on which competition in monopolistically competitive industries depends. As long as some readers value content different from that offered by the dominant papers, this proposal rewards a "new" paper for satisfying their desire. It thereby directly empowers consumer/reader preferences more than the Kaldor proposal does.

The reasons the royal commission gave for rejecting the Kaldor plan either do not apply or apply with much-reduced force to the TA-SR proposal. First, Kaldor's progressive tax was calibrated to apply its high rate to only two identifiable newspapers. The commission objected that the tax would force these two papers to adopt a policy of dramatically limiting circulation—behavior that should hardly be encouraged, particularly by government. Second, the commission objected because the plan created the potential that government might manipulate the variable tax rates to fit the circulation figures of politically favored or disfavored papers.[19] The TA-SR proposal excludes variable rates and punishment for circulation increases, thus not exhibiting the specific dangers noted. Still, like the Kaldor proposal, the TA-SR proposal does create the more general danger, implicit in any special legislation relating to the press, of predictable effects on identifiable enterprises. But in the TA-SR proposal, these effects will only occur because of a normatively defended general principle embodied in the proposal, whose specific political implications will not be certain over time.

Finally, the royal commission was troubled about forcing some papers (specifically two, although only one paper paid for most of the transfer) to subsidize their rivals.[20] This objection arguably reflected a more general view of at least two of the commission's five members. The commission report stated that these members based their rejection of the scheme on the grounds that *"the liberty of the Press includes* not only the freedom of a publisher to publish what he wishes but *the freedom of the reader to read what he wants*, subject only to the ordinary law."[21] They found no justification to "distort [   ] these freedoms and deny [   ] to some readers *the*

---

* A policy evaluation of product differentiation and resulting competition depends on both normative and empirical considerations. Empirically, product differentiation might merely produce specialized sports and financial papers. Alternatively, it might lead to papers with different editorial and writing styles, different news philosophies, and different partisan commitments. Whether this second type of diversity is socially desirable raises somewhat different normative issues than does the first—questions relating to the desirability of various forms of social conflict and cultural diversity.

right to buy the newspaper of their choice"[22]—a consequence that they attributed to Kaldor's proposal. If this concern amounts to an objection to
any governmental interference with the media marketplace, their complaint would be inconsistent with many existing aspects of both British and
American law (see chapter 5). On the other hand, if it is a narrower objection to interfering with reader choice, an objection that arguably applies to
the Kaldor plan's effect on the two large-circulation papers, the objection
simply does not apply to the TA-SR proposal. The merit of the TA-SR
proposal is that it reduces advertiser influence while increasing reader influence on newspaper content. It is designed precisely to promote the freedom (and opportunity) for readers "to buy the newspaper of their choice"
and "to read what [they] want."

Progressive Tax on Advertising

Several American media commentators have proposed placing a progressive tax on advertising. These proposals responded to the commentators'
conclusion that newspapers' dependence on advertising revenues was a
major cause of the decline in competitive-newspaper towns.[23] That general
conclusion, of course, is supported by the analysis in this book.

An initial design issue for these proposals is to choose the basis of progressivity. Progressivity could increase directly with amount of advertising
revenue,[24] with circulation,[25] or with proportion of the entity's revenue
that comes from advertising.[26] Only the last seems plausible. As long as
the tax applies in cities of different size, the same amount of advertising
revenue or the same circulation corresponds to very different degrees of
economic viability. Hence, basing progressivity on the absolute amount
of revenue or on circulation makes little sense. In contrast, progressivity
that increases the more (proportionately) the paper receives its revenue
from advertising rewards a paper for obtaining revenue by satisfying readers and for providing those readers with a product for which they are willing to pay.[27]

The TA-SR proposal presented above resembles this progressive tax.
Without using graduated rates, the TA-SR plan progressively increases the
burden on the paper as the proportion of the enterprise's revenue coming
from advertising increases. This occurs because the greater the proportion
of the newspaper's revenue that comes from advertising, the larger the
newspaper's tax burden compared to its circulation revenue subsidy. Nevertheless, three primary objections to this progressive tax proposal show
ways in which the TA-SR proposal is superior.

First, the immediate effect of the progressive tax on advertising is to siphon revenue from the mass media and thereby to reduce the revenue available to support for the press. This result is objectionable even though it stems from a government program intended to serve the desirable purpose of increasing the possibility of competitive papers. In contrast, all revenue generated by the TA-SR proposal's tax goes back to subsidize newspapers valued by readers. By leaving the advertising revenue within the media system, the TA-SR proposal avoids reducing the total media product available to readers.[28] The TA-SR proposal should also better promote competition since the subsidy/tax combination more effectively creates a direct benefit for satisfying diverse reader desires.

This difference leads to the second point, the characterization of each proposal's purpose. The progressive tax on advertising is easily described as embodying a desire to suppress, or at least burden, papers dependent on advertising—a restrictive purpose that may be hard to sell either politically or constitutionally. In contrast, the TA-SR plan is best described as an attempt to enhance the role of readers' desires in controlling the type of content produced, a principle perfectly consistent with democratic, market, and free speech values. Any marginal reduction in revenue going to the press as a result of the TA-SR plan is more an unfortunate by-product than a central premise of the scheme.[29] This point is very important. It means that the TA-SR proposal, like the Newspaper Preservation Act, even if it disadvantages particular papers, should be viewed as an attempt to enhance the functioning of the press rather than merely to burden problematic portions of it. Such a legitimate affirmative purpose should be crucial to the constitutionality as well as the desirability of the scheme.

Third, progressive rates surely invite overt manipulation and political abuse in the design of the rate structure. Of course, the danger of manipulation decreases as the number of papers covered increases—and, therefore, the problem is minimized if rates are chosen at the national rather than state level. In contrast, the TA-SR proposal uses a flat tax rate and flat subsidy rate, generating a form of progressivity much less subject to manipulative abuse.

The Swedish Plan

Like the United States, most Western democracies have seen a steady decline in newspaper competition. In Sweden, for a long time the most newspaper-reading country in the world (recently passed by Japan), the total number of papers peaked at about 240 around 1920. After 1950, there was a steady decline from around 210 papers to about 150 in 1970.[30] Swedes found this distressing. They view their partisan, diverse daily newspapers as a cornerstone of their democratic political culture.[31] Virtually all Swedish papers are associated with one or another of the five parliamentary political parties.[32] Swedes believe that lack of alternatives in newspapers could undermine political competition.

Swedish analysts concluded that papers failed because of lack of advertising revenue. According to their findings, to be economically viable—that is, to get a necessary level of advertising—a paper needed a high penetration in the area of its issuance; it needed subscriptions from at least 50% of the households in order to be indispensable to advertisers.[33] Even some papers with large circulations failed when their readership was spread over too large an area. Preservation of competition required outside support for papers with low household coverage. Further, the support would have to be permanent—or at least persist until a paper increased its penetration, which, given market saturation, was often unlikely.[34]

In 1971, Sweden implemented a "production subsidy," supported by a tax on advertising, designed to preserve competition.[35] The subsidy worked—the decline in newspapers stopped.[36] A key element of the program is that it provides subsidies only for papers with low coverage (i.e., household penetration) in the place of issue.[37] In addition, to be eligible, normally the paper must carry general news and information, have the character of a newspaper, be published at least once a week, have a minimum circulation, carry less than 50% advertising, and be sold mainly by subscription (an eligibility requirement that excludes the Swedish evening tabloids).[38] The method of calculating the amount of subsidy is significant. The subsidy is directly proportional to the amount of newsprint devoted to editorial copy.[39] This criterion excludes support for advertising content. Instead, the subsidy varies directly with increases in circulation and with increases in space devoted to editorial content. Finally, although the commentary seems not to count this as a policy benefit, the subsidy is supported by a 10% tax on general advertising, which is reduced to 3% for newspaper advertising.[40]

The Swedish plan has obvious merit—it appears to have sustained competition. It also bears important similarities to the TA-SR plan recommended here. Both the Swedish selective production subsidies and the TA-SR proposal recognize that newspapers' dependence on advertising is a key threat to the maintenance of competition in the existing market environment. Both use an allocation criterion that avoids direct support of advertising and that, in different ways, rewards emphasis on editorial content. The Swedes' newspaper subsidy rewards increased editorial content directly; TA-SR's subsidy of circulation revenue rewards satisfaction of reader, money-backed preferences. Likewise, by financing the subsidy with a tax on advertising, both plans at least marginally decrease the role of advertising in newspapers' finances. Swedish commentators note that weak papers in Sweden would "prefer a pricing policy by which the greater share of revenues were derived from the circulation market . . . [but were] unable to alter newspaper pricing policy on their own."[41] Like the TA-SR proposal, the effect of the Swedish advertising tax and its method of allocating subsidies was to decrease the role of advertising in all papers' financing (given the tax), and especially in weak papers (given the subsidy).

Still, the two approaches contain significant differences, and these differences indicate why the TA-SR plan proposed here is preferable, at least for the United States. The Swedes developed their selective-subsidies plan for the limited purpose of maintaining competition that otherwise was undermined by newspapers' overwhelming dependence on advertising. Thus, only papers whose lack of market penetration resulted in inadequate advertising revenue received subsidies. The Swedish subsidy is not specifically designed to discourage an advertising focus nor to provide an incentive for greater emphasis on responding to readers' interests. In contrast, the TA-SR plan is designed to redirect all papers' financial calculations away from serving advertisers and toward serving readers. For this reason, the TA-SR plan provides the subsidy to all circulation-revenue-producing papers rather than only to particularly endangered papers. This structural change implements a more principled goal. Rather than trying to identify and save a few unsuccessful, competitive papers within an otherwise accepted market environment, the TA-SR proposal tries to create a different market environment that is more hospitable to the purposes of a free and democratic press. Within that restructured environment, TA-SR does not attempt to prop up papers that fail because of inadequate reader interest.

Other differences follow from this initial difference between the narrow purpose of the Swedish program and the broader aim of the TA-SR proposal. In the TA-SR proposal, most elements follow relatively mechanically once the tax rate is set. In contrast, the Swedish subsidy program is very complex, requiring numerous additional decisions and using different subsidy criteria depending on the paper's penetration rate,[42] circulation size, and publication schedule. Those designing the Swedish program recognized the vital need to make the grant process as objective as possible in order to prevent political manipulation of the press, and the Swedes apparently believe that they succeeded.[43]

Nevertheless, the Swedish scheme's complexity clearly holds the potential for partisan design of threshold amounts and varying benefits. Virtually no evidence suggests that partisan manipulation has occurred, or that even opponents of the subsidy program have made such a charge. Still, the distribution of subsidies is interesting. The Social-Democrats (the socialists) are generally supported by 40% to 50% of the electorate and constitute the largest parliamentary party,[44] although only about 16% (by circulation) of the press is affiliated with them, as compared to about 73% affiliated with the bourgeois parties.[45] Of the five parliamentary parties, the Social-Democrats pushed the longest and hardest for subsidies in the media marketplace—and Social-Democratic papers have received 55% of the subsidies.[46]

Thus, despite the proven usefulness of the Swedish program, the TA-SR proposal embodies a more basic and general principle of promoting readers' preferences over those of advertisers. It attempts to create a better environment for a free and democratic press, but then lets papers succeed or fail on their own. This more general, principled goal also suggests a simpler plan with less potential for political manipulation.

Proposed Revenue-Oriented Media Taxes

With occasional exceptions like Huey Long's "tax on lying," which was carefully designed to apply only to the opposition press in Louisiana,[47] raising revenue is the primary purpose of most modern taxes on advertising or on the press. In response to continuing budget crises, legislative bodies increasingly eye these major economic activities as potential sources of tax revenue.[48] In 1987, Florida adopted, but then quickly repealed, legislation that applied its sales tax to advertising.[49] California followed in 1991 with an extension of its sales tax to cover newspapers but then, under heavy lobbying pressure, repealed the tax as it applied to ad-supported "free" papers.[50]

These tax revenue proposals generally take one of four forms: (1) they apply the state's sales (or use) taxes to previously exempt publications; (2) they apply the state's sales tax to advertising, often as part of an extension of the sales tax to a broad range of services; (3) they reduce income tax deductibility of advertising by treating it, for example, as a capital expense and requiring that it be amortized;[51] (4) they deny (or reduce) income tax deductibility of advertising for specific, usually harmful, products like tobacco or alcohol.[52] Of these, the fourth type, related to discouraging promotion of specific products, raises a policy issue that is beyond the scope of this study; although economically complex and apparently theoretically justified,[*] the third, which was briefly pushed by the Bush administration and persuasively advocated by Harvard economist Lawrence Summers,[53] creates basically the same type of consequences for the media as the second, and therefore will not be specifically considered.

Both the media and advertising agencies vehemently and usually effectively oppose these taxes.[54] The American Advertising Federation claims credit for helping defeat proposals in twelve states to tax advertising in 1990,[55] trumpeting the ad industry's "reputation of fighting and winning fights."[56] Advertising agencies even plan to launch a major advertising and public relations campaign to convince the public of the social value of advertising.[57]

State newspaper associations have also been relatively successful at getting exemptions for their product. Only nine of the approximately forty-four states with sales taxes apply them to newspapers.[58] Still, these exemptions are not safe. For example, with the support of the Democratic legislative leadership, Republican governor Pete Wilson in 1991 got California to extend its sales tax to various items including newspapers.[59]

Although understandable as states scramble for tax revenue, application of the sales tax to newspapers or magazines is undesirable from the perspective of a democratic press. Sales taxes on either subscriptions or single-copy sales reduce both media revenue and reader influence over the media. States that exempt newspapers and magazines from sales tax act in a manner supportive of First Amendment values, while sales taxes like California governor Wilson's move in precisely the wrong direction. Predictions that the states are much more likely to adopt new taxes on newspaper circulation than on newspaper advertising indicate extreme perversity from the policy perspective of a democratic press.[60] In contrast, application of a sales tax to advertising, like Florida's ill-fated tax, would have some beneficial effects for a free press. It would marginally reduce the influence of advertisers on content. By increasing the comparative role of circulation revenue, the tax on advertising should encourage product differentiation and diversity in the media, and correspondingly have some tendency to encourage competitive media offerings.

---

[*] Rather than relating to an immediate sale, much advertising can be viewed as an investment in the future—as an attempt to create "good will" or product recognition. Hence, for tax purposes, it would seem reasonable to capitalize at least part of advertising expenditures, depreciating them over a period of years. Summers suggests that the existing system of deductibility results not only in the loss of tax revenue but also in the arguably undesirable consequence of favoring investment in intangibles as opposed to tangible capital that would seem more directly related to jobs, productivity, and international competitiveness.

The merit of taxing advertising rather than readers' purchases has been recognized elsewhere. In Europe, the press commonly receives tax exemptions and other subsidies.[61] The sale of newspapers is normally exempt from the Europeans' value-added tax (VAT)—an exemption similar to typical sales tax exemptions here. Nevertheless, most European countries apply their VAT to advertising in the press.[62] The policy analysis in this book supports the European practice. The sales of newspapers and periodicals ought to be exempted from sales taxes. Taxes should be applied, if at all, to advertising.

Still, the problem with the revenue-oriented tax on advertising, from the perspective of the press,[63] is that it takes income from the press. In this respect, the TA-SR proposal is preferable. Like revenue taxes on advertising, TA-SR reduces the influence of advertisers, but unlike the revenue taxes which reduce media resources, TA-SR returns the revenue to the press in a manner that intensifies the influence of readers.[64]

COMBATING ADVERTISERS' CENSORSHIP

Advertisers, not governments, are the primary censors of media content in the United States today. Or perhaps it should be said that advertisers are second after the media themselves, the "gate-keepers," which engage in self-censorship for both good and bad reasons. Advertisers effectively restrict the circulation of media content that they do not like and are often even able to get their preferred content to appear as nonadvertising content.

The direct legal response would be to prohibit advertisers' exercise of influence, but this is easier said than done. Law has never been very effective in preventing bargaining parties from reaching outcomes that the parties find optimal. Black or gray markets in drugs, sex, or rationed consumer goods—or here, in influence over media content—result. Rent control drives owners' attempts to extract value from renters underground: owners skimp on upkeep or services, exact special payments, and so forth, in order to effectively charge closer to market rates. Economists show that governmental attempts to prevent market exchanges that the parties find optimal are partially circumvented, with the parties' coping behavior often causing a waste of resources.

The above might paint too bleak a picture of the possible use of law. Complaints about resources wasted in parties' circumventing regulations apply mostly when the regulatory aim is to redistribute wealth of a specific sort from one contracting party to the other. But in the case of prohibiting advertiser influence on media content, the intended behavioral change is unrelated to redistributing wealth between advertisers and media enterprises. Rather, as with antitrust legislation, the goal is to block a particular type of result. This goal is advanced by making achievement of the parties' aim more costly. Costs of circumvention partially deter the unwanted behavior. These costs make purchase of influence over nonadvertising content somewhat more difficult and more expensive. With this in mind, I will consider three levels of legislative response to advertisers' control, moving roughly from the more easily justified to the most controversial regulations.

Advertiser Censorship

First, advertisers sometimes intentionally block or try to block communications. Tobacco companies prevent publication of reports on the dangers of smoking by threatening to withdraw advertising. Revlon retaliates against *Ms.* for publishing a front-cover picture of Soviet feminists who were not wearing makeup. Proctor & Gamble announces a threat to retaliate against broadcasts criticizing its purchase of El Salvadoran coffee, withdrawing ads from a station that breaks rank (examples from chapter 2).

This censorship by advertisers accomplishes little other than to reduce the perspectives and information available to the public while increasing the media's slant toward commercial values. Legislation should outlaw an advertiser's attempts to use its economic relationships with a media enterprise to influence the enterprise not to print or broadcast content that it would otherwise choose to present. The advertiser's restraint on press freedom resembles corporate agreements that restrain trade, violating the antitrust laws; but it is more objectionable—the activity restrained is trade in communication.[65] There is little reason to allow this use of economic power to censor others' speech and to block the public's access to information or viewpoints.

Some firms may criticize this analysis of their behavior. Communications to which the advertiser objects sometimes are demonstrably false and should never be published. This fact is not a reason, however, to give advertisers censorship powers that others, without such economic leverage, do not have. Much better would be a more broadly effective system of identifying and deterring false stories. Like other private parties, the advertiser can communicate "true" information to the media enterprise. This communication will usually suffice to end the presentation of the false material. Of course, sometimes the media enterprise will not be convinced; and at other times, it may have an economic or ideological reason to continue presenting the false information. Regardless of whether the advertiser would then have a tort remedy against the media enterprise for its knowingly or recklessly false presentation, this scenario is sufficiently unlikely, as compared to cases of advertisers' abuse of power, that its possibility does not justify permitting advertisers to use their economic power to "censor" the media.

It will often be difficult to prove that subtle retaliatory behavior by advertisers was a response to disliked content. As long as advertisers are free to choose not to advertise in publications of which they disapprove, interpretations of a withdrawal of advertising will be equivocal. Without incriminating statements by Revlon, *Ms.* would be unable to prove a legal violation. When a media enterprise "knows" what it cannot prove, the advertiser will have circumvented the legal rules while effectively applying pressure on the media. Still, overt cancellation of all tobacco advertising after a story on the dangers of smoking should constitute a prima facie legal case. Likewise, Proctor & Gamble would not be able to publicly announce its threat to withdraw advertising from stations that broadcast a particular item. In any event, these proof problems can be put aside here—at worst they will make the law less effective. Although too much should not be expected, this prohibition should strengthen the hand of the media in living up to their own proclaimed norms. The legal prohibition would formalize the norm of noninfluence and could operate marginally to change advertisers' behavior, thereby making the press marginally "freer."

Intentional Control or Influence over Nonadvertising Content

The above discussion proposed a restriction on behavior that had two elements—an intention of the advertiser and an effect of excluding content. Initially, a more general prohibition of advertisers' influence over nonadvertising content might seem a straightforward proposition. Nevertheless such a complete prohibition would not be feasible (and sometimes might not even be desirable). Advertiser influence is so built in to the market context that not only is it often difficult to prove, but advertiser influence frequently occurs without the advertiser's inducing it by any specific act, sometimes even without the advertiser's wanting it.

The lead sentence of the *New York Times*'s story about the dismissal of Gabriel Rotello, the editor and founder of the gay and lesbian magazine *Outweek*, asserted that the magazine had been trying to attract "main-

101

stream advertisers."[66] Rotello said he was dismissed because the publisher wanted *Outweek* to be less political, noting " 'resistance by advertisers who do not want to be in a journal that reflects the political values that they do not subscribe to.' "[67] Both the firing and the move away from politics appeared to be attributable to advertisers' influence.[68] Proving it, however, would be more difficult. The publisher of *Outweek* explained that he had dismissed Rotello because the magazine was getting stale. Even if it could be shown that the publisher fired Rotello in order to change the magazine in a way that would please advertisers, this may have merely represented the publisher's own judgment about what would attract advertisers. Possibly no advertiser ever suggested that the magazine should change—or even wanted it to. If advertisers had avoided the magazine because of its political orientation, that does not necessarily mean they attempted to change it—they just did not want to be a part of it. If readers can favor magazines whose values they respect, it might be asked what is objectionable about advertisers' doing likewise.*[69] Advertisers' patronage of magazines they like does not constitute a conscious attempt to exercise influence.† Of course, structural changes could be devised that would limit the economic influence apparently inherent in advertisers' patronage choices. The British Labour party once supported a proposal to treat newspapers' advertising revenues as a common pool to be distributed on a basis other than advertisers' choice of the media enterprises in which to advertise.[70] This pool and a centralized distribution of revenue would remove the ideological control that the advertisers exercise over the press. A similar goal, but related only to the influence of a peculiarly influential advertiser, the government, is implicit in certain countries' practice of requiring that government advertising support all newspapers equally.[71] Still, it may be unreasonable to require corporate advertisers to patronize publications with which they disagree.

---

* This question might be answered in various ways. For example, the answer might track the judicially accepted arguments for limiting corporate involvement in political campaigns and rejecting the constitutional status for commercial enterprises' associational rights. The proper interest of commercial enterprises should be seen as *only* their interest in communicating their commercial message to the public. Or, at least, their other interests should be subject to regulation when action based on those interests would produce objectionable social structures.

† Compare the illegal gratuities statute, stating that any "public official, . . . [who] otherwise than as provided by law for the proper discharge of official duty, directly or indirectly . . . receives . . . anything of value personally for or because of any official act performed or to be performed by [him]," is guilty of accepting an illegal gratuity. See 18 U.S.C. 201(c)(1)(B) (1988). To whom and why would one make campaign contributions if not "for or because" of what the person has done or has promised to do?

Whatever the real reasons for Calvin Klein's placement of its very large, unconventional, 116-page "polybagged outsert" (ad supplement) in the October 1991 issue of *Vanity Fair*—Calvin Klein said it was because *Vanity Fair* was "the hot book"—the *New York Times*'s story reporting the placement noted that in 1987 *Vanity Fair* had published an "adulatory cover story" about Mr. Klein and his wife.[72] This comment in the *Times* (or the predictable industry gossip to the same effect) inevitably sends a strong message to other magazines about the type of stories that will eventually turn out to have been wise—that is, profitable. None of these events—the original *Vanity Fair* story, the placement of the supplement, or the *Times*'s story—necessarily involves any objectionable behavior, but the overall effect increases the sway of advertising over content. The press is simply not as free to serve its constitutionally valued functions if the need to please present or potential advertisers significantly influences its choice of what people, products, or activities to glamorize and what stories to report.

These examples illustrate influence that is not only virtually impossible to prove but also possibly unintentional, the influence being built into the structure of interaction. In these circumstances, the law should not hold advertisers responsible.

Even advertisers' *intentional* attempts to influence nonadvertising content are incredibly varied in nature and offensiveness. As a sampling, consider: (1) advocacy campaigns in which businesses (as well as others) seek improved quality of media or improved media presentation of particular issues unrelated to the businesses' specific products—for example, companies (that engage in advertising) join others in advocating that media provide better coverage of economic news or in a public outcry demanding that the media treat rape victims with greater respect; (2) public relations and information campaigns about the business itself or its products, including more "news"-oriented information such as Proctor & Gamble's provision of what it considered accurate information about its coffee purchases or about the origins of its corporate logo; (3) "infomercials," usually program-length pieces with format designed to imitate regular television programming but created by the advertiser and intended to promote the advertiser's products; (4) "product placements,"[73] that is, payment to programming producers to include branded products in a movie or video programming;[74] (5) use of its leverage as an advertiser to influence programming on which its advertising will appear, including sponsorship of Public Broadcasting programs wherein the sponsor dictates elements of the content—at least the program's subject matter and sometimes more;

and (6) use of this economic leverage to influence programming on which the firm does not advertise.

Of the types of influence listed above, reasons to object are most obvious when the advertiser intentionally uses its economic power—for example, payments or threats to end paying relationships (advertising)—to influence nonadvertising content. This suggests as a possible rule a ban on a company's intentionally using its economic power to influence media's nonadvertising content. This rule, however, would not be self-interpreting.

Surely, a corporation should be able to tell the world about itself—it may have a public, even a legal, duty to release some information about itself and its products. But when it does so, when the firm supplies the media with "free" videos or press releases or news conferences, it uses economic resources to influence media content.* From the media's perspective, the firm's "information transfers" can be as economically beneficial as if an advertiser gave money to the media entity to cover the expenses of writing or taping a favorable report on the firm or its products. The newspaper prints the press release rather than hire a reporter and writer. The nightly news does not bother to announce that its report on nuclear power is composed solely of a video given to it by a local utility company. The networks did not announce that much of their video material of events in Kuwait during the period leading up to our 1991 invasion of Iraq was supplied by a Washington-based public relations firm indirectly paid by the emir of Kuwait.[75] Nor were the networks able to note, because they did not know, that many of the videos they were given and that they then broadcast presented "outright misinformation"—for instance, videos purportedly but falsely showing Iraqi troops firing on peaceful Kuwaiti demonstrators.[76]

Although the FCC requires that broadcasters identify all commercial sponsors, in a controversial decision, it declared that this did not apply

---

* Advertisers and their public relations firms carefully prepared and offered to newscasters about four thousand video news releases ("VNRs") in 1991. The same aspect of this activity—the VNR's capacity to obtain access to the media and, as news, to be more believable than paid commercials—both creates the VNRs' appeal to their corporate or political sponsors and makes them objectionable from the perspective of a free press. First, well-made, "picture rich" VNRs can effectively chase out of the nightly news more important stories that are "picture-poor" and, for the stations, more expensive. Second, to the extent that their source is not identified, VNRs are implicitly deceptive. Nevertheless, "roughly 80 percent of the country's [television] news directors acknowledge [using the] material at least several times a month"—and predictions are that reliance on VNRs by news departments will increase. See David Lieberman, "Fake News," *TV Guide*, Feb. 22, 1992, 10, 16.

when a station broadcast a "program" supplied by a toy manufacturer and featuring a company product because the station had "paid" for the program by giving the toy producer two minutes of advertising time during other children's programming.[77] The advertiser used its economic resources to get both its product-promoting show and two minutes of ads on television, but in FCC doublethink, the product show did not constitute advertising or sponsorship since the broadcaster paid the toy company by giving time for advertisements. Here and in the case of press releases and video news releases, the firm (the advertiser) neither directly pays the station for influence nor threatens withdrawal of advertising, but does use its economic resources to provide the media with something the media value (that is, supplies programming that they otherwise would have to spend money to get) and thereby successfully influences the station's broadcasts.

These examples should begin to illustrate that advertiser influence is an incredibly complex phenomenon and unlikely to be wisely regulated with general principles or all-encompassing rules. Still, I propose a general principle. An advertiser should be barred from intentional use of its economic resources to influence nonadvertising content *unless* the advertiser is identified to the public in a manner that suggests its influence—for example, by being an identified advertiser on a program or by being identified as the source or supplier of the content when it produced the content and the media merely printed or broadcast it. Although this principle has most obvious application to broadcast or video material, possibly it should also be applied to print in the form of a requirement that the source be identified when a print medium essentially reprints an enterprise's press release. In a sense, this proposal merely extends the earlier proposal to prohibit advertisers from using their economic power to censor content to which they object. Here the prohibition applies to all use of economic power to engage in intentional influence—however, it recognizes that sometimes this intentional influence should be acceptable, but only if the influence is identified.

The requirement that sources of influence be identified would require, for example, identification of the source or sponsor of infomercials[78] and of product placements. Program-length commercials not identified as such and paid product placements are basically identical to the paid "reading notices" that appeared in newspapers around the turn of the century: each presents a message or image chosen by an advertiser in a context designed to mislead the public about the advertiser's control of the content. In addition, each practice implicitly suggests to the public that media professionals, journalists or program creators and directors, formulated the commu-

105

nication for their own professional or artistic reasons. "Reading notices" were effectively outlawed by the 1912 act which denied second-class postage rates to periodicals that did not clearly identify the inserts as advertisements. Prohibition of unidentified "product placements" or "infomercials" merely applies this rule to the broadcast and video media. An appropriate implementation would be to require at the beginning and end of a video program an announcement that the inclusion of particular products constitutes a paid advertisement, or, better, to require a subtitle at the time the product appears. A similar requirement should also apply to program-length commercials. Without identification of material as advertiser-sponsored, many of these advertising techniques could be interpreted as "misleading" trade practices, already illegal and subject to FTC control.[79] Likewise, product placements of cigarettes in movies arguably require health warnings and, if broadcast, violate the existing ban on cigarette advertising on television. With these problems in mind, the tobacco industry informed the FTC that it would cease buying placements in films.[80]

More difficult are situations, such as those of press releases and "video news releases" discussed above, in which the firm uses its financial resources to influence content but does not *directly* pay the media firm for the influence—rather, it subsidizes certain content, thereby making it advantageous to the media entity to choose to present that material. In one sense this is no different from direct payments—that is, both formally leave the media entity free to decide what to present and only tilt the economics of the choice. In another sense, however, this form of influence is more limited. At most, it reduces the cost to the media of presenting content. Direct payments, however, can be as high as the advertiser chooses and can in themselves constitute profit for the media entity. Moreover, supplying information to the media is not only often appropriate but may sometimes be legally required. Possibly, these forms of influence that avoid direct payments should be left unregulated.

Nevertheless, the public could hardly be hurt, and would often be served, if the media were required to identify content that corporate sponsors used their resources to influence. Just as newspapers typically identify stories provided by the Associated Press with a symbol such as "[AP]" at story openings, they could identify any substantially reprinted press releases with markings such as "[General Motors]." The public would also be served by a requirement that news programs' broadcasts of video provided by corporate public relations departments include written subtitles during the broadcast identifying the corporate source. This proposal hardly seems radical. The editors of *TV Guide* have recommended that "when a TV news organization includes film or tape prepared by an out-side source in a broadcast, the label 'VIDEO SUPPLIED BY [COMPANY OR GROUP NAME]' be visible for as long as the material is on-screen."[81] The social interest arguing against identification of the commercial source of information is hard to imagine.

In the end, it is difficult to decide whether the law ought to establish rules for these forms of influence that do not involve actual payments by the outside source. The problem is one of line drawing. Intuitively most cases seem easy. Although all news sources in a sense use their economic resources to provide the media with information, nondisclosure often seems appropriate, especially given some constitutional and plenty of pol-icy arguments that reporters ought to be able to keep sources "confiden-tial." The typical cases for nondisclosure are those in which a reporter's own efforts are the primary basis of a story or in which an individual seeks out the media in contexts that suggest personal or ideological reasons for anonymity. These seem quite distinguishable from situations in which public relations departments produce news releases or videos, and ano-nymity serves only profit concerns.[82] Required identification should only apply to the latter cases. Possibly, given that the requirement of identifica-tion should apply in quite diverse and changing contexts, an agency, maybe the FTC, should develop specific guidelines. Existing laws already embody some identification requirements.[83] This proposal merely carries those rules a slight step further.

All Advertiser Influence over Nonadvertising Programming

Unintentional influence—as well as ubiquitous opportunities for hard-to-prove intentional influence—are built into the structure of interactions be-tween advertisers and the media. If this unintentional influence is to be reduced, the structure or subject matter of interaction must be changed.

The most obvious locus of advertisers' influence involves the specific programming on which its ad appears—the program or editorial content that it "sponsors." The advertiser chooses to advertise on "Murphy Brown" and not program X, or on "Thirty-something" but only if there is no scene involving homosexuality. Advertisers' concerns are similarly evi-dent in print—ranging from the choice of publications in which to ad-vertise, to choice of type of editorial material that should appear close to the ad (e.g., the financial section, the science section), to concerns about the specific content with which it chooses to be associated (to advertise adjacent to).

107

The *New Yorker* commissioned a well-respected environmental author, John Mitchell, to write a ten-thousand-word "advertorial" for its Earth Day issue. According to Mitchell, who eventually demanded that his name be taken off the article, his piece was first cut to five thousand words, then kicked upstairs to the "marketing gurus," where it was turned into a piece of "pap," made upbeat, with criticism of government and industry largely removed.[84] If the marketing department had made the changes only after showing the piece to potential advertisers who objected to certain portions, this would involve advertisers' consciously using their power to influence content. But what apparently happened here, and in several examples discussed earlier, is that advertisers influenced content without any conscious intent but through the structure in which media decision making occurs.

Whether this possibly "unintentional" type of influence should be permitted is debatable. It is easy to argue that enterprises should not be permitted to use their economic power for the purpose of restricting the speech of others. But a firm (and sometimes the public) may view programs on which it advertises as in some sense the advertiser's own speech. Advertisers obviously have a different and generally greater economic interest in the content of video programming and, maybe to a lesser extent, of print content surrounding their ads than they do in media content in general. Before considering whether or to what extent this type of influence should be permitted, I will survey methods of restricting the influence.

The most direct legal response would be to prohibit this influence—but what behavior would have been prohibited? A ban on influence could be partially implemented if the law permitted broadcasters or publishers to tell advertisers only general things about the programming or print content that would surround their ads, prohibited prescreening for advertisers, and outlawed advertisers' making suggestions directly to the writers, publishers, broadcasters, or producers about either specific stories or general programming and editorial content. Such a law would require great changes in industry practices but would probably be only marginally effective. At most, it would get at overt influence. The media entity risks a loss of good will or, more specifically, the loss of enterprises' willingness to advertise at a given price if stories or programs contain "surprise" elements to which the media entity knows the advertiser would object. As long as advertisers pay the bills, considerable influence seems unavoidable.

Regulatory difficulties may differ in print and broadcast media. Surely, in broadcasting the point at which advertisers exercise the most influence is in their control over ad placement. Two approaches to reducing advertiser influence attack this placement control in broadcasting.

First, the law could prohibit selling advertising time within particular programs or time slots. Instead of placing ads on particular programs, advertisers would be required to place ads on some other basis. The law could restrict advertisers to purchases of access to viewers with payment based on a negotiated rate per demographically specified viewer.[85] However, informal understandings could defeat this rule. Broadcasting business managers' competition with other stations or networks would lead them to be very solicitous of an advertiser's easily discovered preferences. Broadcasters could place ads on the basis of "informal" information concerning advertisers' programming wishes. To combat this, broadcasters could be required to schedule ads using a computer program designed, for example, to maximize revenues given advertisers' varying payment rates for viewers of different demographic groups. To the extent that this criterion was not determinant, randomized placements would be required. Of course, sufficiently timid broadcasters could still design their entire programming to conform to their perceptions of advertisers' generic preferences—trying to become, for instance, "XBC—the upbeat, buying-mood network!"

Alternatively, the law could take another tack. It could try to sever the connection between advertisers and specific shows. Out of a concern for program integrity,[86] as well as to prevent overcommercialization and to restrict advertisers' influence, some European countries require all advertising to occur in limited blocks that do not cut into individual programs.[87] For example, a broadcaster could be restricted to one block of five (or ten) minutes of advertising each hour, with a rule that the advertising block not break into an individual show unless that show lasts longer than sixty minutes, and then only as an intermission occurring at least twenty minutes before the show's end. This requirement would substantially disconnect advertising and program content.

The primary objection to these proposals is likely to be financial. Broadcasters would object to block advertising. It limits the time available for advertising. (FCC guidelines limiting advertising minutes per hour were abolished as part of the Reagan administration's deregulation agenda; at the demand of Congress, limits were reestablished for children's programming.)[88] Advertisers, and hence broadcasters, would also fear that people would stop watching during these blocks, although the European experience suggests that commercial broadcasting can successfully operate using restricted blocks of advertising.[89] As for the semirandom ad-placement proposal (which considers only demographics in placement), advertisers would have both legitimate and less legitimate objections. The very existence of the present system indicates, unsurprisingly, that advertisers economically value the opportunity for program selection. Of course, the critic argues that advertisers' interest in surrounding ads with content calculated to produce buying moods and designed to avoid offense to any potential customers prostitutes broadcasting to its paymaster. Even if advertisers will pay for this result, the practice should be disallowed. A policy-based evaluation of the legitimacy of advertisers' demographic interests is more equivocal. These interests tilt media content undemocratically, but as long as advertisements are thought to serve some valuable social function, it may seem appropriate that ads be broadcast to the audience most likely to be interested in them. Any other policy would be wasteful.

There are, however, sometimes policy-acceptable reasons for advertisers to associate their ads with particular programming, reasons that have nothing to do with censorship. First, sometimes advertisers affirmatively wish to promote high quality programming, a wish that presumably deserves praise, not legal obstacles. Decision-makers at Texaco may be proud of more than fifty years of Metropolitan Opera broadcasts. Xerox's proclaimed policy is to sponsor programs designed "to stretch the mind, to inspire, to stir the conscience and require thought." Xerox says that its "programs should try to advance TV over what it has been."[90] (Erik Barnouw observes, interestingly, that generally such enlightened sponsorship policies of major corporations, including Xerox, IBM, Mobil, and Exxon, reflect considerations including "an image-protection strategy, relat[ed] to antitrust perils" and, in some cases, an attempt to appeal to particularly "sophisticated customers.")[91] Second, advertisers design some commercials specifically for particular programming. This has two dimensions. Either the coherence of the ad or the relevance of the advertised product could build on the programming. Commercials for tennis rackets or commercials for any product containing an endorsement from a tennis star make more sense during a broadcast of Wimbledon than of "Murder She Wrote."

On balance, however, the evils of censorship associated with advertisers' determining which program they sponsor probably outweigh the practice's benefits. All norms of the journalistic and creative communities deny the propriety of advertisers' control over content. Entertainment writers and news personnel in broadcasting consistently reject the legitimacy of advertiser influence even as media enterprises submit. Journalists and writers should use their professional skills to report news and create entertainment that they think has the greatest worth—material that gives the people what they want or need.[92] Chapter 2 illustrated that advertisers' control often reduces diversity and restricts the presentation of challenging, sobering, or partisan programming even when such programming is capable of attracting audiences. If not *too* costly in terms of decreasing advertising revenue, either the proposal for block-broadcast of ads or that for semirandom placement of ads would render the media freer and potentially more diverse.

Countervailing considerations are real, but weak. Denying advertisers the power to mesh ads with particular programs is probably not a major social cost. Despite real fans of Anheuser Busch's "Bud Bowl," which was designed specifically for broadcast on the Super Bowl, its absence is a small price to pay for reducing advertisers' power to censor. More troublesome is the loss of advertisers' opportunity to sponsor "classy," high-prestige shows, but this too is probably not too great a cost.[93]

If rationales for advertiser-controlled placement are sufficiently important, exceptions to the above proposals could give them some scope. The censorship implicit in advertiser control is nullified if this control is restricted to a few shows that become, in part, the advertiser's "speech."[94] Advertisers could be permitted to avoid random placement by paying a 10% "placement" sales tax. In order to keep this revenue within the communications system, it could be allocated to public broadcasting.[95] Likewise, an exception to block scheduling of ads could be permitted. Advertisers could pay to be associated with a particular program, with sponsorship noted at the show's beginning and end. If the rules for pricing these sponsorships are properly defined,[96] they would provide an incentive to sponsor "prestige" shows, which often increase broadcast diversity and possibly broadcast quality.

In summary, advertiser influence over programming content is usually objectionable but cannot be entirely eliminated. Various reforms could, however, reduce that influence. Each reform has real costs but, tentatively, each proposal offered in this section seems merited.

Tax on Advertising to Fund Noncommercial TV and Radio

Broadcasters' inability to sell broadcast content directly to viewers leads to market failures that arguably cause underproduction[97] as well as advertiser-oriented distortions[98] in video production.[99] Public broadcasting can partially correct these market failures. Additional justifications for public broadcasting usually repeat non-market-based arguments favoring governmental financial support for public education and public culture—concerns to enhance the media's potentially beneficial role in the process of value formation and in humanistic development.[100] I will not canvass the arguments for public broadcasting, but all proposals eventually must face the question of how public broadcasting should be supported. Two policy concerns are central: the support should not be too stingy in amount; and it should promote quality without leaving public broadcasting vulnerable to political or ideological censorship by either government or private bodies, but should still assure that the system's decision-makers act responsibly. No funding approach will be perfect. I will briefly compare four frequently suggested revenue sources with a fifth advocated here: significant reliance on revenue from a dedicated tax on advertising in commercial broadcasting and video distribution. Of course, any actual system is likely to rely on a combination of sources—and this can be a strength if it promotes some degree of responsiveness while reducing (nothing can eliminate) the danger of improper influence, a danger implicit in an entity's power to eliminate any particular source of funding.

Presently, public broadcasting in this country receives revenue from sources that can be categorized variously but that I will describe as: (1) private—including both viewers and noncommercially controlled foundations; (2) commercial—basically the same corporations that advertise on commercial broadcasting; and (3) regular governmental appropriations, made from general revenues. In addition, public broadcasting in many countries relies heavily on a special form of government support: (4) dedicated revenue from a sales tax on broadcast receivers or from annual fees paid by viewers for possession/use of receivers.

Reliance on private contributions will not produce revenue commensurate with the value of public broadcasting's programming. "Free rider" problems and solicitation costs prevent viewers' contributions from providing anything close to the value that viewers actually find in public television programming. And viewers certainly cannot be expected to pay for the public good externalities of public broadcasting. Private foundation support may fill a portion of the gap but again cannot be expected to be adequate. Corporate contributions exhibit both problems listed above: they are insufficient in amount and create dangers of censorship. All the evils associated with advertising discussed in chapter 2, problems that partially explain the need for public broadcasting, are introduced by extensive reliance on corporate contributions. Corporate support is additionally troublesome because it relies on the same source, and thus gives power to the same group, that dominates the more influential alternative—commercial broadcasting. Thus, all serious studies of public broadcasting conclude that significant government support is essential.[101]

Government funding can take various forms—for example, the third or fourth option listed above. Presently, in the United States it comes from appropriations from general tax revenues. These funds partially compensate for market failures in the provision of broadcasting and admirably move toward a more efficient level of expenditures. Nevertheless, reliance on general tax revenues has two distinct disadvantages. First, the existing glut of repetitive video programming may make it difficult to sell politically the notion that we have so little TV that we need to devote scarce public tax revenues to the field. Second, and more important, it is difficult to entrench annual expenditures from general tax revenue in a manner that avoids constant political scrutiny. The result is acute vulnerability to political retaliation for critical programming, which spawns timidity and a status quo orientation.[102]

The press's vulnerability to governmental censorship leads countries to constitutionalize their guarantee of a free press. But given the inevitable tension between institutional independence and the media's need for government support,[103] the response to this danger must involve more than negative constitutional guarantees. Government support of the media is granted in all developed countries—but the notion of freedom requires affirmative legislative efforts to include within their support programs structural features that will reduce the danger of censorship. The existing public broadcasting system in the United States serves as an illustration. A variety of structural features have been designed to reduce, and other devices could further reduce,[104] both the opportunity and the incentive for government censorship or partisan manipulation. Public broadcasting surely needs government support structured to reduce the twin dangers of inadequate financing and improper censorship.

As an element of a possible solution, consider a dedicated revenue source that provides public broadcasting with all the revenue from (1) an annual fee for receivers or a sales tax applied to television and radio receivers,[105] or (2) a tax on advertising in commercial broadcasting (or on advertising in all commercial video products, including broadcasting, cable, movies, and videocassettes). Since they rely on money that either consumers or advertisers willingly spend within video-oriented markets, these dedicated taxes avoid the appearance of "wasting" scarce general tax revenues on more television. More importantly, both proposals respond to the two dangers noted above. After setting a sensible tax rate that would provide an appropriate revenue stream, either system could operate without any immediate impetus for annual legislative reconsideration. Either form of dedicated tax would provide a more stable and less politically vulnerable revenue stream than do annual appropriations from general revenues.

A tax on advertising has several advantages over annual fees for or taxes on receivers. First, the advertising tax is likely to be less regressive. Of course, both taxes benefit those people who watch—when they watch—public broadcasting.* But in a society in which virtually all households have a television, an annual receiver license fee amounts to a charge leveled on everyone independent of income.[106] Such a regressive poll tax is apparently popular only with Margaret Thatcher. In contrast, an advertising tax burdens only those who benefit from the advertising itself, and in proportion to the amount they benefit. This does not have the obvious systematic regressivity of a tax on receivers. Second, an advertising tax could provide significant revenue needed for public broadcasting.[107] According to *Broadcasting Yearbook*, in 1989 public broadcasting had an income of $1.55 billion of which 17%, about $263 million, came from the federal government.[108] With broadcast advertising revenues that year of $29.7 billion,[109] a 6% tax rate would have produced $1.78 billion (this ignores any reduction of demand for advertising caused by the tax). Third, like the TA-SR proposal for the print media, this tax reduces advertiser control over broadcasting in favor of control by more independent, professional bodies whose mission is to serve the public. But unlike the TA-SR proposal's effect of tilting influence toward readers and away from advertisers throughout those media, this proposal creates an independent parallel medium—leaving advertising to rule in commercial broadcasting.

In addition to reflexive opposition from the advertising and commercial broadcasting industries, two arguments of "principle" could be leveled against the dedicated advertising tax. First, the video and broadcast advertising tax will presumably cause some erosion of advertising expenditures in broadcasting.[110] If commercial broadcasting is inadequately supported at present, this tax would worsen the situation. Despite its economic logic, however, the claim that we spend too little on commercial broadcasting seems dubious.[111] But let us put these assertions aside and

---

* The main arguments for public television relate to adding diversity and a voice independent of advertisers—that is, for its contributions to a democratic society. Still, public television most immediately benefits those who watch (and those who produce) it. A study in 1977–1978 found that two groups watched public broadcasting more than the societywide norm of 26% who watched at least once a week: African Americans (31%) and the relatively wealthy (31%), an interesting grouping (Ronald E. Frank and Marshall G. Greenberg, *The Public's Use of Television: Who Watches and Why* [1980], 175).

accept the claim that too little is spent on broadcasting; the policy analysis must compare the costs from a decline in total revenue spent on broadcasting and the benefits from (an assertedly) better allocation of the revenues within broadcasting due to the dedicated tax. Although my conclusion will inevitably be contested, the benefits seem likely to be significant and the costs slight.

Second, the proposal imposes a special tax on a form of communication. Some might claim that doing so always makes the tax objectionable, and perhaps unconstitutional. Special taxes are sufficiently manipulable that they should always be troublesome. Although the advertising tax is not overtly viewpoint-biased, the only reason for the dedicated tax is a judgment that it would result in a better mix of broadcast content, with comparatively less spent on commercial television and comparatively more on public television. It can be argued that the government has no business making these content judgments and that these determinations should be left to the market—an equation of freedom of the press with "free" markets. Such a broad argument is, however, economically misguided and historically myopic. Above, I described the failure of "free" markets to supply either the content that people want or that democracy requires; that is, the constraining force of advertising causes the free market to be neither economically efficient nor democratically responsible. Therefore, I argued that reducing the sway of advertising can make the press "freer." Historically, we have never relied on an unadorned free market: state intervention to structure the market or promote better press outputs has been a constant. Virtually no one uniformly objects to all these governmental interventions—but only to those interventions the critic specifically dislikes. When tested on the merits, both the dedicated tax and the public broadcasting support are desirable interventions and, I will argue in chapter 5, constitutional.

A NEW STATE COMMUNICATIONS ENVIRONMENT

Pragmatically, battles for some of the legislation proposed here might be best fought at the state level. Certainly, a state could itself effectively implement most of the proposals, and possibly could do so in a simpler and more rational manner.

For example, a state could eliminate the exemption from the state sales tax generally given to advertising. It could then dedicate the proceeds to improving the state's communications environment. Tax revenues collected from newspaper advertising could subsidize newspapers' circulation revenue. Tax revenue collected from advertising in broadcasting could fund public television and public radio outlets within the state. A fixed portion of the tax revenue from other advertising expenditures could provide increased support for public-access cable channels. Remaining revenue from the advertising tax could go to a bipartisan commission, somewhat like existing state endowments for the arts and the humanities, to fund both ongoing and experimental nonprofit communication forms, including theaters and concerts.

As a practical matter, progressive state legislatures are potentially a more receptive audience for many of these proposals. The extensive political organization needed to push for reform may be more possible in individual states. If, over time, local experiments appeared beneficial, other states or the federal government could adopt similar measures. Of course, reliance on state innovations also presents problems. Most obviously, small states could be subject to political blackmail—boycotts by the advertising industry.

No easy passage can be expected no matter how meritorious the proposals. In Sweden, a tax-and-subsidy scheme was first seriously proposed by the first Parliamentary Commission of the Press of 1963 but was then soundly rejected. The newspaper industry forcefully argued that the proposal would violate constitutional guarantees of press freedom.[112] Only after almost ten years of debate and reflection was this initial rejection reversed, with selective subsidies receiving widespread support. A consensus developed in Sweden behind a new press policy: state intervention and support are viewed as necessary to the maintenance of a free press that properly performs its functions in a democracy.[113] Reform is unlikely to come any more easily or quickly here.

As people develop an agenda for a better communications environment, they must also recognize that the proposals advanced here are only a part of the story. Proposals presented and defended in this chapter respond only to ways that advertising restricts the democratic functioning of a free press. This hardly represents a complete program of democratic reform. Other factors than advertising, such as the concentration of ownership, may restrict or undermine the democratic free press. Therefore, additional legislative responses—and also nonlegislative political responses by individuals and groups[114]—are needed and are possible. For example, greater "contractual newsroom democracy" or legislative protection of rights of journalists within the media enterprise might be a useful response to the tendency for ownership to be concentrated.[115] Much more commonly discussed, various citizen-access proposals have been a mainstay on progressive media agendas. These may be best seen as a response to ownership concentration. Certainly, these access proposals merit attention. Many locales presently require cable systems to provide one or more community-access channels.[116] The potential of community access in cable may be susceptible to nurture. Some commentators have viewed the fairness doctrine, currently rejected by the courts as inconsistent with statutory mandates, as a desirable way of promoting access in broadcasting.[117] I suspect that some forms of access to at least some media could lead to provision of important information to the public, could be the locus of citizen community involvement, and could provide mobilizing communications that could lead to more active citizen involvement generally in civic affairs and politics.[118]

On the other hand, these access proposals have limits. The vast majority and the most important of our mass media communications are likely to be best developed and presented by media professionals. These paid professionals should be able to engage in reporting, creating, editing, and presenting media communications on a scale and with a quality that unpaid citizen involvement would not reproduce. Even if cable access systems or nonprofit community radio should be promoted by government policy and could be expected to add valuable elements to the media realm, they are likely to remain on the margin of the mass media—that is, they are unlikely to serve as a substitute for the advertising-oriented mass media discussed in this book. Thus, the reforms advanced in this book would still be needed.

The Constitutionality of Taxation or Regulation of Advertising

It would be strange indeed . . . if the grave concern for freedom of
the press which prompted adoption of the First Amendment
should be read as a command that the government was without
power to protect that freedom. . . . Surely a command that the
government itself shall not impede the free flow of ideas does not
afford non-governmental combinations a refuge if they impose
restraints upon that constitutionally guaranteed freedom. . . .
Freedom of the press from governmental interference under
the First Amendment does not sanction repression of that
freedom by private interests.[1]
(*Justice Hugo Black*)

THE FIRST AMENDMENT provides that "Congress shall make no law
. . . abridging the freedom of speech, or of the press." "Speech" and "the
press" could be read as merely referring to different methods of expression.
Alternatively, and I think more persuasively, they could be understood to
refer to quite different concerns. Free speech is easily seen as a fundamental
personal right, a guarantee of individual liberty, a person's right to be expressive. In contrast, "the press" could refer to an institution or set of
humanly created entities. The only persuasive (secular) reasons to give
constitutional protection to an institution are instrumental judgments that
doing so will serve human values. History, political theory, and the practice
of other countries suggest that the Press Clause is best understood as a
structural provision designed to protect an institution (or a category of
enterprises) because of its contribution to various forms of human good—
in particular, the press's contribution to checking governmental abuses
and its provision of perspective and information useful to people in their
self-defining activities.[2] This instrumental, structural understanding is illustrated by the popular image of the press as a "fourth estate," playing a
crucial role in our system of government and complementing the legisla-

118

tive, executive, and judicial branches. This institutional approach, how-ever, does not itself determine whether the Press Clause should receive one or another doctrinal reading in relation to the issues raised by the policy proposals in chapter 4.[3]

A Broad or Narrow Reading of the Press Clause

The Press Clause can be read broadly or narrowly on various axes—"broad" meaning in this discussion an interpretation that justifies invali-dating more rather than less government action. Elsewhere I have argued for a particular broad or "special rights" reading of the Press Clause. Spe-cifically, I argued that in addition to granting the press the same broad right to speak as it assures to any private individual, the Constitution also mandates that the press receive special "defensive" protection against gov-ernmental intrusion into its operations, such as protection against com-pelled disclosure of confidential sources or against third-party search war-rants.[4] (The narrow view on this axis is that the Press Clause provides the press with no special rights.) These special protections are those needed to protect the borders, the integrity, of the press as an institution from gov-ernment intrusion. The instrumental argument is that these special rights prevent the government from interfering with the institution in a manner that could undermine the press's ability to perform those of its functions that justify constitutional protection—especially its "fourth estate" role of providing a check on government and maybe its democratic role in provid-ing the public with an independent source of information and opinion.

On the axis of concern in this book—governmental taxation or struc-tural regulation—a "neutrality" reading would be broadest; it would pro-hibit any special treatment of the press, any special taxes and regulations, and any differential treatment.[5] A narrower reading, which I will call the "bad-purpose" reading, would only prohibit special governmental treat-ment of the press that has some specific, objectionable aspect—for exam-ple, the impermissible purpose of trying to undermine the institution's capacity to inform the public. Along this axis, I will argue for the narrower reading. But note that a person's choice between these two readings is likely to turn on an evaluation of the primary threats to, and the significant needs of, a democratic free press.

Either public or private power can threaten press freedom. A possible definitional argument, of course, could be that only government can limit

119

press freedom—that action of a private power is "by definition" an exercise of freedom. But this definitional approach avoids the question that should be a matter of inquiry—that is, what form of press most relates to human or democratic freedom? As long as the press is understood as an institution valued for serving various human purposes, its freedom is best conceived of as dependent on circumstances under which it would be "free" to serve these purposes. From this perspective, the definitional argument is wrong as well as uninteresting. If one person owned all the presses in the country and ordered that the press print nothing or only print a narrow range of views, few would argue that the country had a free press in any meaningful sense. Press freedom requires that this arrangement be broken up: requires, for instance, antitrust laws applied to the press whether or not they apply elsewhere.

A single-minded fear of government abuse requires, however, that all special treatment of the press be condemned. Even special privileges or "subsidies" are objectionable. They allow government to manipulate the press by threatening to take away the privileges or promising new benefits. The carrot combined with the possibility of its withdrawal could create a dependent, docile institution. Mark Hertsgaard suggests that the Reagan administration manipulated the press by granting (or promising) benefits, while the Nixon administration relied on burdens or threats of burdens. The former approach quite clearly secured the more favorable treatment.[6] Governmental power either to bestow favors or to impose burdens creates a real danger that the press will pull punches to curry favor.

A broader view of threats to a free press sees private power and market processes as significant potential obstacles to the press's capacity to serve the needs of a democratic society. This broader understanding of the dangers leads to the narrower, bad-purpose interpretation of the Press Clause. This interpretation's central premise is that government intervention can either promote or undermine press freedom. A properly acting democratic government would intervene only to promote freedom, but history shows that governments often intervene improperly. By providing for judicial review under the Press Clause, the Constitution allows a partially independent institution, the judiciary, to evaluate the propriety of executive and legislative interventions, and to strike down those that it concludes serve an improper purpose. This, it is hoped, maximizes prospects for freedom. The legislature will sometimes, not always, be wise enough to intervene to increase freedom. The courts likewise will sometimes, not always, be wise enough to catch the occasional improper legislative interventions. Unlike the neutrality interpretation, the bad-purpose reading allows normal dem-

120

ocratic processes to promote freedom but retains judicial review to check governmental abuse.*

A broad understanding of the press's needs, like the broad understanding of threats to freedom, leads to the "narrow" bad-purpose interpretation of the Press Clause. Any institution needs many resources to function effectively. The market, operating within the general legal framework, might routinely provide these resources. However, a democratic society may be better served if the press receives a variety of special privileges or opportunities. Only the bad-purpose interpretation of the Press Clause permits these grants.[7] Advocates of the neutrality interpretation must assume that special provisions are not needed, not useful, or more dangerous than they are worth.

The neutrality reading would be supported if a press, unregulated except by generally applicable rules and taxes,[8] creates a proper, "undistorted" or "unbiased" marketplace of ideas while any government intervention causes distortions or biases. Then, the First Amendment might be understood to impose "a special obligation on government to avoid disrupting the integrity of the information market."[9] The constitutional flaw in differential taxes would be that "they distort the competitive forces that animate [the press]."[10] However, unlike the arguments for the "neutrality" interpretation based on the government's being the only relevant threat to press freedom, this "nondistortion" rationale is unsupportable. In practice, the government participates massively in the information marketplace and virtually no one thinks that all aspects of this participation are bad.[11] At least since Jerome Barron forcefully argued for a First Amendment right of access to the press largely on the ground that the existing marketplace of ideas is overwhelmingly biased toward large corporate centers of power,[12] few in legal academia have imagined that the actual media marketplace is neutral or unbiased. Theoretically, the notion of an unbi-

---

* Unlike some European constitutions, ours gives the press legal (judicial) protection only from "governmental action"—that is, governmental restrictions on its freedom. A constitutional regime that did not maintain our "governmental (state) action" requirement (or public/private distinction) might offer the press constitutional protection from both governmental and private threats. Quite obviously, use of such a constitutional standard to identify unconstitutional actions, particularly private restrictions on that freedom, would require development of a more precise theory of what constitutes both the press and its freedom. Although the danger of private restrictions on freedom is real—demonstrating that has been a major point of this book—the identification of what counts as a private abridgment of freedom and, within limits, what counts as the "press" arguably should be left to legislative bodies. Under this pragmatic view, legislative remedies for private threats would not be constitutionally required but also should not be outlawed by the First Amendment's Press Clause.

ased or neutral information context lacks clear meaning. There are no un-contested criteria of neutrality.[13] The appropriate content (or structure) of the information marketplace will necessarily be contested and most justifi-ably depends on political choice. Rather than the doctrinaire assertion that some "unregulated" market is neutral, the more meaningful concern is that the system which some would describe as an *unregulated* market pro-duces characteristic, objectionable tilts as compared to other market or other institutional configurations.

This book's claim is that private power, and particularly advertisers' power, poses a major threat to press freedom. This claim requires rejection of the neutrality interpretation of the Press Clause since that interpretation would thwart effective responses to these threats to freedom. The alter-native, the bad-purpose interpretation, still leaves plenty for the Press Clause to do. The bad-purpose reading is premised on the view that both private and public restrictions of press freedom can be serious problems. This insight suggests a number of doctrinal elements. First, government regulations having bad purposes would be outlawed; all governmental ef-forts to censor or to burden media because of their content should be invalidated. Second, the bad-purpose reading would rule out gratuitous burdens on the press. Such burdens could be understood as implicitly hav-ing a bad purpose. The objection could also be that the gratuitous burdens are inconsistent with the Constitution's implicit attribution of an especially high value to the press. For example, even without evidence of a bad pur-pose, it arguably should be impermissible to impose a *special* tax on the press justified *merely* on the grounds that the tax provides revenue. Given the press's constitutionally recognized value, the government should not treat the press as a special font of tax revenue. Third, governmental pur-poses to make the press operate more effectively or to protect it against private threats to its freedom should rank as not only permissible but highly desirable.

This just begins a sketch of the bad-purpose interpretation. Settling on the most useful doctrinal criteria for identifying unconstitutional govern-ment treatment of the press is not easy. For example, when are rules spe-cially directed at the press adequately justified? Maybe the best view is to permit any special rules not shown to have a bad purpose. Alternatively, since general rules—that is, rules which treat the press and other organiza-tions the same—will usually suffice as responses to most social issues, and since bad purposes are often difficult to identify, maybe constitutional doc-trine should permit special rules for the press only when the rules are rea-sonably seen as promoting a free, democratic press. Or, as another example

CONSTITUTIONALITY

of a doctrinal issue, should there be bans or at least heavy presumptions against particular types of governmental interventions? The bad-purpose reading might adopt these "per se" approaches if experience or reason suggests that certain types of interventions are especially dangerous to press freedom or involve contexts where bad purposes are especially hard to identify. Thus, taxes directed only at the press may seldom be needed to serve a legitimate purpose—a broader tax would always be more effective at raising revenue—but may be sufficiently dangerous that these taxes should be banned for prophylactic reasons.

Despite questions about how the bad-purpose interpretation should be elaborated, as a description of existing law it clearly wins over the neutrality interpretation. The United States has always intervened in the media marketplace, heavily as a participant that produces its own media output but also prominently in ways directed at influencing the content and availability of the constitutionally protected "private" press.[14] The government gives many benefits specifically to the press—often to individual media enterprises. Huge subsidies in the form of second-class mail privileges (given to newspapers and periodicals, but only those not primarily designed for advertising), special facilities for use by reporters, protective shield laws that restrict courts' right to force reporters to disclose confidential sources, tremendous revenue from government advertising (often expended on favored media enterprises), selectively granted interviews with valuable governmental newsmakers, press releases given specially to the media, access to governmentally controlled space where admission depends on having a governmentally issued press card—these are among the routine special treatments of the press. Other governmental interventions, such as the Civil War tax on advertising, the ban on broadcasting tobacco ads, or any other restriction on advertising freedom with the consequent reduction in advertising revenue, drain resources available to the press. Some special benefits, such as government advertising or grants of interviews, are routinely used to manipulate press content, often for partisan reasons. None of these special privileges or burdens, however, has been found to be per se impermissible. Rather, courts more carefully intervene only if they find that the government grants or withholds these benefits for an impermissible reason.[15]

Many forms of state intervention simply are not seen, here or anywhere else in the world, as inconsistent with press freedom. A study of the press of sixteen Western democracies found all countries, including the United States, had at least a moderate level of state intervention.[16] Observers recognize that the interventions are usually unobjectionable, often contributing to a free press's capacity to serve a democratic society. Sweden, the first country to establish freedom of the press, a value it takes very seriously,[17] has the highest level of state intervention in the press among Western democratic countries. Yet virtually no one charges that censorship occurs there (except with respect to motion pictures).[18] Largely as a result of governmental intervention, Sweden has a much higher rate of newspaper competition than does the United States. Swedes are also twice as likely as people here to purchase a newspaper, often purchasing two competing newspapers.[19]

The neutrality interpretation might adjust to these practical realities and only condemn those special governmental interventions that impose burdens. Arguably, the stick presents the greater danger. To reject inducements or "bribes" may be easier than to oppose an effectively enforced prohibition. Thus, governmentally imposed burdens on or prohibitions of the press's communications represent the greater interference with press freedom. Still, historically, prohibitions on publication or purposefully repressive taxes have often become an overt target of massive popular resistance, while the coziness of support, of "bribes," is often more insidious, often both internally ignored and generating little public indignation.

More relevantly here, this doctrinal adjustment cuts the heart out of the neutrality reading. By accepting apparently benign interventions as properly serving the free press, thereby allowing special treatment even though it poses the specter of dependence and manipulation, the neutrality view loses its coherence. It now resembles the bad-purpose interpretation, or better, might be called the "bad-effects" interpretation, which tries to identify the circumstances of intervention or the types of intervention that threaten press freedom. However, the case law rejects even this revised version of the neutrality reading. When the purpose is acceptable, the courts have upheld even regulations that disadvantage the press or, worse, that selectively disadvantage some elements of the press.

In *FCC v. National Citizens Committee for Broadcasting*,[20] newspapers challenged FCC regulations that barred a newspaper from receiving a license to operate a broadcasting station within the newspaper's circulation area. These ownership restrictions applied only to newspapers. The Court, emphasizing that not everyone will be able to obtain a broadcast license,[21] upheld the restrictions. It explained that "the regulations are not content related; moreover, their purpose and effect is to promote free speech, not to restrict it."[22] This good purpose, and lack of a bad purpose, apparently justified differential, *negative* treatment of newspapers. The Court held that "the regulations are a *reasonable* means of promoting the public interest in diversified mass communications; *thus* they do not violate the First Amendment."[23]

The FCC also crafted rules that required divestiture of newspapers' ownership in sixteen "egregious" cases while allowing other newspaper/broadcaster combinations to continue, thereby targeting a small group of media enterprises for specially negative treatment. Despite this discrimination among newspapers, the Court upheld the rules as a "rational" way to promote the public interest in this communications arena. In fact, the Court found that the regulation's reasonableness was "underscored" by the possibility of waivers.[24] Thus, in this situation, the possibility of differential treatment among newspapers, although only for the good purpose of promoting the public interest in a better communications marketplace, apparently added to the regulation's acceptability. Although the case might be limited because it involved the constitutionally unique realm of broadcasting, the Court clearly sanctioned more burdensome treatment of newspapers than of other license applicants. And it sanctioned differential treatment among newspapers as long as no bad purpose was shown and a good purpose, related to improving the communications sphere, was served.

In 1946, the Court approved a labor law exemption for newspapers that published weekly or semiweekly and had a circulation, primarily within the county of publication, of less than three thousand.[25] Although the law treated different papers differently, the Court found *Grosjean v. American Press* (a differential tax case discussed below) inapplicable because the exemption was "not a 'deliberate and calculated device' to penalize a certain group of newspapers."[26] In a sense, this distinction resembles many to be found in various regulations—for example, those distinguishing between the postal rates available to different publications. In this case and others, although the Court does not permit bad purposes, legitimate purposes apparently justify differential treatment.

Similar reasoning led the Ninth Circuit to uphold the Newspaper Preservation Act. The act exempts failing newspapers from otherwise applicable antitrust restrictions on forming a "joint operating agreement" (JOA).[27] Challengers argued "that certain newspapers are treated differently, i.e., preferentially"[28] in that some newspapers get the advantage of JOAs to create a media juggernaut that threatens those papers' actual or potential competitors. Members of Congress opposing the act had made the same point: "[The Act] will preserve certain newspapers but will stifle competition in ideas by crippling the growth of small newspapers and preventing successful establishment of competing dailies."[29] The act treats newspapers differently from other businesses by partially exempting them from the antitrust laws; it also clearly favors some papers and disadvantages other existing and potential competitive papers in the area by allowing two papers to form a JOA, thereby gaining market power. Still, with quite superficial reasoning,[30] the court upheld the act. It implicitly accepted differential treatment among newspapers, even though this treatment disadvantages some media enterprises, making them worse off than if the special legislation did not exist. The Court required only an acceptable purpose—in this case, the policy of preserving editorial diversity.

Even if the Court *generally* upholds governmental action specifically directed at the press as long as the government's purpose is acceptable, in certain contexts, specifically taxation, the dangers of abuse may be sufficient and the need for special treatment may seem sufficiently remote that the Court would apply a prophylactic rule barring all differential treatment.[31] The rule would be, as Justice Thurgood Marshall suggested, that "freedom of the press prohibits government from using the tax power to discriminate against individual members of the media or against the media as a whole."[32] Until very recently, this approach conformed to a plausible reading of the case law.

In *Grosjean v. American Press Co.*,[33] the Court struck down a 2% gross receipts tax on those newspapers with a weekly circulation above 20,000. According to Senator Huey Long, the law was a "tax on lying."[34] The circulation criterion exempted all but 13 of about 124 publishers in the state, but the 13 large-circulation papers included all 12 papers that had "ganged up" on the senator.[35] In *Minneapolis Star v. Minnesota Commissioner of Revenue*,[36] the Court struck down a "use tax" imposed on the cost of paper and ink products consumed in the production of newspapers. The tax exempted the first $100,000 expended on ink and paper, thus effectively exempting all but 14 of the 388 paid-circulation papers in the state, leaving the largest paper to pay about two-thirds of the money raised by the tax.[37] The Court objected both to imposing a special tax on newspapers and to discriminating among the papers.[38] In *Arkansas Writers' Project v. Ragland*,[39] the Court invalidated the application of a general sales tax that exempted all but a few magazines, which were identified on the basis of content. These cases, particularly the two most recent, contain language suggesting that any tax imposed uniquely on the press or discriminating among elements of the press would be struck—or certainly would require a compelling justification to be sustained.

Then, in its 1991 decision in *Leathers v. Medlock*,[40] the Court upheld a tax on cable providers that did not apply to newspapers or other mass media. Given the Supreme Court's acceptance of the state court's conclusion that cable and satellite pay-television are effectively the same medium, by allowing the exemption of satellite services, the Court even upheld differential tax treatment within a single medium.[41] It arguably jettisoned its earlier principles. The Court asserted, "That [a part of the press] is taxed differently from other media does not by itself . . . raise First Amendment concerns. . . . A tax that discriminates among speakers is constitutionally suspect only in certain circumstances";[42] this is hard to reconcile with its statement four years earlier, "Our cases clearly establish that a discriminatory tax on the press burdens rights protected by the First Amendment. . . . Selective taxation of the press—either singling out the press as a whole or targeting individual members of the press—poses a particular danger of abuse by the State."[43]

Nevertheless, despite some broad dicta,[44] the earlier cases should not have been interpreted to support a broad nondiscrimination principle. Rather, these cases are more consistent with the bad-purpose reading of the Press Clause—namely, that bad purposes in regulating the press are impermissible but good purposes can justify special treatment of the press, especially if the purpose is to improve the press's functioning. The only reason constitutional restraints often seem more stringent in the tax than in the regulatory context is that, historically, differential tax treatment could seldom be explained as serving a good purpose.

Louisiana's 2% "tax on lying" certainly had an illicit purpose—to burden content and publishers that Huey Long did not like.[45] The Minnesota tax presents a more difficult issue. The most obvious purpose of any tax is to raise revenue, but the Court persuasively argued: "Standing alone, . . . [this interest in raising revenue] cannot justify the special treatment of the press, for an alternative means of achieving the same interest without raising concerns under the First Amendment is clearly available: the State could raise the revenue by taxing businesses generally, avoiding the censorial threat implicit in a tax that singles out the press."[46] The special tax was not needed to serve any good purpose. This argument basically explains *Minneapolis Star*.

Despite its broad dicta, *Arkansas Writers' Project* also supports the bad-purpose reading. The magazines targeted by the sales tax—three magazines at most paid the tax[47]—were identified specifically by content, which made the differential treatment presumptively objectionable.[48] Beyond the discrimination and its content basis, Arkansas's key failing was that it could not offer a plausible, acceptable purpose to explain the differential treatment.[49] The Court repeated the objection to the revenue-raising purpose that it had made in *Minneapolis Star*,[50] and then considered Arkansas's claim that its legitimate purpose was "to encourage 'fledgling' publishers." Finding the tax exemption both "overinclusive and underinclusive" in relation to this purpose, the Court implicitly rejected the applicability of the offered justification; it was just implausible as an understanding of the exemption's purpose.[51] Still, encouraging fledgling publications amounts to an attempt to improve, expand, and diversify the media marketplace. This is precisely the type of purpose that the Court has approved in regulatory cases. The most interesting aspect of the Court's analysis is that, without deciding the issue, the Court admitted that this purpose might justify the tax if it had been "narrowly tailored to achieve that end."[52] In other words, even before *Medlock*, the Court may have been less committed to a nondiscrimination principle than to a requirement of a proper purpose justifying differential taxation. The cases merely illustrate that in the tax context the state routinely fails to provide such a justification.

PROTECTED COMMERCIAL SPEECH?

The discussion so far has examined newspapers' possible claims that a special or discriminatory tax or regulation violates their press freedom. Depending on how the "press" is conceptualized, regulation or taxation *of advertising* might not even raise a question of the press's freedom. The point of freedom of the press might be to allow people who want to publish and people who want to receive press communications to do so— assuming the would-be publishers have sufficient resources (this recalls A. J. Liebling's famous remark: "Freedom of the press is guaranteed only to those who own one"),[53] and assuming the would-be recipients can convince (pay) the press to provide them with the communications. Under this view, press freedom encompasses the editors' freedom to publish any content they choose (including the *messages* now contained in advertisements), and may encompass the commercial transaction between the publisher and the reader (or viewer) since that is part of their freedom of gaining assess. However, press freedom would not include the commercial transaction between the publisher and the advertiser. That transaction does not involve the press's own decision of what to print but the advertiser's attempt to get the press to print something, to act as the advertiser's agent for communications. Regulation of that transaction is aimed not at the press's communicative choices but at those of the advertiser. A regulation of or tax on advertising, like income taxes and other economic regulations that apply to the press, only affects the press's ability to obtain economic resources. The press has no constitutional right to demand a tax or regulatory regime favorable to its financial needs. Even though cigarette advertising was the largest source of revenue for television and radio, the congressional ban on advertising cigarettes over the electronic media, which eliminated this revenue, did not infringe press freedom.[54] Of course, even on this understanding of the press, if the *purpose* of the regulation or prohibition of advertising was to undermine the press as an institution, the law would be unconstitutional. The proposals advanced in chapter 4, however, are better characterized as having the purpose of strengthening the press as an institution.

Still, whether or not regulation and taxation of advertising should be seen as regulation of the press, chapter 4's proposed regulation and taxation of advertising clearly implicate *advertisers'* possible constitutional rights. For several years after the Supreme Court's mid-1970s decisions that first found commercial speech to be protected by the First Amendment,[55] advertisers' free speech claims had considerable legal force. More recent Court decisions, however, make a shambles of the notion that commercial speech receives significant constitutional protection. The Court has adopted a four-part test that permits the government to enact even "paternalistic" regulations aimed at preventing the commercial speaker from providing nonmisleading information, if the regulation directly advances a substantial governmental interest. The Court in 1980 indicated that it would uphold a ban on an electrical utility's advertisements that promoted electrical usage, presumably even if the prohibited ads were entirely true and promoted only lawful uses of electricity, as long as the ban applied only to those promotions that were contrary to the state's conservation goals.[56] More dramatically in 1986, the Court upheld Puerto Rico's prohibition of casino advertising directed at the local population. The ban purportedly served the paternalistic purpose of reducing demand for gambling by local residents, even though their gambling at the casinos was legal in Puerto Rico.[57] Similarly, the Court has upheld a restriction on corporate political speech and association that would be impermissible if applied to individuals.[58]

This does not mean that any regulation of commercial speech will automatically be upheld. In 1993, the Court in a 6–3 decision struck down a city's order to remove the 62 freestanding newsracks used for distributing "commercial handbills" while the city left untouched the 1,500 to 2,000 newsracks used to distribute traditional newspapers.[59] The Court emphasized that "the distinction between the commercial speech and noncommercial speech . . . bears no relationship whatsoever" to the aesthetic concerns behind the city's regulation and that there was nothing special about the commercial speech as a cause of the problem. That is, the Court found no "reasonable fit" between the city's interests and its regulation. Of course, this decision provides no support for invalidating any of the regulations proposed in this book since all the proposed regulations do relate directly to problems caused by advertising.

These recent cases hint that the Court's protection of commercial speech may now be virtually limited to the requirement that the regulation be a reasonable means to advance the governmental interest plus the Court's original "consumer-protection"-oriented decisions, such as those striking down bans on advertising drug prices or lawyers' services. These restrictions on commercial speech harmed consumers while benefiting segments of the pharmacy or legal profession by limiting the effectiveness of competition, usually price competition.[60] Although possibly commercial speech should never have been protected at all,[61] under current doctrine any good policy justification for a tax or regulation should defeat an advertiser's First Amendment claims.

APPLICATION OF CONSTITUTIONAL PRINCIPLES

Chapter 4's policy proposals should withstand constitutional attack. Still, the certainty of this conclusion depends on the detailed design of the proposals.

First are the various proposals to tax advertising. Such taxes are arguably like the Stamp Act taxes that, according to the Court in *Grosjean v. American Press Co.*, helped prompt adoption of the First Amendment.[62] The Court's historical claim has surprisingly little support in most histories of the Press Clause. In a later dissenting opinion, Justice Reed argued that an examination of sources relied on by the Court in *Grosjean* reveals no support for the claim that the Stamp Act influenced the adoption of the First Amendment.[63] Possibly because of a focus on seditious libel in their principal historical works, neither Leonard Levy nor David Anderson describes a concern about the Stamp Act as playing any role in the adoption of the First Amendment.[64] Although England's imposition of a Stamp Act, which applied to both newspapers and newspaper advertising, helped radi-

calize the colonial press and stirred opposition that contributed significantly to the American Revolution, the colonists' opposition to the Stamp
Act revolved primarily around the "no taxation without representation"
issue.[65] Still, Massachusetts's 1785 stamp tax on newspapers and its subsequent tax on newspaper advertisements, with which the state quickly replaced the initial stamp tax, generated strong opposition both in Massachusetts and in commentary from other states precisely on the ground that
the tax was an "unconstitutional restraint on the Liberty of the Press."[66]
Massachusetts's repeal in 1786 of its advertising tax was treated as a great
victory for "Freedom of the Press."[67] Certainly this history supports the
notion that stamp taxes, including advertising taxes of the time, violated
prevalent early conceptions of press freedom, thereby lending support to
the general linkage suggested in *Grosjean*. This history does not speak,
however, to the question of whether the problem was with all taxes on the
press or only with specific taxes—and if the latter, to the question of what
criteria make them objectionable. Specifically, the history is mute concerning the validity of taxes that do not have an objectionable, unconstitutional
purpose to undermine press freedom. Whether or not this history con-
demns taxing the press merely for revenue purposes, it surely says nothing
about taxes on advertising enacted affirmatively to support a reasonable
conception of press freedom.

The tax most vulnerable to challenge would be one that applied
uniquely to, or at a higher rate to, advertising in the media and that applied
to only some segments of the media. The Court has never upheld such a
tax. In *Leathers v. Medlock* , the Court allowed Arkansas to treat different
media differently, but the tax on cable services was identical to the tax on
many other items; thus the tax did not single out the media or any segment
of the media industry for a unique burden. But even though such a
uniquely burdensome tax has not been upheld, the issue remains open. No
such tax has been defended on a legitimate ground that could provide a
rationale for the differential treatment. The taxes in *Grosjean*, *Minneapolis
Star*, and *Arkansas Writers' Project* lacked plausible, legitimate rationales
for their differential treatment of portions of the press. In contrast, chapter
4's proposed taxes on advertising serve, and have a purpose to serve, First
Amendment values. Both the tax and the subsidy in the TA-SR proposal
perfectly fit the important goal of making the press more responsive to its
readers by reducing advertising's value and increasing circulation sales'
value to the media, thereby leading any profit-oriented press to focus its
decision making more on the needs and interests of its readers and less on

131

the interests of its advertisers. Of course, the Court regularly invalidates laws that censor press content.[68] And the Court has struck down laws for imposing a direct burden on an editor's decision to publish particular messages, for example, Florida's law giving a potential candidate a right to force a newspaper to print his or her reply to newspaper criticism.[69] But the Court has never struck down a tax or regulation that was designed to improve press functioning by structural regulation.[70] The legitimate justifications of improving press functioning should suffice for upholding all the tax proposals discussed in chapter 4.

Even if the Court would strike down a uniquely media-oriented advertising tax, it would likely uphold a more broad-based tax. Probably the tax would be sufficiently general if it applied to all advertising (including direct mail, billboard, point-of-purchase display ads and promotions, free shoppers, and advertising supplements) and not just advertising in the media or in one component of the media.[71] There would also be significant policy advantages in adopting this broader tax. Taxing only advertising in newspapers, for example, would cause some advertisers to shift some of their expenditures on newspapers to other advertising media, and this would result in a net reduction in newspapers' revenue. In contrast, a tax on all advertising expenditures would greatly reduce these shifts in advertisers' allocation of advertising expenditures.[72] If all the tax revenue went to subsidize newspapers (or newspapers and other mass media), the broader advertising tax would probably increase net newspaper or media revenue. Thus, even though a narrow tax probably meets constitutional requirements, this broader tax is more clearly constitutional and makes the most policy sense.[73]

Finally, there is the unlikely possibility that the courts would read the Press Clause to rule out even a broad advertising tax, possibly on the ground that the tax discriminated against commercial speech.[74] A version of the tax proposals presented in chapter 4 could still be upheld. A general sales tax that included advertising among the taxed sales is unquestionably constitutional. The government could tax advertising at the general sales-tax rate and still allocate the tax revenue to support the subsidy plan.

The subsidy portion of chapter 4's TA-SR proposal (or the subsidy for public broadcasting) causes no constitutional problems. Even content-oriented government subsidies, such as grants by national endowments for the arts and humanities, are often acceptable. A subsidy based on circulation revenue should be even more acceptable since it creates no issue of content discrimination, with its latent danger of censorship. The one significant policy concern (although implausible as a constitutional objection) is that the subsidy could make the press too dependent on the government. The press might become timid out of fear of losing the subsidy or might be manipulated by promises or threats regarding the subsidy. This concern is real and troubling.* As long as subsidies or any other form of special benefits are permitted, this danger cannot be entirely eliminated. However, as far as I know, this reasoning has never been the basis of a Court decision striking down a subsidy scheme. The government has always provided extensive press subsidies. Some of these benefits, especially discretionary access to official sources and government advertising, have even been consistently used to manipulate the press. A subsidy based on circulation revenue allows for little administrative discretion. In this respect, it is most like forms of subsidy that have been least susceptible to manipulative abuse. Unless all versions of subsidy are ruled unconstitutional, which is virtually unthinkable, the subsidy scheme proposed here should withstand constitutional challenge.

The regulatory proposals suggested in chapter 4 are also constitutional. These regulatory proposals amount to prohibiting nonmedia entities from using economic leverage to affect media content, at least unless the media enterprise identifies the affected content as an advertisement. A restriction on advertisers' influence on nonadvertising content was imposed in a limited fashion as early as the 1912 postal legislation, which denied special mailing privileges to papers that published advertising not clearly marked as an advertisement.[75] Like this early law, the proposals in chapter 4 do not restrict but indeed support editorial control over the publication's editorial content.

A comparison of two landmark Supreme Court decisions related to freedom of the press illustrates the same point. In *Miami Herald Publishing Co. v. Tornillo*,[76] the Court invalidated a law that required newspapers to

---

* This danger is the origin of the oft-noted problem of bias resulting from reporters' dependence on their governmental sources. I. F. Stone is famous for the view that reporters should not become cozy, should not drink cocktails, with those on whom they are reporting, especially with those in power. See, e.g., Lee and Solomon, *Unreliable Sources*, 103. This dependence explains, for example, why a local television station will *sometimes* choose not to broadcast graphic pictures of police brutality. Retired television anchor Roger Grimsby put it bluntly: "A reporter has to remain in the good graces of the police." Rewarding the station for killing the brutality pictures, the police provided a tip that enabled the station to give the public award-winning pictures of the police acting effectively (Lew Irwin, "Cops and Cameras: Why TV Is Slow to Cover Police Brutality," *Columbia Journalism Review*, Sept.–Oct. 1991, 15, 16–17).

print replies of political candidates whom the newspaper had criticized. In *Associated Press v. United States*,[77] the Court upheld the government's application of the antitrust laws to prevent AP and member newspapers from agreeing to deny nonmembers news generated by the AP or its member papers. Essentially, the Court in *Associated Press* allowed the government to outlaw use of private power (even by members of the media) to restrict the speech of media entities or to restrict the availability of news to others. That is, the government was permitted to regulate private power when it was used to limit a newspaper's speech. Rather than interfering with or punishing an editor for editorial choices, as did the invalidated right-to-reply law, restrictions on advertiser influence are versions of laws that prevent nongovernmental combinations from using economic power or wealth to restrain press freedom—the type of law the Court upheld in *Associated Press*.

Analogous to the antitrust laws that prohibit agreements in restraint of trade, laws to restrict advertisers' influence over suppliers of media content prohibit agreements in restraint of publication (or prohibit the use of economic leverage to achieve goals of this sort). Chapter 4's proposals prohibit the advertiser from restraining the media enterprise's decisions to print or broadcast anything other than what the media entity would independently choose. On the facts, the antitrust analogy and the proposals made here are even closer. In *Associated Press*, the antitrust laws were interpreted to prohibit media entities from entering into agreements with other media entities to restrict their own speech. Here the proposals are to prohibit advertisers from using their power in their interactions with media entities as a means to restrict the media's speech. If freedom of the press is seen as essentially the freedom of media to decide what to provide to their audiences, the advertiser influence that causes the media not to speak as they would otherwise choose, using the words of Justice Black, is a "nongovernmental combination" that "impede[s] the free flow of ideas," a "repression of that freedom by private interests."[78]

Tornillo is the central decision offering even potential support for a constitutional challenge to proposals limiting the time broadcasters can devote to advertising, requiring the media to identify paid-for content as advertising and to identify the advertisers, or requiring partial randomization of ad placement or block broadcasting of ads. Each of these proposals controls an element of the media presentation—each could be said to let the government into the editorial office. The Court in *Tornillo* gave two grounds for its holding. The more persuasive, and narrower, basis of the holding was the Court's argument that requiring newspapers to print a response to the paper's own speech "exacts a penalty on the basis of the content of a newspaper."[79] Not only is this penalty itself unconstitutional; it has the objectionable consequence that "editors might well conclude that the safe course is to avoid controversy. Therefore, . . . coverage would be blunted or reduced."[80] This ground of decision creates no obstacle for any of the reforms offered here. None of these proposals penalizes the paper for any of its choices of content. This narrow ground of decision also makes unnecessary *Tornillo*'s alternative, broader basis—the impermissibility of the statute's "intrusion into the function of editors."[81]

Even this broader basis of decision does not require invalidation of the policy proposals. First, editors' control over editorial choices does not necessarily mean they have the same authority over advertising. The function of the editor preeminently covers the medium's own speech. It is a separate question how much control the editor should have over space or time the editor (or publisher) opens up to sell to others for their speech. The Constitution may give editors complete freedom over their own speech and still permit them to be restricted with respect to how they perform as an agent for advertisers' speech. Moreover, none of the proposals requires editors to perform this role—they do not compel that advertisements be published or broadcast. Second, the compelled speech implicit in identification requirements, possibly because of its factual nature, has generally been thought to raise less of a constitutional problem than the compelled statement of opinion or ideological viewpoint that was involved in *Tornillo*.[82] Finally, the identification requirement is clearly constitutionally acceptable as applied to advertiser-influenced content. No recent developments in commercial speech doctrine question the propriety of the Court's suggestion in *Virginia State Board of Pharmacy v. Virginia Citizens Consumer Council*: "It . . . [may be] appropriate to require that a commercial message appear in such a form, or include such additional information, warnings, and disclaimers, as are necessary to prevent its being deceptive."[83]

Both the proposal to regulate the amount of broadcast advertising and to limit it to set blocks between programs and the proposal to mandate randomized placement of broadcast advertising are probably justifiable on grounds described above. Moreover, their application only in the broadcast context, given the Court's willingness to treat broadcasting as more subject to regulatory control than the print media, makes them even less vulnerable to attack.[84] The Court has hinted that it would uphold a mandate that broadcasters accept issue-oriented advertising if required by Congress (or the FCC).[85] It presently upholds mandatory access for candidate campaign ads.[86] These interferences are at least as intrusive into broadcasters' "editorial" freedom as the proposals made here. Likewise, earlier FCC restrictions on overcommercialization and current congressional limitations on advertising time during children's programming[87] provide support for the proposal to limit the amount of broadcast time devoted to advertising. The purpose of reducing advertiser influence over programming provides sufficient justification for these regulations.

. . . . .

The heart of this book is chapter 1 and 2's examination of the way advertising undermines the free and democratic nature of the press, and chapter 4's recommended legislative responses. Chapters 3 and 5 were defensive. Chapter 3 explained that although economic theory supports or at least is consistent with the critique of advertising's effects on the media, economic theory cannot solve the normative issues raised concerning the proper structure of the media. Chapter 5 argued that, despite inevitable assertions to the contrary, the policy proposals do not conflict with the Constitution.

This suffices as a recap. The next question follows Lenin: "What is to be done?"[88] That is a question each reader must decide, and the answers appropriately vary. One thing I want to do is to move on, to study the impact that the distribution and nature of ownership and the distribution of control between owners and media professionals have on the democratic quality of the press. Activists may want to promote media reform. Journalists and editors may want to increase their already strong commitment to keep their journalistic and creative decisions free of even subtle or indirect advertiser influence. The claim of this book, however, is that individual efforts of journalists and editors cannot succeed adequately given the existing economic and legal framework. A better, freer, more democratic press requires structural change. This structural change should be put on the agenda of progressive politics. The call is for everyone to support useful reform. Recent taxes like California's on newspaper sales should be opposed. Applications of sales taxes to advertising are wisely supported. But more dramatic proposals like those offered in chapter 4 should be entertained.

Given a generally healthy, almost reflexive tendency of journalists and editors, writers and producers, to keep the government out of their house, support for legal reform is likely to be grudging, at best, from this group. Still, because of knowledge about the media, organizational focus on the media, interest in the media's quality, and belief in the media's importance, this group's leadership is central. Out of a concern for both press freedom and a more democratic society, I must hope that this group— journalists and editors, writers and producers—will come to see that the problem of keeping their house clean, of both government and commercial influence, requires not just their own professional integrity but structural change, structural change for which their support is likely to be crucial.

✩ *Mathematical Appendix* ✩

GIVEN A FEW simplifying assumptions, the effects of TA-SR on a newspaper's cover price can be described mathematically. First, I assume a linear relation between circulation and ad revenue and a negative linear relation between cover price and circulation. I adopt as definitions:

p = cover price

n = circulation sales; n is assumed to be a linear function of cover price, $n = n(p)$.

$n(p) = n_1 - n_2 p$, where:

   n_1 = circulation if $p = 0$

   n_2 = marginal change in circulation as price changes

np = circulation revenue

c_1 = fixed costs

c_2 = marginal cost of each additional paper sold

a = ad revenues and is a function of circulation, $a = a(n)$.

$a(n) = a_2 n = a_2(n_1 - n_2 p)$, where:

   a_2 = additional ad revenue for each paper sold.

$\P$ = profit

total cost = $c_1 + c_2 n$

total revenue = $a + np = a(n) + n(p)p$

profit = total revenue minus total cost, or:

$$\P = a(n) + n(p)p - c_1 - c_2 n$$

Then tax advertising at rate k, and subsidize circulation revenue at rate s:

$$\P = (1 - k)a(n) + (1 + s)n(p)p - c_1 - c_2 n$$
$$\P = (1 - k)(a_2)(n_1 - n_2 p) + (1 + s)(n_1 - n_2 p)p - c_1 - c_2$$
$$(n_1 - n_2 p)$$
$$\P = (1 - k)(a_2 n_1) - c_1 - c_2 n_1 + p[(1 - k)(-a_2 n_2)$$
$$+ (1 + s)(n_1) + c_2 n_2] + p^2[(1 + s)(-n_2)]$$

Then take derivative with respect to price and set equal to 0.

$$0 = (1 - k)(-a_2 n_2) + (1 + s)(n_1) + c_2 n_2 - 2p[(1 + s)(n_2)]$$

To maximize $\P$, solve for p:

$$p = \frac{a_2 k}{2(1+s)} + \frac{c_2 - a_2}{2(1+s)} + \frac{n_1}{2n_2}$$

In order to find whether the effect of the tax and the subsidy on the profit-maximizing price causes the price to go up or down, take the derivative of p with respect to k and then with respect to s. First:

$$\frac{dp}{dk} = \frac{a_2}{2(1+s)} > 0, \text{ therefore the tax causes an increase in the profit-maximizing price.}$$

Rearranging terms,

$$p = \frac{c_2 - a_2(1-k)}{2(1+s)} + \frac{n_1}{2n_2} \quad \text{and then:}$$

$$\frac{dp}{ds} = \frac{c_2 - a_2(1-k)}{-2(1+s)^2} = \frac{a_2(1-k) - c_2}{2(1+s)^2}$$

Thus, the subsidy would cause the profit-maximizing cover price to decrease if $a_2(1-k) - c_2 < 0$, and to increase if > 0. That is, the higher marginal ad revenue (a_2) is in comparison to marginal cost (c_2), the more likely the subsidy would cause an increase in cover price.

Ann Lofaso, Adam Litke, and Reed Shuldiner assisted in this appendix; any errors are those of the author.

☆ *Notes* ☆

PREFACE

1. But see Elizabeth Blanks Hindman, "First Amendment Theories and Press Responsibility: The Work of Zechariah Chafee, Thomas Emerson, Vincent Blasi and Edwin Baker," *Journalism Quarterly* 69 (1992): 48.

2. See Project Censored, "The Top 10 Censored Stories of 1990," *Utne Reader* 46 (1991): 61.

3. C. Edwin Baker, *Human Liberty and Freedom of Speech* (1989).

INTRODUCTION

1. Despite the historical importance attributed to the Stamp Act by the Supreme Court in Grosjean v. American Press Co., 297 U.S. 233, 245–49 (1936), the British and Massachusetts stamp acts' relevance to the First Amendment may be somewhat more complex. See chapter 5.

2. See Act of July 1, 1862, ch. 119, § 88, 12 Stat. 432, 472–73; Frank L. Mott, *American Journalism: A History, 1690–1960* (1962), 398.

3. See An Act Relating to Taxation, 1987 Fla. Laws ch. 6 (repealed 1987); Steven M. Cohen, "A Tax on Advertising: First Amendment and Commerce Clause Implications," *New York University Law Review* 63 (1988): 810.

4. See Steven W. Colford and Julie Liesse, "Marketers Dodge Bush Tax Bullet," *Advertising Age*, Oct. 29, 1990, 1.

5. See Richard J. Barber, "Newspaper Monopoly in New Orleans: The Lessons for Antitrust Policy," *Louisiana Law Review* 24 (1964): 503, 553 (examining the impact of antitrust policy on the newspaper industry, and suggesting that in view of its limitations, "progressive tax levies on advertising revenue" would be more effective in reducing reliance on advertising as a source of revenue); Thomas E. Humphrey, "The Newspaper Preservation Act: An Ineffective Step in the Right Direction," *Boston College Industrial and Commerce Law Review* 12 (1971): 937, 951–54 (noting that the Newspaper Preservation Act will not stop the anticompetitive trend and proposing a progressive tax on newspaper advertising revenue).

6. See below, chapter 5.

7. See Valentine v. Chrestensen, 316 U.S. 52 (1942); Posadas de Puerto Rico Assocs. v. Tourism Co., 478 U.S. 328 (1986); Board of Trustees v. Fox, 492 U.S. 469 (1989).

8. See C. Edwin Baker, *Human Liberty and Freedom of Speech* (1989), 194–224.

9. Advertising provides this country's daily newspapers with 60% to 80% of their revenue, and broadcasters with virtually all of theirs.

Newspapers' dependence on advertising revenues varies quite dramatically from country to country. In the mid-1970s, the percentage of newspaper revenues that came from advertising was approximately 83% in Switzerland, 71% in West Germany, 50% in Sweden, 41% in Great Britain, and 33% in France. See Royal Commission on the Press, *Final Report Appendices* (1977), app. C, 105–6 (hereafter cited as *Royal Commission*).

10. The German Constitutional Court suggests that legislative bodies have a constitutional obligation to prevent broadcasters' access to advertising from inordinately undermining newspapers' advertising. See *North-Rhine/Westphalia Broadcasting Law*, 82 BVerfGE 238, 1991 NJW 899, 907 (holding that the purpose of the broadcasting statute of North-Rhine/Westphalia—the protection of the economic basis of the press against dangers resulting from commercial broadcasting—supports the constitutionality of the law); *Lower Saxony Broadcasting Law*, 73 BVerfGE 118, 180 (1986) (F.R.G.) (noting that the danger that advertising in private broadcasting will result in the press's losing an essential source of financing is relevant under constitutional law, since that would affect the constitutional protection of the press as an institution, that is, the existence and effectiveness of a free press); *FRAG*, 57 BVerfGE 295, 341 (1981) (F.R.G.) (raising but not deciding whether advertising in private broadcasting needs regulation in order to protect the press).

11. Robert J. Samuelson, "The End of Advertising?" *Newsweek*, Aug. 19, 1991, 40.

12. Michael Schudson, *Advertising: The Uneasy Persuasion* (1984), 209–38.

13. See, e.g., James Curran, "Mass Media and Democracy: A Reappraisal," in James Curran and Michael Gurevitch, ed., *Mass Media and Society* (1991), 82–117.

14. Baker, *Human Liberty and Freedom of Speech*, 229–34, 250–55.

15. See, e.g., Vincent Blasi, "The Checking Value in First Amendment Theory," *American Bar Foundation Research Journal* (1977): 521.

16. See, e.g., Alexander Meiklejohn, *Political Freedom: The Constitutional Powers of the People* (1965).

17. Of course, many additional specific qualities could be listed as appropriate elements of a free and democratic press. See, e.g., Michael Gurevitch and Jay G. Blumler, "Political Communications Systems and Democratic Values," in Judith Lichtenberg, ed., *Democracy and the Mass Media* (1990), 269, 270 (listing eight nonexclusive functions or goals for democratic media).

CHAPTER I
ADVERTISING: FINANCIAL SUPPORT AND
STRUCTURAL SUBVERSION OF A DEMOCRATIC PRESS

1. Leo Bogart, *Press and Public*, 2d ed. (1989), 50–51; see also 166–67; and see James N. Dertouzos and William Trautman, "Economic Effects of Media Concentration: Estimates from a Model of the Newspaper Firm," *Journal of Industrial*

Economics 39 (1990): 1, 6n.13 (support for assumption that consumers value news and advertising content equally on the margin).

2. U.S. Department of Commerce, "General Summary," *1987 Census of Manufactures* (1991), table 1, code 2711, p. 1–114. Generally, estimates vary and, of course, change over time. See, e.g., Christopher Sterling and Timothy B. Haight, *The Mass Media: Aspen Institute Guide to Communication Industry Trends* (1979), 119 (75.1% in 1972, citing Census of Manufacturers); Ben H. Bagdikian, *The Media Monopoly*, 3d ed. (1990), 115 (75% of daily paper revenues from advertising); Peter J. S. Dunnett, *The World Newspaper Industry* (1988), 25 (as much as 80% of revenue of the *Wall Street Journal* comes from ads); James N. Rosse and James N. Dertouzos, *Economic Issues in Mass Communications Industries* (1978), 29 (daily papers get 60% to 80% of revenues from advertising), and 44 (representative paper in 1977 obtained 76% of revenue from advertising); Jon G. Udell, *The Economics of the American Newspaper* (1978), 99 (65% to 70% from advertising); George T. Kurian, ed., *World Press Encyclopedia* (1982), 2:975 (dailies receive between 20% and 30% of revenue from circulation sales).

3. One statistical study offers apparent support for the view that advertising contributes only a relatively small subsidy to newspapers' nonadvertising costs. See Lawrence C. Solely, "Does Advertising Lower the Prices of Newspapers to Consumers?" *Journalism Quarterly* 66 (1989): 801. If its conclusions are right, this might mean that there is no need to preserve advertising in order to protect the press's viability; moreover, for purposes of this book, the study's most important implication is that advertisers might not be expected to exercise much leverage over media content. However, its analysis seems fundamentally flawed. Solely's regression crucially relied on the assumption that ad space would be proportional to ad revenue among papers. However, the more that advertising revenue supports a higher-quality editorial product (a product that draws, for instance, an upscale audience), the higher the ad revenue will be for a given space—thus, the regression is likely to have gravely understated the contribution of greater advertising space to greater revenue and hence to support of the editorial product. The analysis seems riddled with other problems in its assumptions and interpretation of observed data, including the curious inclusion of editorial space as an element of both the dependent and one of the independent variables. Moreover, its conclusions seem inconsistent with the accepted wisdom within the industry and with other more direct economic studies of newspaper production. For example, in the 1960s Reddaway found that the quality national London papers which had a cover price of fourpence obtained approximately an additional fivepence per copy from advertising after all the costs of obtaining and including the advertising were subtracted—revenue that provides a huge potential for support of the editorial content. See, e.g., William B. Reddaway, "The Economics of Newspapers," *Economic Journal* 73 (1963): 201, 206.

4. This hypothesized relationship survives today in limited contexts—for example, in papers that, consisting solely of classified advertising, are sold to readers but permit advertisers to advertise for free.

5. Dunnett, *The World Newspaper Industry*, 39n.7.

6. Bogart, *Press and Public*, 49.

7. For example, in 1960 advertisers provided 48% of the revenue for typical London "popular" dailies but 73% for typical London "quality" dailies; and the advertising rate per copy sold in the "quality" papers was 3.9 times the rate for the "popular" ones (Reddaway, "The Economics of Newspapers," 207).

8. More precisely, the newspaper will lose "marginal purchasers," which will not directly correspond to a loss in readers. Historically, as price goes up, the number of readers per copy tends to increase.

9. If, before the elimination of advertising, the paper could have charged readers a higher price and obtained from readers alone as much as it had obtained from readers plus advertisers, the profit-maximizing paper would have charged something closer to that price and also obtained at least some of its previous advertising revenue.

10. Some magazines make a conscious decision not to take advertising, and others have chosen to take it only on a very limited basis. James Curran documents some ideological or political discrimination against the radical working-class press. See James Curran, "Capitalism and Control of the Press, 1800–1975," in James Curran et al., eds., *Mass Communication and Society* (1979), 195, 218. However, Curran finds much more widespread evidence of discrimination on the basis of the perceived value of the working-class audience, quoting, for example, an anonymous expert in an 1851 *Guide to Advertisers*: " 'Character is of more importance than number. A journal that circulates a thousand among the upper or middle classes is a better medium than would be one circulating a hundred thousand among the lower classes' " (218–19).

11. Edward Herman and Noam Chomsky, *Manufacturing Consent* (1988), 14.

12. In the few remaining American markets where competitive daily newspapers exist, maintenance of competition seems to depend on the two papers' maintaining roughly equal circulation.

13. Curran, "Capitalism and Control of the Press, 1800–1975," 225.

14. Ibid.

15. Ibid. While the *New York Times* was doing fine, the *New York Daily News* was on the brink on financial collapse throughout the 1980s even though it began the decade as the country's second largest newspaper after the *Wall Street Journal*.

16. Competitive papers presumably must split both advertising and circulation available in a community. Thus predictably each would individually have much less money available to spend on editorial content than would a monopoly paper. Surprisingly, available evidence suggests that competition results in each paper's allocating more money for editorial content than it would when and if it became a monopolist. See, e.g., Stephen Lacy, "The Effects of Intracity Competition on Daily Newspaper Content," *Journalism Quarterly* 64 (1987): 281. Lacy found that competition affected a newspaper's budget allocations in the direction of its purchasing more wire services and hiring more reporters to fill a given space. He con-

cluded that "intense competition means a newspaper must spend more money to differentiate itself and to remain a substitute for its competitor" (288).

17. See, e.g., Bagdikian, *The Media Monopoly*, 120–25 (referring to the rise of mass advertising as having occurred during the last two generations).

18. Ibid., 125.

19. See Mott, *American Journalism*, 201. Mott reports that although there were few advertisements in the first, unprosperous papers in the country, "announcements of merchants and traders" filled three to five pages of papers by the middle of the eighteenth century (56), and he notes that "front pages were more or less filled with advertising" until the 1850s (298).

20. Robert Atwan, "Newspapers and the Foundations of Modern Advertising," in John W. Wright, ed., *The Commercial Connection* (1979), 9, 14.

21. See Michael Schudson, *Discovering the News: A Social History of American Papers* (1978), 14.

22. See ibid., 22.

23. See ibid., 18–19 (noting that "sources of income that depended on social ties or political fellow feeling were replaced by market-based income from advertising and sales" and that "patent medicines became the mainstay of the advertising columns").

24. *Congressional Globe*, 37th Cong., 1st sess. 1487, 1860 (statement of Representative Colfax).

25. See, e.g., Mott, *American Journalism*, 201 (noting the especially high ratio of advertising to space because of low advertising rates); S.D.N. North, *History and Present Condition of the Newspaper and Periodical Press of the United States* (1881), 88 (noting that colonial printers were apparently glad to get what they could for advertising and that advertising space in the six-penny New York dailies of the first half of the nineteenth century "was not only sold at very low rates, but often given away").

26. Bogart, *Press and Public*, 49.

27. Ibid., 504.

28. Schudson, *Discovering the News*, 93 (citation omitted).

29. Dan Schiller, *Objectivity and the News* (1981), 185 (citation omitted).

30. Alfred M. Lee, *The Daily Newspaper in America* (1937), 748–49. This report of a roughly 5% increase each decade from 1879 to 1929 combines newspapers and other periodicals; after 1909, Lee also listed percentages for newspapers, which tended to be 1% to 4% higher than for the combination, reaching a high of 74.3% of newspaper revenue in 1929. Lee's data were relied upon, but mistranscribed, in Sidney Kobre, *The Yellow Press and Gilded Age Journalism* (1964), 309. Schudson reported that the portion of newspaper revenue from advertising increased from 44% in 1880 to 55% in 1900 (*Discovering the News*, 93). Schudson also cites a different study which found that advertising revenue as a percentage of newspaper revenue rose from 49% in 1879 to 64% in 1909 (206n.13).

31. Sterling and Haight, *The Mass Media*, 119, 157; U.S. Department of Commerce, "General Summary," *1987 Census of Manufactures*, 1–114; U.S. Department of Commerce, *U.S. Industrial Outlook '92* (1992), 25–3.

32. See "Memo from the Publisher," *1992 Editor and Publisher International Yearbook*; Rosse and Dertouzos, *Economic Issues in Mass Communications Industries*, 48 (citing James N. Rosse et al., "Trends in the Daily Newspaper Industry 1923–1973," in *1978 Editor and Publisher International Yearbook*); John C. Busterna, "Trends in Daily Newspaper Ownership," *Journalism Quarterly* 65 (1988): 831, 833; Raymond B. Nixon and Jean Ward, "Trends in Newspaper Ownership and Inter-Media Competition," *Journalism Quarterly* 38 (1961): 3, 5.

Different studies report slightly different numbers. Numbers taken from *Ayer Directory* tend to be the highest, followed by those from the *Census of Manufactures*; the lowest come from *Editor and Publisher*, which includes only English-language papers. See Sterling and Haight, *The Mass Media*, 19–20, 22. Rosse's study, which reports a decline in dailies from 1,977 in 1923 to 1,589 in 1978, is routinely cited. Nixon and Ward report 850 dailies in 1880; 2,202 in 1910; 2,042 in 1920; 1,744 in 1945; and 1,763 in 1960. Busterna reports a decline from 2,042 in 1920 to 1,657 in 1986. Apparently the number of dailies peaked around 1910.

33. Without supporting data, one study indicates that this trend has been observable since 1890. See Paul Neurath, "One-Publisher Communities: Factors Influencing Trend," *Journalism Quarterly* 21 (1944): 230, 240.

34. See Rosse and Dertouzos, *Economic Issues in Mass Communications Industries*, 56 (figures for 1978); Busterna, "Trends in Daily Newspaper Ownership," 833 (figures for 1960 and 1986); Nixon and Ward, "Trends in Newspaper Ownership," 5 (figures for 1910–1960); Albert Scardino, "The Media Business," *New York Times*, May 29, 1989, sec. 1, p. 35 (figures for 1989). Different studies give slightly different numbers. Although apparently not describing new competition but rather a different way of counting, *Facts about Newspapers* (1992) (Newspaper Association of America) reports that there are thirty-seven cities with competing, separately owned papers, but this included nineteen cities where the papers operated under a joint operating agreement (26). In contrast, Stephen Lacy reports that by 1982 only twenty-three cities had "two or more separately owned and operated daily newspapers" ("Competition among Metropolitan Daily, Small Daily and Weekly Newspapers," *Journalism Quarterly* 61 [1984]: 640).

35. See Busterna, "Trends in Daily Newspaper Ownership," 833 (deriving figures from total number of noncompetitive dailies); Nixon and Ward, "Trends in Newspaper Ownership," 5 (same).

36. See Rosse and Dertouzos, *Economic Issues in Mass Communications Industries*, 58.

37. See, e.g., Bruce M. Owen, *Economics of Freedom of Expression* (1975), 75 (price data on papers from 1851 to 1970); Sterling and Haight, *The Mass Media*, 169 (prices from 1966 to 1975); *'89 Facts about Newspapers* (1989), 5, 20 (prices up to 1988) [SRI # A2350–4 1989].

Without precisely defining the relevant time period, James N. Rosse endorses the per-page calculation and reports that "the relative importance of circulation revenues has declined as subscription rates (corrected for the number of pages) have failed to rise as fast as cost indices" (*Economic Limits of Press Responsibility*, Studies in Industry Economics no. 56 [Stanford Dept. of Economics, January 1975], 18).

38. See, e.g., Nixon and Ward, "Trends in Newspaper Ownership," 11.

39. Stephen Lacy, "Effect of Intermedia Competition on Daily Newspaper Content," *Journalism Quarterly* 65 (1988): 95, 99, 96. A study of Canadian newspaper markets in 1971 purports to find "no relationship between daily newspaper household penetration and television viewing, radio listenership and monthly magazine subscriptions" (Gerald Alperstein, "The Influence of Local Information on Daily Newspaper Household Penetration in Canada," *ANPA News Research Report #26*, May 23, 1980, 2). An earlier American study investigated whether, during the 1930-to-1940 period, the decline of newspaper competition could be explained by the presence of a radio station in the community, but found the evidence did not support this hypothesis. See Neurath, "One-Publisher Communities," 238–41.

40. Rosse and Dertouzos, *Economic Issues in Mass Communications Industries*, 54; U.S. Department of Commerce, *Statistical Abstract of the United States 1991*, 111th ed. (1991), 556.

41. See Rosse and Dertouzos, *Economic Issues in Mass Communications Industries*, 54: Benjamin M. Compaine, *The Newspaper Industry in the 1980s: An Assessment of Economics and Technology* (1980), 29; Walter Potter, "Amid Uncertainty, Forecasters Look for Signs of Recovery," *presstime*, Jan. 1992, 18.

The number of readers per copy is also relevant. If competition contributed to a desire for the media product and if that desire translated into more readers per copy, then a decline in competition combined with a constant number of papers sold per population might mask a true decline in readership. James Curran reports that in England, the typical number of readers per copy of national newspapers in the 1970s was 2 to 3, compared with approximately 20 readers per copy of cheap unstamped (untaxed), radical working-class papers in the 1830s, and probably even more readers per copy, with estimates as high as 50–80, of the more expensive, stamped radical papers published during the middle of the nineteenth century ("Capitalism and Control of the Press, 1800–1975," 202 and n.13).

42. U.S. Department of Commerce, *Statistical Abstract of the United States 1991*, 845.

43. William B. Blankenburg, "Structural Determination of Circulation," *Journalism Quarterly* 58 (1981): 543, 548.

44. Ibid., 548–49. During the 1965-to-1975 period, New York, Chicago, Boston, Washington, and Newark each lost one or more papers. Although surviving papers in these cities gained an average of 8.6% in circulation, in each city total circulation declined, the average decline being 21.8% (Udell, *The Economics of the American Newspaper*, 103–4).

45. See John Tebbel and Mary Ellen Zuckerman, *The Magazine in America, 1741–1990* (1991), 365, 373. Relying on reports of Magazine Publishers of America covering an estimated 1,707 consumer magazines, these data are also reported in Albert Scardino, "Magazines Raise Reliance on Circulation," *New York Times*, May 8, 1989, sec. D, p. 11. Depending on how magazines are defined or how the category is identified, somewhat different results would be obtained. For "general and consumer periodicals," the U.S. Department of Commerce reports the advertising revenues to be about 52% in 1972, 49% in 1977, 55% in 1982, and 51% in 1987 ("General Summary," *1987 Census of Manufactures*, 1–114, table 1, code 2721).

46. Tebbel and Zuckerman, *The Magazine in America*, 373.

47. Deirdre Carmody, "Despite Gloom, Start-ups Are Booming," *New York Times*, Oct. 28, 1991, sec. D, p. 8. Using a different base, another study reported the average newsstand price of $2.65 in 1990 to have increased 8.6% over 1989 (*U.S. Industrial Outlook '92*, 25–7.

48. Scardino, "Magazines Raise Reliance on Circulation"; Tebbel and Zuckerman, *The Magazine in America*, 373. Many factors influence media trends, so explanations other than that offered here are, of course, possible.

49. Carmody, "Start-ups Are Booming."

50. Ibid.

51. U.S. Department of Commerce, *Statistical Abstract of the United States 1991*, table 934. As this source indicates, these papers accounted for 13.8% of paid daily newspaper circulation.

52. Dunnett, *The World Newspaper Industry*, 67; they accounted for about 6% of total circulation.

53. Kurian, *World Press Encyclopedia*, 2:977 (median return-on-sales for publicly owned newspaper-owning firms at 9.6% compared to 4.8% for Fortune 500 companies). Rosse seems to be the one dissenter from this view. Although his reports suggest profitability that appears somewhat higher than the average for U.S. manufacturers, his conclusion is that, "on average, return to investment among dailies is not greatly different from that earned by similar sized comparably risky firms in competitive industries" (*Economic Limits of Press Responsibility*, 7).

54. Bogart, *Press and Public*, 45.

55. Compaine, *The Newspaper Industry in the 1980s*, 18–20; see also Sterling and Haight, *The Mass Media*, 163, 166. Bagdikian, who describes newspapers as "fabulously profitable," reports returns on equity of 17.1%, with only five other industrial groups having higher returns (*The Media Monopoly*, 119, 265n.119).

56. U.S. Department of Commerce, *U.S. Industrial Outlook '92*, 25–4.

57. See Bagdikian, *The Media Monopoly*, xi, 119. "Mass advertising" is distinguishable from other forms. According to Bagdikian, it has arisen over the last two generations and consists of that advertising purchased mainly by large regional and national merchants aiming at an audience spread over wide geographic areas. Bag-

dikian argues that the large, chain retail outlets have used mass advertising to "kill off" smaller, locally owned stores (120–23).

58. Ibid., 122.

59. Ibid., 123.

60. Humphrey, "The Newspaper Preservation Act," *Boston College Industrial and Commerce Law Review* 12 (1971): 937, 951 (quoting Thurston Twigg-Smith, *Hearings on S. 1312 before the Subcomm. on Antitrust and Monopoly of the Senate Comm. on the Judiciary*, 90th Cong., 1st sess., 1967, pt. 2, 613).

61. Ibid.

62. Randolph E. Bucklin, Richard E. Caves, and Andrew W. Lo, "Games of Survival in the US Newspaper Industry," *Applied Economics* 21 (1989): 631, 636.

63. Ibid. Bucklin reported Rosse's finding that smaller-circulation dailies' first-copy costs were 40% and, surprisingly since the portion of costs that are first-copy costs should go down as the size of the paper increased, reported a study by Wagner "that for mass circulation papers first-copy costs are about half of total costs." However, Wagner's actual comment, made in an offhand manner, was that "setting-up" costs, which she contrasted to "running-off costs," "often account for half of total costs" (Karin Wagner, "The Newspaper Industry in Britain, Germany, and the United States," *National Institute Economic Review* 95 [1981]: 81). Wagner's findings are not comparable to Rosse's for at least two reasons. First, the comment, while not referring to any evidence, apparently applied to British papers, and the main point of the article was to show and explain that productivity was much lower, and hence first-copy costs were much higher, in Britain than in the German or American newspaper industries. Second, it is not clear what costs Wagner was including as first-copy costs, so comparisons with Rosse are impossible. Moreover, Wagner does specifically find that increased circulation has the expected effect of causing a reduction of unit costs (82–83).

64. Compaine, *The Newspaper Industry in the 1980s*, 18–20.

65. Sterling and Haight, *The Mass Media*, 164, 166.

66. Surprisingly, Peter Dunnett asserts that "there is little evidence for either significant economies of scale or diseconomies of scale when based *on a per copy basis* in the newspaper industry" (*The World Newspaper Industry*, 48 [emphasis added]). Advertising and editorial space both may generally go up along with increases in circulation and, depending on what Dunnett means by his remark, this could contribute to the result he reports. Dunnett argues that the single copy is the appropriate unit of comparison since it is the product people buy. He finds diseconomies of scale in newsprint, production, advertising sales, and distribution; no significant economies of scale in editorial content; and some evidence of economies of scale in administration costs (43–48).

67. See Rosse and Dertouzos, *Economic Issues in Mass Communications Industries*, 63–64.

68. For example, Bucklin supports Rosse's characterization and finds "results [that] certainly support the general indications that the trend toward monopoly in

US central-city newspaper markets is largely inevitable" (Bucklin, Caves, and Lo, "Games of Survival," 646). See also Kurian, *World Press Encyclopedia*, 2:979 ("economics of scale have played a pivotal role in the dominance of one-newspaper towns").

69. Rosse and Dertouzos, *Economic Issues in Mass Communications Industries*, 63–64. This economic condition makes the model of monopolistic competition the appropriate economic model to analyze the industry (21–26). See generally Edward H. Chamberlin, *The Theory of Monopolistic Competition* (1960).

70. See Rosse and Dertouzos, *Economic Issues in Mass Communications Industries*, 63.

71. See ibid., 64.

72. Bucklin, Caves, and Lo, "Games of Survival," 637–38 (emphasis added). Bucklin here notes that "formal theories of ruinous competition assume a homogeneous product."

73. See James N. Rosse, "The Decline of Direct Newspaper Competition," *Journal of Communication* 30 (1980): 65, 67 ("fundamental long-run cause of newspaper failure is loss of effective newspaper market segmentation").

74. Ibid., 69–70.

75. Bagdikian, *The Media Monopoly*, 125. He also argues: "Pursuit of advertising . . . reduced the media's responsiveness to reader desires. Publishers became more dependent on advertising revenues than on reader payments" (176).

76. See generally Bucklin, Caves, and Lo, "Games of Survival," 634n.3, 636 (stating that "to the extent that [the interdependence of advertising and circulation demands] amplifies the effect of changes in output upon profits, predation will become more likely").

77. Although newspapers are generally oriented toward a relatively affluent, undifferentiated audience, advertiser interests in special segments of this group influence both newspaper content and layout. Many of newspapers' specialized sections have advertisers for particular product consumers in mind—a food section for grocery ads, a science section for computer advertisers, a real estate section for real estate advertisers. Fashion would undoubtedly be less of a news item without department store advertisers.

78. Michael Schudson, *Advertising: The Uneasy Persuasion* (1984), 236.

79. Reddaway, "The Economics of Newspapers," 207.

80. Ibid., 206–7. This compares to a cover price of 2 ½*d*. for the "popular" and 4 *d*. for the "quality." The "qualities" derive greater profits from advertising because they allocate more pages per issue to advertising as well as charging higher rates. In Reddaway's "representative" papers, advertising represented 8 of 19 pages in the quality, and 5 of 14 pages in the smaller popular paper (207).

81. Reddaway, making the same point as Rosse, argues that monopolistic competition in an industry with great economies of scale, like the newspaper industry, is likely to lead to a small number of producers in each product class. However, Reddaway notes that there is no logical limit to the number of product classes (ibid., 218).

82. Bagdikian, *The Media Monopoly*, 178.

83. Gerald J. Baldasty and Jeffrey B. Rutenbeck, "Money, Politics and Newspapers: The Business Environment of Press Partisanship in the Late 19th Century," *Journalism History* 15 (1988): 60, 63.

84. Ibid., 68n.1.

85. Hazel Dicken-Garcia, *Journalistic Standards in Nineteenth-Century America* (1989), 48–49, 114–15.

86. Ibid., 114.

87. Baldasty and Rutenbeck, "Money, Politics and Newspapers," 62.

88. Ibid., 68.

89. Ibid., 63, 65.

90. Ibid.

91. Ibid., 65 (quoting *The Newspaper Maker*, Apr. 18, 1895, 4).

92. Ibid. (footnotes omitted).

93. Ibid., 66.

94. Harlan S. Stensaas, "Development of the Objectivity Ethic in U.S. Daily Newspapers," *Journal of Mass Media Ethics* 2 (1986): 50.

95. Marion T. Marzolf, *Civilizing Voices: American Press Criticism 1880–1950* (1991), 123.

96. Stensaas, "Development of the Objectivity Ethic," 53, 55.

97. Ibid., 55. The view that the introduction of the telegraph and news services contributed significantly to the rise of objectivity is also disputed in Schudson, *Discovering the News*, 34–35. But cf. Donald Shaw, "News Bias and the Telegraph: A Study of Historical Change," *Journalism Quarterly* 44 (1967): 3, 31 (suggesting that increased use of telegraph news by newspapers correlated to declining levels of bias).

98. In contrast, if the cause of the trend away from political party papers had been, for example, a desire that the papers adopt a more opinionated advocacy style or become more adversarial to all holders of power, objectivity (at least in the form that it has taken in American journalism, where objectivity means basically quoting and seldom challenging government sources) would not have been the result.

99. Dicken-Garcia, *Journalistic Standards*, 229.

100. Mark Hertsgaard, *On Bended Knee: The Press and the Reagan Presidency* (1989), 78 (quoting William Greider).

101. Marzolf, *Civilizing Voices*, 121 (quoting George Juergens, *News from the White House: The Presidential-Press Relationship in the Progressive Era* [1981], 6).

102. See, e.g., Bagdikian, *The Media Monopoly*, 125, 133.

103. Anthony Smith, *Subsidies and the Press in Europe* (1977).

104. Bogart, *Press and Public*, 243 (citing study by Roper for the Television Information Office).

105. Ibid., 244.

106. Ibid., 245–46.

107. Guido H. Stempl III, "Where People Really Get Most of Their News," *Newspaper Research Journal* 12 (Fall 1991): 2, 4.

108. John P. Robinson and Mark R. Levy, *The Main Source: Learning from Television News* (1986), 232. See also John P. Robinson and Dennis K. Davis, "Television News and the Informed Public: An Information Processing Approach," *Journal of Communications* 40 (1990): 106. Justin Lewis, director of the Center for the Study of Communication at the University of Massachusetts at Amherst asked both heavy TV news viewers and others factual questions with clear ideological slants, and found generally that heavy TV news users were more likely to get the facts wrong and got them wrong in a conservative direction— e.g., they were "five times less likely to know that the Sandinistas' human rights record was an improvement over the Somozas'" ("What Do We Learn From the News?" *Extra!* Sept. 1992, 16, 17 [publication of Fairness and Accuracy in Reporting]).

109. Robinson and Levy, *The Main Source*, 234.

110. There seems to be little scholarly writing on weeklies. Lacy, for example, observes that media economists have generally neglected weekly newspapers (Stephen Lacy and Stephen Dravis, "Pricing of Advertising in Weeklies: A Replication," *Journalism Quarterly* 68 [1991]: 338).

111. These numbers come from Sterling and Haight, *The Mass Media*, 21–22; roughly comparable numbers are reported in U.S. Department of Commerce, *Statistical Abstract of the United States 1991*, 561, table 932. Using different sources, both Bogart (*Press and Public*, 53) and the U.S. Department of Commerce (*U.S. Industrial Outlook '92*, 25–4) report about 1,000 fewer.

112. See *1991 Facts about Newspapers*; U.S. Department of Commerce, *U.S Industrial Outlook '92*, 25–4.

113. Bogart, *Press and Public*, 54–55.

114. C. David Rambo, "Free Circulation Newspapers," *presstime*, Jan. 1988, 22, 28.

115. Historically, the "country" weekly may have been the rural alternative to the city daily. During the last quarter of the nineteenth century and first quarter of the twentieth, the nature of the weekly and the daily increasingly diverged (Irene Barnes Tauber, "Changes in the Content and Presentation of Reading Material in Minnesota Weekly Newspapers 1860–1929," *Journalism Quarterly* 9 [1932]: 281). Although the last thirty years of increasingly free, typically urban/suburban weeklies represents another turn in the nature of weeklies, it hardly returns them to being substitutes for the daily.

116. A study of a sample of weeklies in 1960 and 1980 showed that during this period, paid circulation among the sample increased 65.5% while free circulation increased 172% (Eugenia Zerbinos, "Analysis of the Increase in Weekly Circulation, 1960–80," *Journalism Quarterly* 59 [1982]: 467). Bogart reports that between 1977 and 1988, weeklies' paid circulation declined almost 20% from 25,655,000 to 20,896,000 while free weeklies increased their circulation almost 90% from 11,659,000 to 21,994,000 (*Press and Public*, 54).

117. See, e.g., Rambo, "Free Circulation Newspapers," 22, 28.

118. Morris Janowitz, *The Community Press in an Urban Setting*, 2d ed. (1967), 131, 142, 144.

119. Ibid., 66, 146.

120. Ibid., 67.

121. Ibid., 25, 66n.7.

122. Ibid., x, 216.

123. See, e.g., ibid., 219.

124. Ibid., 60, 61, 75–77, 171.

125. Ibid., 171.

126. Ibid., 35–36, 81.

127. Ibid., 78. Janowitz suggests that reports on labor unions are so rare partly because unions are not organized on a geographical basis while the papers are.

128. Ibid., 89, 208.

129. Ibid., 172.

130. Rosse, *Economic Limits of Press Responsibility*, 21.

131. Janowitz, *The Community Press*, 133.

132. Similar conclusions might be reached in relation to the form of industry organization described by James Rosse in *Economic Limits of Press Responsibility* as an "umbrella" structure, where as many as three levels of smaller-circulation papers—those in larger satellite cities, suburban newspapers, and then various weekly publications—exist under the umbrella "shade" of a metropolitan regional paper. Rosse argues that it is because "advertisers are interested in audiences" (14), that competition will not exist within a level—monopoly existing there—but only between levels. Moreover, the heavy competition between levels is mostly over advertising revenue. Rosse describes and predicts many consequences for this umbrella structure of competition. Still, the competition will only in some places result in people's having a choice among daily papers, and then not of papers of the same level—that is, papers having comparable resources and serving similar functions. Competition between levels may influence advertising rates, but its main effect on content is not to increase diversity of perspective; rather the competition is likely to reinforce the trend toward objective nonpartisanship and the emphasis on the type of news for which a paper of that level has a comparative advantage. Rosse's main point is that this type of umbrella competition constrains the capacity of the press to make choices other than those dictated by the market—for instance, it may limit a paper's ability to choose to act responsibly. There is, however, little in his theory of competition to alleviate the policy concerns of those disturbed by the increased local monopoly status of daily newspapers.

133. *A.A.N. News: The Quarterly Newsletter for the Association of Alternative Newsweeklies*, Fall 1992, 9, 26, 31–32. At the 1992 convention, only seven of twenty-three applicant papers were admitted (9).

134. Albert Scardino, "Alternative Weeklies on the Rise," *New York Times*, May 29, 1989, sec. 1, p. 35.

135. Laureen Kessler, *The Dissident Press* (1984), 21, 44. This book provides

useful references to other sources for all the dissident presses. See, e.g., Roland E. Wolseley, *The Black Press, U.S.A.* (1971).

136. Kessler, *Dissident Press*, 90. The classic in this area is Robert E. Park, *The Immigrant Press and Its Control* (1922).

137. Kessler, *Dissident Press*, 117.

138. Ibid., 150. See especially David Armstrong, *A Trumpet to Arms: Alternative Media in America* (1981). Some of the underground papers took no advertising and existed on subscription income. Like the current "alternative papers," many—although typically subsisting on minimal budgets—were distributed free, especially when they began, and depended o*sn advertising and benefactors for revenue, although the advertising was of a sort unlikely to impose pressure on the paper to become more traditional (Robert Glessing, *The Underground Press in America* [1970], 89–92).

139. Kessler, *Dissident Press*, 151.

140. Ibid., 125.

141. Ibid., 84.

142. Ibid., 106.

143. Ibid., 114.

144. Ibid., 108.

145. William S. Sullins and Paul Parsons, "Roscoe Dunjee: Crusading Editor of Oklahoma's *Black Dispatch*, 1915–1955," *Journalism Quarterly* 69 (1992): 204, 206.

146. Stephen Lacy, James M. Stephens, and Stan Soffin, "The Future of the African-American Press," *Newspaper Research Journal* 8 (Summer 1991): 13–14.

147. Sullins and Parsons, "Roscoe Dunjee," 212.

148. Kessler, *Dissident Press*, 45.

149. Ibid., 46.

150. Cf. William B. Blankenburg, "Newspaper Scale and Newspaper Expenditures," *Newspaper Research Journal* 10 (Winter 1989): 97, 101: "If news-editorial quality can be equated with expenditures, then it's better to have a single large daily than two half its size." But see Gerald L. Grotta, "Consolidation of Newspapers: What Happens to the Consumer?" *Journalism Quarterly* 48 (1971): 245–50. Grotta found that consumers derived no benefits and experienced some apparent losses when local newspaper competition was eliminated.

151. See Barry R. Litman and Janet Bridges, "An Economic Analysis of Daily Newspaper Performance," *Newspaper Research Journal* 7 (1986): 9, 10.

152. See, e.g., Robert M. Entman, *Democracy without Citizens* (1989), 91–101 (arguing that since regressions indicate that competition has little effect on content, the concern with the trend toward one-newspaper towns may be overdrawn); John C. Schweitzer and Elaine Goldman, "Does Newspaper Competition Make a Difference to Readers?" *Journalism Quarterly* 52 (1975): 706, 710 (finding that, in general, the content of competitive papers is very similar and that the presence of competition does not matter much to the audience).

153. A recent article about increasing newspaper readership gave as examples the *Leesburg [Fla.] Daily Commercial*, which reportedly increased paid circulation in a few months from 17,505 to 30,805, and the *Spartanburg [S.C.] Herald-Journal*, which increased circulation from 47,661 to 55,404 during the 1985–1987 period. Both papers underwent redesign, expanded the newshole (keeping it above 50% compared to a reported industry average of 37% of space), and increased the editorial staff, from 24 to 38 at the *Daily Commercial* and 36 to 54 at the *Herald-Journal* (Gene Goltz, "Reviving a Romance with Readers Is the Biggest Challenge for Many Newspapers," *presstime*, Feb. 1988, 16, 19–20).

154. See Litman and Bridges, "An Economic Analysis of Daily Newspaper Performance," 23.

155. Lacy, "The Effects of Intracity Competition," 288.

156. Litman and Bridges, "An Economic Analysis of Daily Newspaper Performance," 24n.8.

157. See Lacy, "The Effects of Intracity Competition," 282–83 (reviewing research on the relationship between competition and content).

158. A table of turnout in recent national elections in twenty-four industrialized democracies placed the United States twenty-third, ahead only of Switzerland, where national elections are not very competitive and where the federal government plays a minor role as compared to that of the cantons. See Frances Fox Piven and Richard A. Cloward, *Why Americans Don't Vote: Turnout Decline in the United States, 1960–1984* (1989), 5. A turnout of 55.1% in the 1980 presidential election in the United States compares very unfavorably to the following typical European rates around 1980: 90.7% (Sweden), 90.4% (West Germany), 90.4% (Italy), 85.9% (France), and 75.9% (Great Britain). See Walter Dean Burnham, *The Current Crisis in American Politics* (1982), 183.

159. Burnham, *The Current Crisis in American Politics*, 184; Piven and Cloward, *Why Americans Don't Vote*, 15.

160. See, e.g., Dicken-Garcia, *Journalistic Standards*, 97 (indicating that the tradition of newspaper partisanship persisted long after a weakening of formal commercial ties to parties in the middle of the century).

161. Michael E. McGerr, *The Decline of Popular Politics* (1986), 135.

162. See ibid., 116–20.

163. Ibid., 121.

164. Ibid., 122. McGerr also describes the other movement in the press during this period, the rise of sensationalism, and argues that it was a different means to a similar result. Rather than making politics inaccessible, sensationalism made politics irrelevant, a "matter of gossip about personalities" (127). See also W. Russell Neuman, Marion R. Just, and Ann N. Crigler, *Common Knowledge: News and the Construction of Political Meaning* (1992), 76, 82–83, 106, 115.

165. See Bagdikian, *The Media Monopoly*, 179–80. See generally Gaye Tuchman, "Objectivity as Strategic Ritual: An Examination of Newsmen's Notions of Objectivity," *American Journal of Sociology* 77 (1972): 660 (analyzing how report-

ers rely on the conventions of objectivity as a means of insulating themselves from the "dangers" of their profession).

166. Michael Parenti, *Inventing Reality: The Politics of the Mass Media* (1986), 51 (quoting Jack Newfield, "Honest Men, Good Writers," *Village Voice*, May 18, 1972).

167. Schudson offers similar criticisms: that the content, form, and process of objectivity are all biased in a manner that reinforces the status quo and official viewpoints (*Discovering the News*, 184–86).

168. Hertsgaard, *On Bended Knee*, 67 (quoting former *Washington Post* assistant managing editor William Greider). See also Herman and Chomsky, *Manufacturing Consent*, 18–25.

A study of national and foreign news stories in the *New York Times* and the *Washington Post* examined 1,146 front-page stories, excluding local stories, in sample weeks from 1949 to 1969. The study found that the executive branch of the federal government dominated the news, accounting for about 38.5% of the stories. See Leon V. Sigal, *Reporters and Officials: The Organization and Politics of Newsmaking* (1973), 124. Official sources, a category encompassing the judiciary, Congress, state and local government officials, and officials of foreign governments and international agencies, accounted for 78% of the total. People who represent most of the world—typical citizens, combined with oppositional leaders, scholars, labor leaders, political activists, environmentalists, etc.—accounted for only about 16.5% of sources (119–130). This bias reflected to a significant degree differential reporter practices. Routine channels (as opposed to informal or reporter enterprise channels) produced 58% of the stories' sources and were primary in 71% of the stories (121–22). Nongovernmental sources, however, constituted only 11.3% of the sources in routine channels but 28.8% of the sources in reporter enterprise channels (126). A more recent study of front-page stories in 1979–1980 confirmed Sigal's results, again finding that a "disproportionate share of news is coming from elite sources," especially from government and executives. See Jane D. Brown et al., "Invisible Power: Newspaper News Sources and the Limits of Diversity," *Journalism Quarterly* 64 (1987): 45, 51.

169. See Hertsgaard, *On Bended Knee*, 66–69.

170. Marzolf, *Civilizing Voices*, 128–29 (providing a general critique of objectivity); see also Schudson, *Discovering the News*, 167–68 (explaining that during the McCarthy era "reporters were angry that the conventions of their work required them to publish 'news' they knew to be false, but they did not abandon the conventions").

171. Christopher Lasch, "Journalism, Publicity and the Lost Art of Argument," *Gannett Center Journal*, Spring 1990, 1.

172. See ibid., 2. Lasch may have placed the date of the decline of argument a little late. According to Dicken-Garcia, "the idea as the reason for newspaper items diminished steadily from being dominant in the earliest decade [of the nineteenth century] to virtual nonexistence by the 1890s" (*Journalistic Stan-*

dards, 229). By the 1850s, although the press remained highly partisan, the early emphasis on ideas on every page of the paper had given way to an event-orientation (71, 82, 88).

173. Robert A. Hackett, "Decline of a Paradigm? Bias and Objectivity in News Media Studies," *Critical Studies in Mass Communication* 1 (1984): 239, 252.

174. Ibid. (quoting Maaret Koskinen).

175. Ibid.

176. Ibid., 253.

177. Presently, the best investigative journalism may come close to this goal, but the journalists' commitment to objectivity arguably leads their moral content, which both reinforces and shapes community values, to be less reflective than it ought to be. See Theodore L. Glasser and James Ettema, "Investigative Journalism and the Moral Order," in Robert K. Avery and David Eason, eds., *Critical Perspectives on Media and Society* (1991), 203.

CHAPTER II
ADVERTISING AND THE CONTENT OF A DEMOCRATIC PRESS

1. Ben H. Bagdikian, *The Media Monopoly*, 3d ed. (1990), 153; Martin A. Lee and Norman Solomon, *Unreliable Sources* (1990), 59.

2. Michael Schudson, *Advertising: The Uneasy Persuasion* (1984), 210; see 230–33. Elsewhere I have argued that, within a market economic system, the way advertising "creates" the world reflects market forces rather than individual value choices. These market forces ought to be brought under human control, which would require, among other things, subjecting advertising to regulation based on egalitarian political choice. I also present a more general justification for not equating "free markets" with human freedom (although, of course, free markets of varying scope may be important, chosen elements of a free society). See C. Edwin Baker, *Human Liberty and Freedom of Speech* (1989), 194–24.

3. Michael Parenti, *Inventing Reality: The Politics of the Mass Media* (1986), 67 (citing J. S. Henry, *From Soap to Soapbox: The Corporate Merchandising of Ideas, Working Papers*, May/June 1980, 55 [emphasis deleted]).

4. Erik Barnouw, *The Sponsor* (1978), 84–86.

5. Bagdikian, *The Media Monopoly*, 162–63.

6. "Pleasantville's Velvet Trap," *Publisher's Weekly*, June 17, 1968, 49.

7. Lee and Solomon, *Unreliable Sources*, 75.

8. Gloria Steinem, "Sex, Lies and Advertising," *Ms.*, July/Aug. 1990, 18, 19–20.

9. Ibid., 18–19, 25–26.

10. Wayne Walley, "War Bleeds Nets of Millions a Day," *Advertising Age*, Jan. 21, 1991, 1, 54.

11. Steinem, "Sex, Lies and Advertising," 25.

12. See, e.g., Bagdikian, *The Media Monopoly*, 45, 155; Mark Hertsgaard, *On*

Bended Knee: The Press and the Reagan Presidency (1989), 87–90; Lee and Solomon, *Unreliable Sources*, 98–99.

13. See Les Brown, *Television: The Business behind the Box* (1971), 196–203. Brown observed that "good documentaries were bad business for broadcast companies that had allowed themselves to become extensions of the advertising industry" (197).

14. Les Brown, "Sponsors and Documentaries," in John W. Wright, ed., *The Commercial Connection: Advertising and the American Mass Media* (1979), 265.

15. Barnouw, *The Sponsor*, 137.

16. Parenti, *Inventing Reality*, 36.

17. Ibid., 35.

18. Barnouw, *The Sponsor*, 54; Barnouw notes that this view was "expressed again and again."

19. James Aronson, *Deadline for the Media* (1972), 144–45.

20. Barnouw, *The Sponsor*, 57.

21. See Linda Lawson, "Advertisements Masquerading as News in Turn-of-the-Century American Periodicals," *American Journalism* 5 (1988): 81.

22. See ibid., 85.

23. William Kittle, "The Making of Public Opinion," *Arena* 41 (1909): 433, 440–43; Lawson, "Advertisements Masquerading as News," 86–90.

24. Lawson, "Advertisements Masquerading as News," 86.

25. Ibid., 93.

26. Ibid., 93–94.

27. See ibid., 95.

28. Post Office Appropriation Act, ch. 389, § 2, 37 Stat. 553, 554 (1912); see Lewis Publishing Co. v. Morgan, 229 U.S. 288, 316 (1913) (upholding act against a First Amendment challenge). Second-class mailing privileges were a major subsidy for newspapers and magazines; letter mail, for example, was subjected to a rate eighty times higher than a second-class newspaper. See *Lewis*, 229 U.S., 304.

Interestingly, from the beginning of second-class mailing privileges, the government recognized the public policy relevance of subsidizing newspapers desired by readers who were willing to pay for them as opposed to papers principally devoted to advertising. Thus, a 1879 statute limited second-class privileges to papers "having a legitimate list of subscribers . . . [and did not grant the privilege to] regular publications designed primarily for advertising purposes, or for free circulation, or for circulation at nominal rates" (*Lewis*, 229 U.S., 305 [quoting act of Mar. 3, 1879, ch. 180, § 14, 20 Stat. 355, 359]). See also Richard B. Kielbowicz, *News in the Mail: The Press, Post Office, and Public Information, 1700–1860s* (1989); Richard Burket Kielbowicz, "Origins of the Second-Class Mail Category and the Business of Policymaking, 1863–1879," *Journalism Monographs*, no. 96 (1986).

29. Unless otherwise noted, information in this discussion of tobacco advertising is taken from Bagdikian, *The Media Monopoly*, 168–73. Bagdikian finds that the dangers of tobacco were clear and a matter of publicly available knowledge by

1936, although he notes that research in England had earlier pointed to the dangerousness of smoking. However, Bagdikian was "scooped" in 1935 by an American exposé of newspapers' suppression of information about cigarettes' health dangers: George Seldes, *Freedom of the Press* (1935), 50–51.

George Seldes describes numerous cases of advertisers' influencing editorial content in order to advance either product sales or the advertiser's own political agenda (42–61). In addition to noting that the overt influence of patent medicine advertisers over newspapers' editorial positions has been constant throughout the century, he argues that the need to please advertisers caused most of the press to oppose the food and drug law of 1906 (62–66). But cf. Gabriel Kolko, *The Triumph of Conservatism* (1963), 108–10 (support for pure food legislation was overwhelming within the food industry with the exception of the patent medicine and whiskey interests).

Despite popular histories that attribute the meat inspection act of 1906 to muckraking exposés, especially Upton Sinclair's *The Jungle*, Kolko shows that even Sinclair recognized that " 'the Federal inspection of meat was, historically, established at the packers' request' " (103 [quoting Upton Sinclair]). The large meat packers had been pushing for, and getting, increasingly strict inspection standards since the 1880s, initially to avoid having their meat excluded from the European market. Both this concern and a desire to prevent small, legally unregulated packers from gaining a competitive advantage over these large packing operations motivated later extensions of the legislation (98–108).

30. William L. Weis and Chauncey Burke, "Media Content and Tobacco Advertising," *Journal of Communication* 36 (1986): 59, 64.

31. Ibid., 66.

32. R. C. Smith, "The Magazines' Smoking Habit," *Columbia Journalism Review* 16 (1978): 29, 31 (over the previous seven years, magazines that accepted cigarette advertising published no articles giving readers clear information on the dangers of smoking). Another study found some articles about health aspects of smoking in magazines that accepted cigarette advertising but presented overwhelming statistical evidence that such magazines, especially those directed toward women, were less likely to do so if they took advertising (Kenneth E. Warner, Linda M. Goldenhar, and Catherine McLaughlin, "Cigarette Advertising and Magazine Coverage of the Hazards of Smoking," *New England Journal of Medicine* 326 [Jan. 30, 1992]: 305).

33. Warner, Goldenhar, and McLaughlin, "Cigarette Advertising," 305.

34. Weis and Burke, "Media Content and Tobacco Advertising," 63.

35. Ibid., 61–62.

36. Ibid., 63. In a similar situation, more than forty newspapers and magazines refused ads by Car/Puter International, which offers computer printouts of list and dealers' prices for cars. One publisher explained that the major problem with the ad was its competitiveness with automobile dealers (Bagdikian, *The Media Monopoly*, 166).

37. Bagdikian, *The Media Monopoly*, 171.

38. Warner, Goldenhar, and McLaughlin, "Cigarette Advertising," 308.

39. Ibid.

40. See ibid.

41. See Mark Sullivan, "The Patent Medicine Conspiracy against Freedom of the Press," in Arthur Weinberg et al., eds., *The Muckrakers* (1961), 179–94 (reprinting an article that originally appeared in *Collier's*, Nov. 4, 1905).

42. Ibid., 176.

43. See ibid., 184–87, 189–91.

44. Ibid., 182.

45. See ibid., 183.

46. Parenti, *Inventing Reality*, 48. In contrast, in 1901, Adolph Ochs reportedly responded to an advertiser who sought to influence the newspaper's policies: "You seem to wish that *The New York Times* should go about as a mendicant, begging for advertising patronage. We will never do anything of the kind" (Elmer H. Davis, *History of the New York Times, 1851–1921* [1921], 318). Davis argues that "no sane man is likely to suppose that [the *New York Times*'s] policies are affected by the wishes of any advertiser," this being a case where "good business and good morals [are] identical" (316, 322).

47. Parenti, *Inventing Reality*, 49 (quoting Art Shields, *My Shaping Years* [1982], 124).

48. Seldes, *Freedom of the Press*, 43.

49. See "Fruit Growers Pull Commercials to Protest Report by CBS on Alar," *New York Times*, May 7, 1989, 36; see also George T. Kurian, ed., *World Press Encyclopedia*, 2:986–87 (providing an illustrative list of cases in which advertisers withdrew their ads). It is important to remember that withdrawals occur only when the advertisers' implicit censorship has failed to operate effectively.

50. Wendy S. Williams, "Two New Surveys Show the Industry's Reach," *Washington Journalism Review*, Nov. 1991, 24 (confidential survey of forty-two real estate editors).

51. Ibid.

52. Robert G. Hays and Ann E. Reisner, "Feeling the Heat from Advertisers: Farm Magazine Writers and Ethical Pressures," *Journalism Quarterly* 67 (1990): 936, 939.

53. Steinem, "Sex, Lies and Advertising," 22–23 (emphasis deleted).

54. "Brewing Trouble," *Economist*, May 26, 1990, 70.

55. Thomas Palmer, "P & G Will Resume Ads on Channel 7 in '91," *Boston Globe*, Dec. 12, 1990, 73–74.

56. The reasons for refusing the ad were unclear. Many stations have a policy against taking issue-oriented advertising, a policy that may in part reflect advertiser-related concerns but also may represent a holdover from the time when the stations might have feared that the advertisements would create "fairness doctrine" obligations. See CBS v. Democratic Nat'l Comm., 412 U.S. 94 (1973). However,

similar refusals occur in contexts in which the fairness doctrine never applied. For example, all four Chicago dailies refused an ad by a union explaining its picketing of Marshall Fields, one of Chicago's largest retail store advertisers. See Hillier Krieghbaum, "The Impact of Advertising Pressure on the Press," in John W. Wright, ed., *The Commercial Connection: Advertising and the American Mass Media* (1979), 245, 246.

57. Palmer, "P & G Will Resume," 73; Thomas Palmer, "WHDH Demands Issue-Ad Accuracy," *Boston Globe*, Dec. 17, 1990, 26, 27. Proctor & Gamble resumed advertising after WHDH adopted more restrictive policies on accepting public interest ads and after a report the *Globe* commissioned (in part to help secure Proctor & Gamble's return) found that the ad improperly singled out Folgers, although Neighbor-to-Neighbor argued that, to be effective, the boycott needed to be focused. The station's study "did establish, however, that 'there were very substantial links between the El Salvadoran coffee industry and violence and human-rights abuses,' " and that "all major American coffee companies should have been aware of the violence" (27). The draft report cites "former US government officials as saying that Salvadoran death squads have received 'continuous financing from the coffee industry since the late 1970s' " (Richard Higgins, "Ch. 7 is Urged to Release Study on Anti-Folgers Ad," *Boston Globe*, Apr. 16, 1991, 20).

58. See Palmer, "P & G will Resume," 74.

59. Barnouw, *The Sponsor*, 112 (quoting memorandum presented by Proctor & Gamble's general advertising manager in 1965 FCC hearings). In the 1930s, Seldes reports Proctor & Gamble canceling their advertising "with all newspapers which had used a syndicated article telling women how to make soap cheaply at home" (*Freedom of the Press*, 50).

60. Bagdikian, *The Media Monopoly*, 156–57 (quoting memoranda presented at 1965 FCC hearings held to determine how much influence advertisers had on noncommercial content of television and radio).

61. Ibid., 157.

62. Ibid.

63. See ibid. (summarizing testimony of Albert Halverstadt, general advertising manager of Proctor & Gamble).

64. Steinem, "Sex, Lies and Advertising," 26. Proctor & Gamble's concern with the occult may be understandable. During the 1980s, P & G faced constant rumors that the company supported the Church of Satan, and that its trademark, a moon and thirteen stars (which purportedly represent the thirteen original U.S. states), was a satanic symbol. At times during 1982, it was receiving fifteen thousand queries a month concerning its relationship to the Devil. Although it spent hundreds of thousands of dollars combating the rumors and brought suit against some of those involved, a serious outbreak of rumors reoccurred in 1985, leading the company to announce that it would remove the logo from its products. See Sandra Salmans, "P. & G. Drops Logo; Cites Satan Rumors," *New York Times*, Apr. 25, 1985, sec. D, p. 1; see also Lisa Belkin, "Proctor & Gamble Fights Satan

Story," *New York Times*, Apr. 18, 1985, sec. C, p. 3 (reporting that court awarded $75,000 in damages and required public recantations from two Amway distributors who had spread rumor and urged boycott).

65. Steinem, "Sex, Lies and Advertising," 24.

66. See, e.g., Barnouw, *The Sponsor*, 106 (noting that the highly popular and critically acclaimed anthology programs of the 1950s "made sponsors restive").

67. See, e.g., ibid., 120–21 (describing how the sponsors' need for noncontroversial "entertainment" led to the proliferation of spy dramas in the 1960s).

68. See generally Schudson, *Advertising: The Uneasy Persuasion*, 90–106 (explaining that because consumers understand advertising as propaganda, they are less attentive to it).

69. See Kathryn C. Montgomery, *Target: Prime Time. Advocacy Groups and the Struggle over Entertainment Television* (1989), 32, 46–47; Jay Sharbutt, "NBC Chief Urges Advertisers to Support 'Roe,' " *Los Angeles Times*, May 11, 1989, sec. 6, p. 1.

70. Genevieve Buck, "Is This Advertising or Is It a Mission? Only Benetton Knows for Sure," *Chicago Tribune*, Feb. 19, 1992, Style sec., p. 10.

71. Kim Foltz, "Igniting Debates through Ads," *New York Times*, Feb. 23, 1992, sec. 3, p. 6.

72. Paula Span, "Colored with Controversy; Outcry over Benetton Ad Showing AIDS Deathbed Scene," *Washington Post*, Feb. 13, 1992, sec. D, p. 1.

73. Ibid., sec. D, p. 9.

74. Ibid., sec. D, p. 1; William Kissel, "Sending Out Shock Waves: More Clothing Companies Are Using Social Commentary and Jarring Images to Peddle Their Products," *Los Angeles Times*, Aug. 30, 1991, sec. E, pp. 1, 4.

75. Bagdikian, *The Media Monopoly*, 129–30.

76. Montgomery, *Target: Prime Time*.

77. Ibid., 224; see also Patrick M. Fahey, "Advocacy Group Boycotting of Network Television Advertisers and Its Effect on Programming Content," *University of Pennsylvania Law Review* 140 (1991): 647.

78. Barnouw, *The Sponsor*, 48.

79. Ibid., 51.

80. See Don Kowet, "The 'Righteous Indignation' of Donald Wildmon," *Washington Times*, July 12, 1989, sec. E, p. 1; "Pepsi Cancels Madonna Ad," *New York Times*, Apr. 5, 1989, sec. D, p. 21.

81. Laura Malt, "Clear-TV Lifts Clorox Ban," *Electronic Media*, Apr. 30, 1990, 3.

82. Montgomery, *Target: Prime Time*, 158 (quoting Donald Wildmon).

83. Barnouw, *The Sponsor*, 33.

84. See Montgomery, *Target: Prime Time*, 109–18. Although the campaign had some initial success in reducing television violence (but with a corresponding increase in programs revolving around sex), violent programming returned after the pressure subsided (118, 120–21).

85. Baker, *Human Liberty and Freedom of Speech*, 153–54, 190.

86. 458 U.S. 886 (1982). The unanimous opinion in *Claiborne Hardware* seems to adopt a liberty perspective referred to in the last note.

87. "Nestlé's Costly Accord," *Newsweek*, Feb. 6, 1984, 52.

88. Carl B. Boyd, Jr., "Countless Free-Standing Trees: Non-Labor Boycotts after *NAACP v. Claiborne Hardware Co.*," *Kentucky Law Journal* 71 (1983): 899, 900n.9 (characterizing the grape boycott as "as much a social as a labor cause").

89. "Groups Join United Farm Workers' Boycott of California Table Grapes over Pesticide Use," *Daily Report for Executives (BNA)*, no. 245, Dec. 23, 1987, sec. A, p. 1.

90. Whitney v. California, 274 U.S. 357 (1927) (Brandeis, concurring).

91. Hughes v. Superior Court, 339 U.S. 460 (1950). But see Baker, *Human Liberty and Freedom of Speech*, 161–93, 223–24 (implicitly rejecting this notion except when applied to boycotts by business enterprises).

92. An argument might be made that the government could forbid boycotts' attempts to induce behavior that the government could not itself require. Boycotts are clearly a form of association. Although freedom of association normally receives considerable constitutional protection, the government has some power to prohibit associations from doing what the government itself cannot constitutionally require—engaging in membership discrimination. See Roberts v. United States Jaycees, 468 U.S. 609 (1984) (upholding a state statute requiring admission of women into Jaycees). Whether *Roberts* is limited due to the commercial nature of the Jaycees, because the Jaycees is a part of the communities' power structure, or for some other reason needs more attention.

93. A California court protected people's constitutional right to boycott a newspaper's advertisers even though the boycott was designed to change the newspaper's editorial policy. The court noted that this "troublesome" boycott did not involve "government action" but was similar to the power an advertiser can legally exert over newspapers. Environmental Planning & Info. Council v. Superior Court, 680 P.2d 1086, 1092 (Cal. 1984).

94. Although buying power is not equally distributed, a consumer-product boycott's dependence on individual backing makes it much more a matter of popular participation than the typical elite distribution of decision-making power.

95. Barnouw, *The Sponsor*, 136.

96. See ibid., 48–49.

97. Ibid., 136, 136n. Boycotts are not the National Rifle Association's only weapon. A NBC documentary initially presented a need for restrictions on ownership of firearms. Prior to its broadcast, however, the program was dramatically watered-down, despite strong opposition from the president of the news department, because of the N.R.A.'s threat of fairness doctrine complaints. See Robert MacNeil, *The People Machine* (1968), 270–71 (quoted in Edward J. Epstein, *News from Nowhere*, 68–69).

163

98. See Fahey, "Advocacy Group Boycotting," 671, 676.

99. Ibid., 684.

100. Montgomery, *Target: Prime Time*, 8–9.

101. See ibid., 68–69, 85–89.

102. See C. Edwin Baker, "Counting Preferences in Collective Choice Situations," *UCLA Law Review* 25 (1978): 381.

103. Advertisers' practices reflect research findings that are more cautiously stated. A review of the research literature indicates that "in general, mood states seem to bias evaluations and judgments in mood congruent directions" (Meryl P. Gardner, "Mood States and Consumer Behavior: A Critical Review," *Journal of Consumer Research* 12 [1985]: 281, 287). It found that "although context-induced moods may significantly affect consumer response to advertising, there is a dearth of evidence supporting this claim" (296). Still, it suggested that "there may be a general advantage to placing advertisements in contexts which induce positive moods" (294).

104. Bagdikian, *The Media Monopoly*, 160 (citation omitted).

105. Bob Shanks, *The Cool Fire: How to Make It in Television* (1976), 98.

106. Ibid., 98–99.

107. Marvin E. Goldberg and Gerald J. Gorn, "Happy and Sad TV Programs: How They Affect Reactions to Commercials," *Journal of Consumer Research* 14 (1987): 387, 401 (citation omitted).

108. Ibid. (citation omitted).

109. Ibid., 401 (quoting *Advertising Age*, Jan. 28, 1980, 39).

110. Barnouw, *The Sponsor*, 106–7.

111. See ibid., 106–8. Barnouw argues that these new "assembly-line" series are also advantageous because they are more exportable. Their de-emphasis on dialogue in favor of action minimizes translation problems and their simple "good-*vs.*-evil plots [can] be understood anywhere" (108).

112. Dale Kunkel and Bruce Watkins, "Evolution of Children's Television Regulatory Policy," *Journal of Broadcasting and Electronic Media* 31 (1987): 367, 376–78.

113. See Dale Kunkel, "From a Raised Eyebrow to a Turned Back: The FCC and Children's Product-Related Programming," *Journal of Communication* 38 (1988): 90, 102–3; Patrick J. Sheridan, "FCC Sets Children's Ad Limits," *Broadcasting* 119 (Nov. 12, 1990): 33.

114. James Curran, "Advertising and the Press," in James Curran, ed., *The British Press: A Manifesto* (1978), 239.

115. Ibid., 242, 244.

116. Ibid., 240–44.

117. In England, Curran shows that the growth in and current proportion of space devoted to such concerns closely correlates with amount of advertising by related products (ibid., 235–39).

118. Bagdikian, *The Media Monopoly*, 166.

119. Ibid., 136. See also Curran, "Advertising and the Press," 238 (surveys commissioned by newspapers show that these features are among the least read in the paper and apparently do not gratify an intensely felt interest).

120. Edward J. Epstein, *News from Nowhere: Television and the News* (1973), 121; see also 78–130 (describing a large number of ways that general economic considerations influenced news programming content).

121. Fred W. Friendly, *Due to Circumstances beyond Our Control* (1967), 212–65. Telling the story somewhat less sympathetically to Friendly, Epstein notes that CBS had already given Friendly greater leeway to broadcast the hearings live than had been permitted at other networks. Epstein presents the disturbing view that the rules Friendly was challenging—rules Friendly had previously accepted—normally control programming and production decisions concerning network news (*News from Nowhere*, 117–23).

122. See Bill Carter, "Few Sponsors for TV War News," *New York Times*, Feb. 7, 1991, sec. D, p. 1.

123. Ibid., sec. D, p. 20 (quoting Richard Dale, an executive at Deutsch Advertising).

124. See ibid., sec. D, p. 1. In contrast, CNN, with its extensive coverage of Baghdad during the first weeks of the war, which greatly increased its viewership, raised its advertising rates more than fivefold and apparently did not experience the networks' problems with sponsors. See Bill Carter, "CNN Sees Its Concept Paying Off," *New York Times*, Feb. 11, 1991, sec. D, p. 8.

125. Carter, "Few Sponsors for TV War News," sec. D, p. 1.

126. Ibid., sec. D, p. 20 (quoting a CBS executive).

127. Ibid. Apparently, however, CBS's offer was not successful in attracting advertisers.

128. Michael Walzer, *Spheres of Justice: A Defense of Pluralism and Equality* (1983), 103–7. Liberal theory requires and justifies this result. See John Rawls, *A Theory of Justice* (1971), 75–83; C. Edwin Baker, "Outcome Equality or Equality of Respect: The Substantive Content of Equal Protection," *University of Pennsylvania Law Review* 131 (1983): 933, 959–72.

129. Even though there has been no generally recognized constitutional right to demand that the government provide people with information, both federal legislation like the Freedom of Information Act (FOIA), 5 U.S.C. § 552 (1988), and state equivalents, as well as open-meeting laws, implicitly recognize the importance of supplying the public with information. The FOIA provides for the furnishing of copies of documents without charge if "disclosure . . . is in the public interest because it is likely to contribute significantly to public understanding of the operations or activities of the government and is not primarily in the commercial interest of the requester" (5 U.S.C. § 552 [a][4][A][iii] [1988]). However, the FOIA does not have any waiver for indigency of the requester.

130. Barnouw, *The Sponsor*, 73n.59.

131. See ibid., 73.

132. Bagdikian, *The Media Monopoly*, 105–13.

133. See ibid.

134. Bagdikian argued that William Shawn, the editor, was able to maintain this editorial course only because the *New Yorker* was independently owned. The *New Yorker*, economically healthy again by the 1980s, was sold to Newhouse, a media conglomerate, in 1986. Newhouse replaced William Shawn the next year. See ibid., 110, 113.

135. Dunnett, *The World Newspaper Industry*, 28.

136. Curran, "Advertising and the Press," 258.

137. William B. Blankenburg, "Newspaper Ownership and Control of Circulation to Increase Profits," *Journalism Quarterly* 59 (1982): 390, 392 (quoting unpublished report by Lee J. Guittar, "Operational Aspects of Marketing Strategies").

138. Mark Fitzgerald, "A Crossroads of Strategic Options," *Editor and Publisher*, May 11, 1991, 18.

139. Ibid.

140. U.S. Department of Commerce, *U.S. Industrial Outlook '92*, 25–5.

141. John Tebbel and Mary E. Zuckerman, *The Magazine in America, 1741–1990* (1991), 381.

142. Bagdikian, *The Media Monopoly*, 116.

143. Stephen Bates, *If No News, Send Rumors* (1989), 198–99.

144. Bradley Johnson, "L.A. Times Woos Inner City; Editorial Coverage, Not Ads, Drives Launch of Section for Riot Torn Area," *Advertising Age*, Aug. 10, 1992, 26.

145. Blankenburg, "Control of Circulation," 392 (Donald Nizen quoted in *Editor and Publisher*, Jan. 3, 1981, 15).

146. Ellis Close, *The Press* (1989), 17.

147. William B. Reddaway, "The Economics of Newspapers," *Economic Journal* 73 (1963): 201, 207.

148. Ibid., 206.

149. Curran, "Advertising and the Press," 247.

150. Martin Mayer, *Making News* (1993), 84–85.

151. Reddaway reported that the surplus per copy from advertising (the amount obtained from advertisers less the costs to the newspaper of including the advertisement), a surplus available to reduce the price of the paper or to go toward profits, was a halfpenny for the popular paper and fivepence for the quality paper ("The Economics of Newspapers," 206).

152. Blankenburg, "Control of Circulation," 398.

153. According to a careful statistical study, in the 1968-to-1980 period, "the decline in newspaper reading alone can be held responsible for almost two-thirds of net [voter] turnout decline and about one-third of the SES [socioeconomic status]-adjusted total" (Ruy A. Teixeira, *Why Americans Don't Vote* [1987], 88).

CHAPTER III
ECONOMIC ANALYSIS OF ADVERTISING'S EFFECT ON THE MEDIA

1. See Mark S. Fowler and Daniel L. Brenner, "A Marketplace Approach to Broadcast Regulation," *Texas Law Review* 60 (1982): 207, 209–10 (stating that "communications policy should be directed toward maximizing the services the public desires. . . . The [Federal Communications] Commission should rely on the broadcasters' ability to determine the wants of their audiences through the normal mechanisms of the marketplace"); and see 211 (claiming that "in the fully deregulated marketplace, the highest bidder would make the best and highest use of the resource," and discussing Ronald H. Coase, "The Federal Communications Commission," *Journal of Law and Economics* 2 [1959]: 1, 20–21). As chair of the FCC, Fowler implemented most of the proposals contained in his article. See also Revision of Programming and Commercialization Policies, Ascertainment Requirements, and Program Log Requirements for Commercial Television Stations, 49 *Fed. Reg.* 33,588–33,620 (1984) (codified at 47 C.F.R. pts. 0–73).

2. There are many other ways unrelated to advertising that the unregulated market predictably fails with respect to media production and distribution, but these failures are left for a later study.

3. Sometimes otherwise unprofitable specialized publications survive by engaging in a form of "voluntary" price discrimination. They solicit readers to contribute something beyond the subscription price, which the solicitation notes is insufficient to cover the publication's costs. In a recent (Sept. 1991) solicitation letter, the *Nation* reported that it was struggling to stay alive despite the largest readership in its 125-year history. The appeal said: "We depend on the Nation's Associates to provide at least 10% of our very slim annual budget. . . . Unlike most magazines, we can't count on advertising revenue. . . . Most advertisers are too timid or too interested in the status quo." Likewise, *High Country News,* a weekly newspaper that plays a significant journalistic role particularly among environmentalists in the Rocky Mountain states, receives about 35% of its annual budget from readers' contributions (David Hill, "High Country News: Small Paper, Strong Voice," *Washington Journalism Review*, May 1989, 44, 46).

Readers who respond to these contribution requests are giving to the publisher some of the consumer surplus that they would otherwise receive (assuming the publication was able to continue). They also may be contributing because they want others, not just themselves, to be able to continue to receive the publication; that is, they may be internalizing some of the "external" benefit they receive from others' purchasing (and reading) the publication. It should not be surprising that quite partisan publications like the *Nation* or *High Country News* receive relatively little advertising revenue and must make such solicitations. The analysis in the text also suggests that were it not for the role of advertising in reducing the price of "competing" publications, the *Nation*'s chances of commercial success, of continuing even without these special appeals, would increase.

4. It could also depend on the wealth effects of moving from one equilibrium to another. Some economists have questioned whether the indeterminacy produced by the wealth effect destroyed the usefulness of the concept of consumer surplus. The classic study of the issue concluded that these criticisms were overdrawn and that the concept was adequately precise (Robert D. Willig, "Consumer's Surplus without Apology," *American Economic Review* 66 [1976]: 591).

5. This specific problem of competitively produced "inefficiency" applies uniquely to monopolistic competition between declining cost firms. Monopolistic competition roughly describes any situation in which a firm prices at a point where average costs are still declining and sells a product that is in some sense unique but for which other products are plausible substitutes. Monopolistic competition, and hence the possibility of competitively produced inefficiency, may occur more frequently than is commonly implied in introductory economics texts. In contrast, this problem of competitive inefficiencies does not exist in the more commonly presented cases of perfect competition. Here, the efficient level of production (assuming no externalities) is where the firm's marginal costs equal average costs and equal marginal revenue. In this equilibrium position, since average costs equal marginal costs, consumer surplus is irrelevant to the question of what an efficient level of production would be. Moreover, in this situation, the ability to price-discriminate relates only to the distributional issue of the firm's ability to capture for itself wealth that would otherwise be left in the hands of consumers.

6. It may be, however, that the lack of observable price discrimination reflects a relatively flat demand curve rather than an inability to price-discriminate, a point suggested by Professor Michael Wachter.

7. Even here "efficiency" is not an "objective" or determinant concept. Introduction of Paper B has wealth effects (benefiting reader 2, making reader 1 poorer). It is possible that if it were to be introduced only on condition that those who benefited compensated those who were harmed, it would not be introduced. But if those harmed had to pay to avoid Paper B's introduction, they would not do so and the equilibrium would be to have it introduced. See, e.g., C. Edwin Baker, "The Ideology of the Economic Analysis of Law," *Philosophy & Public Affairs* 5 (1975): 3.

8. Bruce M. Owen and Steven S. Wildman, *Video Economics* (1992), 148.

9. Ibid.

10. William Kittle, "The Making of Public Opinion," *Arena* 41 (1909): 433.

11. See Anthony T. Kronman, "Mistake, Disclosure, Information, and the Law of Contracts," *Journal of Legal Studies* 7 (1978): 1.

12. Baker, "Ideology," 16.

13. C. Edwin Baker, "Posner's Privacy Mystery and the Failure of Economic Analysis of Law," *Georgia Law Review* 12 (1978): 475, 481–82.

14. This could be seen as one theme in the recent work on republicanism. See Frank Michelman, "Conceptions of Democracy in American Constitutional Argument: Voting Rights," *Florida Law Review* 41 (1989): 443; see also Baker, "Ideol-

ogy," 40; C. Edwin Baker, "Republican Liberalism: Liberal Rights and Republican Politics," *Florida Law Review* 41 (1989): 491.

15. Ronald K. L. Collins, *Dictating Content: How Advertising Pressure Can Corrupt a Free Press* (1992), 28–30.

16. J. W. Freiberg, *The French Press: Class, State, and Ideology* (1981), 1 (quoting Albert Camus, *Combat*, Dec. 1944).

CHAPTER IV
POLICY PROPOSALS

1. A full analysis would also consider the effect of the tax or regulation on the positive and negative contributions of advertising content itself.

2. Despite the comment in the text, if each advertising medium has its own merits, with purchases in each occurring until price equals marginal value, they may not be readily substitutable. If this is the case, the increased cost in one advertising arena may cause more of an overall reduction of purchases of advertising than an increase in purchases in alternative media. See, generally, Yale M. Braunstein, "The Economics of Advertiser-Supported Television in Adjacent Countries: Consumer Sovereignty, Advertising Efficiency, and National Policy," in *Cultures in Collision* (1984), 152. This point, however, has little significance for the policy purposes of the proposals discussed here.

3. James N. Rosse and James N. Dertouzos, *Economic Issues in Mass Communications Industries* (1978), 36; Christopher H. Sterling and Timothy B. Haight, *The Mass Media: Aspen Institute Guide to Communications Industry Trends* (1978), 122–29; Leo Bogart, *Press and Public*, 2d ed. (1989), 48.

4. Ben H. Bagdikian, *The Media Monopoly*, 3d ed. (1990), 176–79.

5. In a 1987 study, "news about local community" was the kind of item most reported to be "usually read"—specifically, reported to be read by 84% of newspaper readers (and also ranked as the category that readers "most like to read")—compared to second place for "international/world news" at 75%. Both of these did better in the reader reports than categories such as "obituaries" (usually read by 50% of readers), "business/financial" (46%), and "help wanted classified" (43%) (Bogart, *Press and Public*, 320).

6. Classified ads could be defined as ads smaller than a certain maximum size, without display or large type, published in a special section devoted to "classified ads."

7. Bogart, *Press and Public*, 48. As Bogart notes, newspaper advertising is typically categorized as national display, local display (or retail), and classified. In 1988 the respective proportions of revenue from each were 12%, 51%, and 37%; in 1950 the corresponding percentages were 25%, 57%, 18%. The biggest change over the last forty years was a gradual but continual decline in national and increase in classified.

8. This observation may be overly optimistic. Car dealers and real estate agents,

long heavy users of the classified ads, sometimes react with advertising boycotts to newspaper stories describing how to sell a house without an agent or reporting sharp practices among local car dealers. These boycotts usually get results, as well as warning other papers to restrict this useful consumer reporting (Ronald K. L. Collins, *Dictating Content: How Advertising Pressure Can Corrupt a Free Press* [1992], 19–25). See also William L. Rivers, Wilbur Schramm, and Clifford G. Christians, *Responsibility in Mass Communications*, 3d ed. (1980), 116–24; G. Pascal Zachary, "Many Journalists See a Growing Reluctance to Criticize Advertisers," *Wall Street Journal*, Feb. 8, 1992, 1.

9. Bogart, *Press and Public*, 50–51.

10. For the percentage of revenue from advertising and circulation, see chapter 1. The advertising tax could be expected to cause some reduction in advertising, and the increased incentive to receive revenues from circulation would cause that category of revenue to increase. Both of these changes would cause some reduction in TA-SR's percentage subsidy of circulation revenue. The percentages in the text are illustrative. The TA-SR program would regularly readjust the subsidy percentages.

Administration of the program would be relatively easy and could take various forms. For example, each newspaper could include in its yearly or quarterly federal tax returns a charge of 10% of its advertising revenue and a credit of x% of its circulation revenue, with "x" adjusted annually, being based on an estimate of the rate necessary to return to the newspapers as a group the 10% charge on advertising revenue. Papers that received more than an average proportion of revenue from advertising would make an increased tax payment, while those receiving less than the average portion of revenue from advertising would receive a credit, either reducing their income taxes or possibly resulting in a payment from the government.

11. This may not be so obviously so. See Bogart, *Press and Public*, 62–63. George Kurian notes a study that "found that in 59.4% of the cases circulation continued to climb despite an increase in price" (George T. Kurian, ed., *World Press Encyclopedia* (1982), 2:975). Nevertheless, Rosse found a price elasticity of −0.65 for small daily papers between 1954 and 1964—that is, a 10% increase in subscription price would yield a 6.5% decline in circulation (cited in William B. Blankenburg, "Newspaper Ownership and Control of Circulation to Increase Profits," *Journalism Quarterly* 59 [1982]: 392). A study reported by Bogart of "300 papers between 1965 and 1986 shows that a 10% price increase was associated with a 5.5% decrease in daily circulation" (59).

12. William B. Reddaway, "The Economics of Newspapers," *Economics Journal* 73 (1963): 201, 207; James Curran, "Advertising and the Press," in James Curran, ed., *The British Press: A Manifesto* (1978), 229, 247.

13. Constitutional protection of the press is presumably justified because it is thought to serve the people (the readers), not as a means to serve advertisers. Of course, whether the conclusion that freedom of the press is "for the people" leads to such things as access rights for members of the public to present their views or,

alternatively, to protection of the autonomy of the institution, possibly combined with protection of the media professionals, presents a more difficult question of institutional dynamics. See C. Edwin Baker, *Human Liberty and Freedom of Speech* (1989), 250–71.

14. Newspapers designed for relatively impoverished ethnic or racial groups predictably find obtaining ad revenue difficult and, therefore, would benefit by this type of support. See, e.g., Mary A. Sentman and Patrick S. Washburn, "How Excess Profits Tax Brought Ads to Black Newspaper in World War II," *Journalism Quarterly* 64 (1987): 769, 770. Publications without ads would have the merit of not being beholden to that source of income. That is presumably why E. W. Scripps created an ad-less newspaper, the *Chicago Day Book*, which lasted six years from its founding in 1911 and was sufficiently successful that Negely Cochran, Scripps's agent in charge, was convinced that it was a practical venture. Scripps had decreed that the paper was to be "the mouthpiece and the friend of the wage-earners who get small wages . . . [and] the poor man's advocate" (Kenneth Stewart and John Tebbel, *Makers of Modern Journalism* [1952], 270–71). Of course, the TA-SR proposal would reduce the competitive disadvantages that such a paper faces in an advertiser-dominated regime.

15. Certainly, resistance to the proposal by that portion of the newspaper industry which sells papers to its readers would rightly increase radically if TA-SR did not also apply to these "free" papers.

16. C. David Rambo, "Free Circulation Newspapers," *presstime*, Jan. 1988, 22; Bogart, *Press and Public*, 54.

17. Sweden does this, taxing all advertising to support its newspaper subsidy program—in fact, it taxes newspaper advertising at a lower rate than other advertising. See chap. 4.

18. See Royal Commission on the Press, *1961–1962 Report* (1962), 93–95.

19. Ibid., 95.

20. See ibid. (stating that "a statutory levy on two publishers to subsidize their rivals raises difficult issues of principle"). Cf. Minneapolis Star & Tribune v. Minnesota Comm'r of Revenue, 460 U.S. 575, 591–93 (1983) (declaring unconstitutional an ink-and-paper tax that required tax payments by less than 4% of the state's paid-circulation newspapers and that imposed roughly two-thirds of the total tax burden on one large newspaper).

21. Royal Commission on the Press, *1961–1962 Report*, 98 (emphasis added).

22. Ibid. (emphasis added).

23. See Bagdikian, *The Media Monopoly*, 230; Richard J. Barber, "Newspaper Monopoly in New Orleans: The Lessons for Antitrust Policy," *Louisiana Law Review* 24 (1964): 503, 549–53; Thomas E. Humphrey, "The Newspaper Preservation Act: An Ineffective Step in the Right Direction," *Boston College Industrial and Commerce Law Review* 12 (1971): 937, 951.

24. Cf. Humphrey, "The Newspaper Preservation Act," 952. Humphrey's illustrative plan quickly increased progressivity to 80% of advertising revenue over

$60,000. Often his economic analysis seems unpersuasive, like his assertion that "it seems doubtful that an increased newspaper cost [to the reader] will substantially affect newspaper sales." Still, he was right in his general conclusion that the Newspaper Preservation Act has been ineffective at maintaining competition and that a policy of limiting the leading paper's ability to obtain most of the community's advertising revenue is likely to be a more successful way to maintain or create competition (950–54).

25. See Royal Commission on the Press, *1961–1962 Report*, 93–95 (Kaldor proposal). Basing progressivity on circulation makes more sense if each market has its own rate table or if the tax significantly affects only a single market (like London's national dailies). This pinpoint regulation, however, also increases the opportunity for manipulation.

26. This appears to be Bagdikian's proposal, although his entire discussion of specifics was that "beyond a certain level of a company's total budget, advertising spending would be subject to a tax that increases with the excess over the limit" (*The Media Monopoly*, 231).

27. This goal, whether or not effectively promoted, is the purported aim of all the tax schemes. See, e.g., Humphrey, "The Newspaper Preservation Act," 952–53 ("Newspapers would financially depend upon, and have to appeal to, readers who could be attracted by a change in the product, instead of advertisers who could not").

28. Depending on how broadly the tax applies to nonmedia advertising, the TA-SR proposal could even increase the revenue received by the media.

29. The TA-SR proposal does not itself take tax revenue out of the system. Still, this proposal will predictably cause some decline in total advertiser expenditures for advertising in the mass media since it effectively increases the cost of that advertising. Also, the administrative costs of the program must be paid either with this tax revenue or out of general tax revenues.

30. See Karl-Erik Gustafsson and Stig Hadenius, *Swedish Press Policy* (1976), 10–11.

31. See Anthony Smith, *Subsidies and the Press in Europe* (1977), 2, 39 (paper as party organ an "essential prerequisite of democracy"; "the principle engine of democracy"); Gustafsson and Hadenius, *Swedish Press Policy*, 52–59; Göran Hedebro, "Communication Policy in Sweden: An Experiment in State Intervention," in Patricia Edgar and Syed Rahim, eds., *Communication Policy in Developed Countries* (1983), 137, 143.

32. Smith, *Subsidies and the Press in Europe*, 39 (97% of Swedish papers are avowedly political and a high proportion of editors and journalists are active in party organizations); Hedebro, "Communications Policy in Sweden," 142.

33. See Gustafsson and Hadenius, *Swedish Press Policy*, 63.

34. During the first five years of the subsidy program, the competitive situation of newspapers remained relatively stable in the nineteen locations where head-on competition existed. See ibid., 110–12.

35. Sweden also adopted a number of other press subsidies, mostly to serve other, related purposes including encouragement for founding new papers. The production subsidy is the largest in amount and is the one most directly aimed at preserving competition. See Karl-Erik Gustafsson, "The Press Subsidies of Sweden: A Decade of Experiment," in Anthony Smith, ed., *Newspapers and Democracy* (1980), 104, 110–12.

36. Apparently, no "secondary paper" (that is, the weaker paper in a competitive situation) closed during the 1970s; many increased their circulation. See Hedebro, "Communication Policy in Sweden," 143. During the 1980s, the number of Swedish newspapers even showed a slight increase (Lennart Weibull and Magnus Anshelm, "Indications of Change: Developments of Swedish Media 1980–1990," *Gazette* 49 [1992]: 41, 45). Moreover, the new nonsocialist government has indicated an intention "to keep press subsidies on the same level as before" (67). Still, as a percentage of the newspaper industry's revenues, the subsidies declined from 5.5% in 1980 to 3.5% in 1990 (49). As reported by these authors, the main changes in Swedish newspapers during the 1980s have elements of the American experience from the late nineteenth and early twentieth centuries. The contribution of advertising to newspapers' revenue increased significantly (58). At the same time the partisan orientation of the papers' news declined, which paralleled a general weakening of the political parties and increased popular disillusionment with government (43, 64–66).

37. The definition of "low coverage" varied somewhat depending on the type of paper: less than 50% penetration for four- to seven-day-a-week papers with circulation of more than 10,000, less than 60% for similar papers with lower circulation, and less than 30% for one- to three-day-a-week papers. See Gustafsson and Hadenius, *Swedish Press Policy*, 83.

38. See ibid., 82–83.

39. See ibid., 84. There are also minimum and maximum subsidy payments for papers in various categories and a standard amount for low periodicity papers. See Gustafsson, "The Press Subsidies of Sweden," 111. Gustafsson notes that the rate of subsidy has steadily increased since 1971; in 1979, the government gave an additional increase in the rate of support for papers with especially low coverage (less than 21%).

40. Kurian, *World Press Encyclopedia*, 2:836; Hedebro, "Communication Policy in Sweden," 143.

41. Gustafsson and Hadenius, *Swedish Press Policy*, 70.

42. Sweden gives papers with particularly low penetration rates especially high subsidies and also provides for different-sized subsidies in unique situations. One might argue, however, that if these papers cannot stimulate a reasonable circulation or overcome their unique problems, they should be allowed to fail.

43. See, e.g., Gustafsson, "The Press Subsidies of Sweden," 107, 121–22.

44. A nonsocialist party came to power in 1976, but press subsidies continued and, in fact, increased. See ibid., 111, 113.

45. See Gustafsson and Hadenius, *Swedish Press Policy*, 10; Kurian, *World Press Encyclopedia*, 2:828; Hedebro, "Communication Policy in Sweden," 142.

46. Gustafsson, "The Press Subsidies of Sweden," 112–13; Gustafsson and Hadenius, *Swedish Press Policy*, 105. Given the premise that competition is valuable, this result should be expected and accepted since the socialist press in most places was the secondary paper and, despite its electoral power, almost everywhere its papers were in danger of closing.

47. See Minneapolis Star & Tribune v. Minnesota Comm'r of Revenue, 460 U.S. 575, 579–80 (1983) (describing the circumstances of the tax invalidated in Grosjean v. American Press Co., 297 U.S. 233 [1936]).

48. See "Ad Industry Mobilizing against Proposed New Taxes," *Communications Daily*, Aug. 30, 1990, 3; Steven W. Colford, "Ad Groups Mobilize as 6 States Mull Taxes," *Advertising Age*, Mar. 11, 1991, 3.

49. Steven M. Cohen, "A Tax on Advertising: First Amendment and Commerce Clause Implications," *New York University Law Review* 63 (1988): 810, 810–11.

50. Douglas Shuit, "Legislature Winds Up Work of 'Worst Year,' " *Los Angeles Times*, Sept. 15, 1991, pt. A, p. 1; Alex S. Jones, "Newspapers See a Threat Of Spreading Sales Taxes," *New York Times*, Aug. 19, 1991, sec. D, p. 6.

51. In 1990, the Bush administration made a last-minute proposal that companies only be allowed to deduct 80% of their advertising expenditures as a regular business expense, the remaining 20% to be amortized over four years, a proposal the Congressional Budget Office estimated would raise $15.3 billion over five years (Steven W. Colford and Julie Liesse, "Marketers Dodge Bush Tax Bullet," *Advertising Age*, Oct. 29, 1990, 1).

52. See, e.g., "AAF to Take Offensive in Battles against Ad Restrictions," *Communications Daily*, Mar. 13, 1991, 3 (noting that more than thirty proposals have been offered in Congress to restrict or tax advertising for specific products like tobacco or alcohol).

53. George Murdock, "Taxation of Business Intangible Capital," *University of Pennsylvania Law Review* 135 (1987): 1179; Lawrence Summers, "A Few Good Taxes: Revenues without Tears," *New Republic*, Nov. 30, 1987, 14; Colford and Liesse, "Marketers Dodge Bush Tax Bullet,"1.

54. Colford, "Ad Groups Mobilize," 3.

55. See "AAF to Take Offensive," 3. Two states, New Jersey recently and Oklahoma for several decades, have taxed telephone yellow-pages advertising, with a constitutional challenge to the New Jersey law threatened. See Steven W. Colford, "A Taxing Situation," *Advertising Age*, Mar. 18, 1991, S-12; Steven W. Colford, "Yellow Pages Group to Fight N.J. Ad Tax," *Advertising Age*, Oct. 22, 1990, 2.

56. Colford, "A Taxing Situation," S-12.

57. See "Ad Industry Mobilizing," 3; "AAF to Take Offensive," 3. As this article demonstrates, the ad industry presents a well-developed set of arguments against these taxes, arguing, for example, that these taxes will " 'choke [advertis-

ing] and the economy it fuels,' " and suggesting that Florida's short-lived tax resulted in " 'economic devastation' " to industry and state (quoting AAF president Howard Bell).

58. Alex S. Jones, "Ruling Adds to Uncertainty on Newspaper Sales Taxes," *New York Times*, Sept. 24, 1990, sec. D, p. 12. In thirteen states, the sales tax applies to magazines, which in some states sets up the potential for constitutional challenges to differential treatment of newspapers and magazines. See, e.g., Department of Revenue v. Magazine Publishers of Am., 565 So. 2d 1304, 1310 (Fla. 1990) (holding it unconstitutional to apply sales tax to magazines while exempting newspapers; rather than extend the exemption to magazines, the court invalidated newspapers' exemption), *vacated*, 111 S. Ct. 1614 (1991); Southern Living v. Celauro, 789 S.W.2d 251, 252 (Tenn. 1990) (holding the application of sales tax to magazines but not newspapers unconstitutional), *cert. denied*, 111 S. Ct. 1693 (1991). But see Hearst Corp. v. Iowa Dep't of Revenue & Fin., 461 N.W.2d 295, 302–3 (Iowa 1990) (upholding differential tax treatment of newspapers and magazines), *cert. denied*, 111 S. Ct. 1639 (1991). The reasoning of most cases invalidating differential treatment seems contrary to that of the Supreme Court in Leathers v. Medlock, 111 S. Ct. 1438 (1991), which upheld application of a state sales tax to cable television subscriptions while exempting other media. Different tax treatment of newspapers and magazines is likely to be upheld in the future.

59. Robert B. Gunnison and Greg Lucas, "Governor Signs Bills Increasing Taxes," *San Francisco Chronicle*, July 1, 1991, sec. A, p. 1; Robert Reinhold, "California Inches toward Closing Big Budget Gap," *New York Times*, June 21, 1991, sec. A, p. 16.

60. Jones, "Newspapers See a Threat," sec. D., p. 6 (prediction of W. Terry Maguire, general counsel of American Newspaper Publishers Association).

61. See "Appendix C—Press Subsidies in Foreign Countries," in Royal Commission on the Press, *Final Report Appendices* (1977), 93–104; Anthony Smith, *Newspapers and Democracy* (1980), 91–93; Robert G. Picard, "Levels of State Intervention in the Western Press," *Mass Communications Review* 11 (Winter/Spring 1984): 27.

62. According to the study by the British Royal Commission, in the twelve (Western European) countries that had VAT, every country except the United Kingdom applied its value-added tax to advertising in the press, although at a reduced rate in the Irish Republic, Luxembourg, and the Netherlands. The standard VAT rate in these eleven countries ranged from 11% to 20%. The rate applied to advertising ranged from 4% to 20%. None of the twelve, however, applied the full VAT to newspaper sales, and seven did not apply it at all. See Royal Commission on the Press, *Final Report Appendices*, 108, table C.4. Thus, these countries exhibited policies corresponding to those suggested here: although recipient-responsive media serve the public good and, therefore, are properly encouraged by tax exemptions (or subsidies), advertising undermines press freedom and should be marginally discouraged—for example, by taxation.

63. I do not consider issues relating to the increase in the cost of advertising. If we presently have too much advertising, then this effect may also be desirable, but that issue requires an analysis not offered in this book.

64. The tax's effect of increasing the effective price of advertising to the advertiser and, hence, of causing a decline in purchases and in total advertising expenditures would, however, presumably result in some reduction of advertising revenue going to the press.

65. I leave aside the important issues of whether the prohibitions discussed in this section should be enforced by criminal or civil law, and if by civil law, who should be potential plaintiffs—the state, the media enterprise, censored authors or producers, injured members of the public acting as private attorneys general—and what should be the measure of damages. The antitrust laws may provide useful analogies for determining appropriate remedies and potential plaintiffs.

66. See Deirdre Carmody, "Outweek, in a Shake-up, Ousts Its Editor," *New York Times*, June 10, 1991, sec. D, p. 10.

67. Ibid.

68. Contrarily, some people at the "strident" magazine attribute *Outweek*'s subsequent closure to "infighting among its editors and poor management" (Deirdre Carmody, "Gay, Lesbian Press Is Starting to Emerge into the Mainstream," *New York Times*, Mar. 2, 1992, sec. A, p. 1). Still, after suggesting that the currently emerging new gay press had " 'got[ten] away from offending mainstream sensibilities,' " Doug Alligood, vice president of special markets for the ad agency BBDO, is quoted as saying, " 'That had to happen before the advertisers could take the medium seriously.' "

69. See First Nat'l Bank v. Bellotti, 435 U.S. 765, 805–8 (1978) (White, J., dissenting); *id.* (Rehnquist, J., dissenting); C. Edwin Baker, "Realizing Self-Realization: Corporate Political Expenditures and Redish's 'The Value of Free Speech,' " *University of Pennsylvania Law Review* 130 (1982): 646; Victor Brudney, "Business Corporations and Stockholders' Rights under the First Amendment," *Yale Law Journal* 91 (1981): 235.

70. James Curran, "The Different Approaches to Media Reform," in James Curran et al., eds., *Bending Reality: The State of the Media* (1986), 89, 107, 112.

71. For example, Norway requires the government to place the same ads in all 156 Norwegian newspapers unless an ad has only local relevance, and then requires publication in all papers of that locale (Smith, *Subsidies and the Press in Europe*, 51).

72. Stuart Elliot, "Calvin Klein Redefines the Big Buy," *New York Times*, Aug. 28, 1991, sec. D, p. 5.

73. See generally Mark C. Miller, "End of Story," in Mark C. Miller, ed., *Seeing Through Movies* (1990), 186–246 (describing the prominence of product placement in movies and critiquing the effect of this form of commercialism on movie content). Product placements, reportedly costing $10,000 and up, apparently increased dramatically after sales of Reeses Pieces rose 70% following their appear-

ance in the movie *E.T.* See Randall Rothenberg, "Critics Seek F.T.C Action on Products as Movie Stars," *New York Times*, May 31, 1991, sec. D, p. 1. Product placements may be increasing in TV, where they have long been prominent in some countries, especially in Brazilian soaps. See Julia Michaels, "Will We Be Seeing J.R. Plugging Goods on 'Dallas' Soon?" *Wall Street Journal*, Jan. 4, 1989, sec. B, p. 4.

74. Both infomercials and product placements are, like *advertising content*, paid for by an advertiser but, to the extent that their origin is not identified, are presented to the public as nonadvertising content is. Thus, they can be conceptualized either way—as ads or as advertiser control of the media's nonadvertising content.

75. See Morgan Strong, "Portions of the Gulf War Were Brought to You by . . . the Folks at Hill and Knowlton," *TV Guide*, Feb. 22, 1992, 11, 12.

76. Ibid., 13.

77. National Ass'n for Better Broadcasting v. FCC, No. 89–1462, 1990 U.S. App. LEXIS 8517 (D.C. Cir. May 22, 1990) (upholding, in an unpublished opinion, the FCC decision after remand); National Ass'n for Better Broadcasting v. FCC, 830 F.2d 270, 278 (D.C. Cir. 1987) (reversing and remanding FCC's original dismissal of complaint).

78. Just as the ethics of implicitly deceptive "reading notices" were debated at the turn of the century, the merit of broadcasting "infomercials" is controversial today. A National Association of Television Program Executives survey of commercial television executives (859 surveyed, 281 responded) found that 60% thought "infomercials" were bad for television, while reportedly only 6% thought there was *anything* good about them. Still, the infomercials provide a significant portion of most stations' revenues. See Robert Epstein, "Prime-Time Invasion of the Infomercials," *Los Angeles Times*, Jan. 14, 1991, sec. F, p. 1.

Legal regulation of infomercials and product placements might be collectively beneficial to broadcasters as well as to the public. At the turn of the century, many leading publishers concluded that they would suffer economic injury from any public exposure that they published reading notices; these publishers opposed publication of reading notices at least in part for that commercial reason. The same may be true today. Not only have leading producers of "infomercials" attempted self-regulation that requires clear identification of sponsorship, but apparently some station executives worry that when the public, which thinks it is watching a noncommercial program, "then wakes up to what is being pitched, the station's image and business can be hurt" (sec. F, p.9). Since the injury of exposure is likely to be partially "externalized," that is, likely to discredit the medium generally, individual advertisers and broadcasters may be tempted to cheat, knowing that, if caught, they will not bear the full cost. Legal regulation could solve this "public good" problem.

79. See Rothenberg, "Critics Seek F.T.C Action," sec. D., p. 1. The Center for the Study of Commercialism announced that it would petition the FTC to reach this conclusion.

80. Ibid., sec. D, p. 5

81. *TV Guide*, Feb. 22, 1992, 26.

82. The right to anonymously communicate information, persuasively elaborated in Talley v. California, 362 U.S. 60, 64–65 (1960) and Brown v. Socialist Workers '74 Campaign Comm., 459 U.S. 87, 100–2 (1982), is generally assumed not to apply to commercial communications. See Virginia State Bd. of Pharmacy v. Virginia Citizens Consumer Council, Inc., 425 U.S. 748, 771n.24 (1976).

While invalidating various informational-oriented regulations imposed on paid solicitors for charitable contributions, the Court distinguished charitable solicitors from commercial speakers. This distinction was apparently crucial since the Court noted that the overbreadth doctrine is inapplicable in various commercial speech contexts, but then held regulations requiring various informational disclosures by charitable solicitors to be unconstitutionally overbroad. See Village of Schaumburg v. Citizens for a Better Env't, 444 U.S. 620, 638–39 (1980).

83. See 47 U.S.C. § 317 (1988) (requiring identification); 47 C.F.R. § 73.1212 (1991) (requiring broadcasting sponsorship identification); 47 C.F.R. § 76.221 (1991) (requiring cable origination programming sponsorship identification).

The payments to play particular songs on the radio, which produced the "payola" scandals of the 1950s and the congressional and FCC rule-making responses, were merely high-profile versions of "product placements." See Douglas H. Ginsburg, *Regulation of Broadcasting* (1979), 1–7.

84. Michael Hoyt, "Earthly Editing: The Dirt on *The New Yorker*'s Environmental Advertorial," *Columbia Journalism Review*, July–Aug. 1990, 8, 9–11.

85. See Patrick M. Fahey, "Advocacy Group Boycotting of Network Television Advertisers and Its Effect on Programming," *University of Pennsylvania Law Review* 140 (1991): 647, 687–88, 691–96.

86. For an excellent parody of this, see the film *Ladri di saponette* (The icicle thief) (Maurizio d'Nichetti, 1989).

87. See John C. Merrill, *Global Journalism*, 2d ed. (1991), 96.

88. Revision of Programming and Commercialization Policies, Ascertainment Requirements, and Program Log Requirements for Commercial Television Stations, 98 F.C.C.2d 1076 (1984) (abolishing guidelines of a maximum of 16 commercial minutes per hour on the assumption that the market will result in the proper level of commercialization); cf. Action for Children's Television v. FCC, 821 F.2d 741, 749–50 (D.C. Cir. 1987) (remanding FCC decision to abolish commercialization guidelines for children's television). In 1990 concern about overcommercialization reappeared in respect to children's TV when new legislation limited stations to 10.5 minutes per hour of children's programming on weekends and 12 minutes on weekdays (47 *U.S.C.A.* § 303a[b] [West 1991]).

89. For example, the 1987 legislation in Germany that introduced a duel (private/public) broadcasting system allowed much more advertising on the private than on the public channels but still "adhered to the established principle of block advertising for both public and private sectors and stipulated that advertising continue to be kept strictly apart from the rest of the schedule and that it should not

influence program content" (Peter J. Humphreys, *Media and Media Policy in West Germany* [1990], 278–79).

90. Erik Barnouw, *The Sponsor* (1978), 112.

91. Ibid., 66, 111–13.

92. The notion of providing the public with what it needs sounds quite paternalistic, but often the public will expect and even "want" this paternalism. Certainly when someone goes to other professional information-providers such as lawyers, doctors, or clergy, the expectation is that they will use their expertise to provide the information that the client needs, not what some third party, such as the pharmacists, want the client to have. In part because he concludes that "most people 'want to want' the news to be enlightening," Christopher Jencks argues that news media should be operated on a nonprofit basis. See Christopher Jencks, "Should News Be Sold for Profit?" in Donald Lazere, ed., *American Media and Mass Culture* (1987), 564, 564–67.

93. See Barnouw, *The Sponsor*, 111–13; cf. 66 (arguing that image problems of major corporations in the early 1970s and earlier partially explain their sponsorship of highly respected public broadcasting programs); and 150 (noting that corporate-sponsored high quality programs have fostered an image of culture as "focused on matters removed, in time or place or both, from pressing concerns of the American scene").

94. Advertisers are probably most inclined and have the most power to engage in objectionable censorship with respect to shows in which they are initially most equivocal about wanting placement.

95. A 10% placement "charge" kept by the broadcaster would not work. A profit-maximizing broadcaster who controls pricing could turn this into roughly the existing system in which advertisers have to pay more for greater placement control. By denying the broadcaster these tax receipts, the system will be tilted toward random access and will produce a corresponding decline in advertiser censorship power.

96. A broadcaster should be required to sell sponsorships on the basis of a rate per viewer, with the rate set high enough that the market would clear no more than, say, a quarter of its programming. This should encourage advertisers to maximize delivery of consumer surplus per advertising dollar spent, thereby leading to sponsorship of more narrowcast, high-quality programming.

97. See Roger G. Noll, Merton J. Peck, and John J. McGowan, *Economic Aspects of Television Regulation* (1973), 7–19.

98. For example, it is often argued that the dynamics of competition among a limited number of stations or networks will produce an inefficient amount of diversity. See ibid., 58–96. The problems of underproduction and distortion are being partially but not completely solved with the increased prevalence of cable, which has many channels and can sell the media product directly to consumers. But this is only one of a number of predictable market failures in the delivery of broadcast programming, issues that are generally beyond the scope of this study.

99. Bruce M. Owen and Steven S. Wildman, *Video Economics* (1992) provide the best accessible treatment of how industry structure—e.g., the number of available channels, existence of monopoly or competition, and advertiser or viewer support—can be expected to affect program delivery. Although an economic treatment, their book, like this book, makes no attempt to evaluate the value of different industrial or competitive structures from the perspective of the advertiser or of the economy produced by advertising. They implicitly assume that the relevant policy concern is not an abstract total efficiency analysis but rather the delivery of diverse nonadvertising media content to the public, which is more an overt freedom of expression perspective than an efficiency perspective.

100. See generally Carnegie Commission on Educational Television, *Public Television: A Program for Action* (1967), 9; Carnegie Commission on the Future of Public Broadcasting, *A Public Trust* (1979), 101–10.

101. See, e.g., Carnegie Commission, *A Program for Action*; Carnegie Commission, *A Public Trust*; John Wicklein, ed., *Public Broadcasting: A National Asset to Be Preserved, Promoted and Protected* (1988).

102. See John Wicklein, "Time for a Public Broadcasting Overhaul," *New York Times*, Feb. 26, 1989, sec. H, p. 35.

103. Government provides significant, often indirect but virtually nowhere solely indirect, economic support for the media in all Western democracies. See Smith, *Subsidies and the Press in Europe*; Anthony Smith, "State Intervention and the Management of the Press," in James Curran, ed., *The British Press: A Manifesto* (1978), 53; Picard, "Levels of State Intervention."

104. See, e.g., Wicklein, *Public Broadcasting*.

105. In a slight variation, the Working Group for Public Broadcasting suggests a 2% tax on consumer electronics products; it estimated this would provide $600 million in 1989, which was apparently "more than twice that now raised for public-broadcast programs from all sources" (Wicklein, "Time for a Public Broadcasting Overhaul," sec. H, p. 35). In 1986, public broadcasting had a total income from all sources of $1.4 billion, of which about $250 million went into programming. See Wicklein, *Public Broadcasting*, 9.

106. A sales tax on receivers (or consumer electronics) might be preferable to the annual fee. In 1989, sales of TV and radio receivers in this country amounted to approximately $9 billion, compared to commercial broadcasting advertising revenues of $29.7 billion (*Broadcasting Yearbook 1991*, A-3, H-56). Thus, a tax on receivers would have to be about three times the rate of a tax on advertising to produce the same revenue (although this difference decreases somewhat if all consumer electronics are taxed). The receiver tax would be more progressive than a head tax to the extent that wealthy households spend more on televisions (per person) because they have more televisions—approximately 98% of homes have a television and 65% have more than one (A-3)—have more expensive televisions, or replace televisions more often.

107. In its 1979 report, the Carnegie Commission concluded that public

broadcasting needed $1.2 billion in 1979 dollars ($590 million to come from the federal government) while in 1977 it had received $482 million from all sources. The commission proposed a tax on spectrum space (whereas the first Carnegie Commission had recommended a tax on the purchase of TV sets, which it calculated would provide at most $100 to $200 million). It reported broadcasters' advertising revenue, at that time, to be about $8 billion (*A Public Trust*, 93, 98, 103–4, 118, 139–40, 143–45). Thus, in 1979, a 6% advertising tax would have produced about $480 million. The commission recognized various merits of a dedicated advertising tax but rejected the proposal apparently because the commission expected that commercial broadcasters would use payment of this tax to justify reducing their public-service obligations (141). Nevertheless, it is not clear that this argument would succeed—certainly it should not succeed—if public-service obligations are otherwise merited. On the other hand, the Reagan administration's deregulatory revolution largely eliminated these public-service obligations, which, for now, makes the commission's concern irrelevant. Finally, imposition of a spectrum fee is also likely to generate pressures both to further reduce public-service obligations and to increase stations' profit orientation.

108. *Broadcasting Yearbook 1991*, A-3.

109. Ibid.

110. It would be advantageous if this tax were adopted in tandem with the tax on advertising in the print media, or even better, a general tax on advertising and promotion. The broader tax would reduce the incentive to advertisers to leave one medium, thereby reducing its support, for another.

111. Cf. Jerry Mander, *Four Arguments for the Elimination of Television* (1978); Neil Postman, *Amusing Ourselves to Death* (1985). In a fuller investigation of the economics of commercial broadcasting, I hope to show that the nature of monopolistic competition in broadcasting causes wasteful, misdirected expenditures on production and that the industry has significant negative externalities. These observations lead to the view that commercial television's greatest need is for a different decision-making structure and a different competitive environment that could lead to a redirection of the expenditures it does make.

112. Gustafsson and Hadenius, *Swedish Press Policy*, 78–79.

113. See ibid., 52, 57–59, 77–78; see also Gustafsson, "The Press Subsidies of Sweden," 104, 112. More recently, newspaper publishers object primarily to the advertising tax rather than any violation of freedom of press implicit in selective subsidies (see 117).

114. For a good initial source of suggestions of sensible forms of media activism, see Martin A. Lee and Norman Solomon, "Postscript," *Unreliable Sources* (1990), 340–58.

115. See, e.g., Gail Lund Barwis, "Contractual Newsroom Democracy," *Journalism Monographs*, no. 57 (1978).

116. David Atkin and Robert LaRose, "Cable Access: Market Concerns amidst the Marketplace of Ideas," *Journalism Quarterly* 68 (1991): 354 (community ac-

cess channels are viewed by about 16% of the potential cable audience weekly, a higher viewership than that for such cable services as BET, C-SPAN, and Financial News Network, and one that can at times match those of Lifetime, CBN, and Arts & Entertainment).

117. I have criticized the balance prong of the fairness doctrine, which is ill suited to serve access concerns, while recognizing the legitimacy of government intervention in the broadcast or cable realm to promote access (Baker, *Human Liberty and Freedom of Speech*, 259–62).

118. See Douglas Kellner, *Television and the Crisis of Democracy* (1990), 207–15 (describing and advocating public access television). Kellner notes that when done competently, access television produces a quite large audience (224n.11).

CHAPTER V

THE CONSTITUTIONALITY OF TAXATION OR REGULATION OF ADVERTISING

1. Associated Press v. United States, 326 U.S. 1, 20 (1945).

2. Many commentators read the Press Clause this way. See, e.g., C. Edwin Baker, *Human Liberty and Freedom of Speech* (1989), 229–49; Potter Stewart, "Or of the Press," *Hastings Law Journal* 26 (1975): 631, 634 (the primary purpose of the First Amendment's Press Clause was to create a "fourth estate" outside government as a check on the power of the executive, legislative, and judicial branches); cf. David A. Anderson, "The Origins of the Press Clause," *UCLA Law Review* 30 (1983): 455 (the Press Clause was originally viewed primarily as a restraint on governmental abuses); Vincent Blasi, "The Checking Value in First Amendment Theory," *American Bar Foundation Research Journal* (1977): 521 (the "checking function" of free expression on abuses of official power should play a major role in First Amendment adjudication).

The main alternative rejects any special concern with the press as an institution and reads the Press Clause as serving the same purposes as the Speech Clause. The Press Clause merely makes clear that written forms (and maybe other media and various artistic forms) merit the same protection as does speech. See, e.g., David Lange, "The Speech and Press Clauses," *UCLA Law Review* 23 (1975): 77 (freedom of the press is a personal, not an institutional, right); Anthony Lewis, "A Preferred Position for Journalism?" *Hofstra Law Review* 7 (1979): 595 (neither history, precedent, nor constitutional principles support a special status for the press, and a preferred constitutional position would actually work against the organized press's interests); William W. Van Alstyne, "The Hazards to the Press of Claiming a 'Preferred Position,' " *Hastings Law Journal* 28 (1977): 761 (a "preferred" position for the press could lead to licensing and both the press and the public are better served if the Press Clause is not treated as separate from the Speech Clause).

3. Arguably, the Supreme Court currently accepts the press-is-not-special reading of the Press Clause rather than Justice Potter Stewart's institutional, fourth

estate interpretation. Although this prism does not cast as informative a light on the issues discussed here as does Stewart's instrumental/institutional interpretation, it is possible (and maybe easier) to reach the conclusions advanced in this section from the press-is-not-special perspective. See, e.g., Leathers v. Medlock, 111 S. Ct. 1438 (1991). No matter which interpretation is employed, the constitutional conclusions reached here receive case law support.

4. Baker, *Human Liberty and Freedom of Speech*, 245–49.

5. See Randall P. Bezanson, "The New Free Press Guarantee," *Virginia Law Review* 63 (1977): 731. At the very least, the Press Clause would prohibit such rules unless the special rules had compelling rationales and unless the rules were narrowly drawn to fit the rationales precisely.

6. Mark Hertsgaard, *On Bended Knee: The Press and the Reagan Presidency* (1989), 182.

7. Although a judicial decision to uphold the constitutionality of these grants would require rejection of the neutrality interpretation and presumably acceptance of some version of a bad-purpose or bad-effect reading, a contrary *legislative* decision to be neutral, to provide no special benefits to the press, is fully consistent with the bad-purpose interpretation.

8. The Supreme Court has consistently held that generally applicable laws can be applied to the press. I am aware of no modern constitutional scholar who objects to that conclusion. Since these rules can greatly change the content of the press, their acceptability makes a mockery of the notion of natural, undistorted media content.

9. Leathers v. Medlock, 111 S. Ct. 1438, 1453 (1991) (Marshall, J., dissenting).

10. Ibid. Although Justice Marshall made this point while objecting to a tax on cable services but not on newspapers, he more clearly and plausibly relied on doctrinal arguments and policies more like the first reasons mentioned in the text to support a "neutrality" interpretation.

11. See Mark G. Yudof, *When Government Speaks: Politics, Law, and Government Expression in America* (1983); Steven Shiffrin, "Government Speech," *UCLA Law Review* 27 (1980): 565.

12. Jerome A. Barron, "Access to the Press—A New First Amendment Right," *Harvard Law Review* 80 (1967): 1641.

13. See Baker, *Human Liberty and Freedom of Speech*, 37–40 (arguing that there are no criteria for identifying an unbiased marketplace of ideas).

14. In the free press context, free market advocates generally make their claim in terms of objecting to any regulations or taxes aimed specially at the press. When I assert that there has always been governmental intervention in the American media marketplace, I too am referring to intervention specially oriented toward the press. On this, it could have been, but was not, different. The broader notion of an "unregulated" market, in contrast, is pure myth even as an abstract possibility. The existence of a market depends on regulation, at least in the form of choosing one

or another set of rights to protect, and these choices will have significant consequences. See Duncan Kennedy and Frank Michelman, "Are Property and Contract Efficient?" *Hofstra Law Review* 8 (1980): 711.

15. For example, the government cannot deny press passes to media personnel because it does not like the content of their reporting. See Sherrill v. Knight, 569 F.2d 124, 130 (D.C. Cir. 1977) (stating that in addition to the impermissibility of content-based reasons to deny White House press passes, the refusal to grant passes "to bona fide Washington journalists . . . must be based on a compelling governmental interest"); Borreca v. Fasi, 369 F. Supp. 906 (D. Haw. 1974) (stating that a mayor cannot deny a particular reporter access to press conferences on the ground that the reporter was irresponsible, inaccurate, biased, and malicious).

16. See Robert G. Picard, "Levels of State Intervention in the Western Press," *Mass Communications Review* 11 (Winter/Spring 1984): 27, 33.

17. George T. Kurian, ed., *World Press Encyclopedia* (1978), 2:832.

18. See, e.g., ibid., 834.

19. See U.S. Department of Commerce, *Statistical Abstract of the United States 1991*, 111th ed. (1991), 845.

20. 436 U.S. 775 (1978).

21. See ibid., 799.

22. Ibid., 801.

23. Ibid., 802 (emphasis added).

24. Ibid., 802n.20.

25. Mabee v. White Plains Publishing Co., 327 U.S. 178 (1946).

26. Ibid., 184.

27. See Committee for an Independent P-I v. Hearst Corp., 704 F.2d 467, 470 (9th Cir. 1983), *cert. denied*, 464 U.S. 892 (1983).

28. Ibid., 483.

29. Ibid., 481 (quoting *H.R. Rep. No. 1193*, 91st Cong., 2d sess., 1970, *reprinted in* 1970 U.S.C.C.A.N. 3547, 3558).

30. For example, the court responded to the charge of differential treatment by observing that "other newspapers in the Seattle area . . . may participate in a joint operating agreement if they qualify" (*Committee for an Independent P-I*, 704 F.2d, 483). Of course! All differential legislation gives its advantages to the complaining parties if they were different from what they are and, thus, met the qualifying criteria. This empty observation is not enough to remove the charge of discrimination.

The court also gave virtually no response to probably the most questionable aspect of the Newspaper Preservation Act: its grant of discretion to the attorney general to decide whether to approve an application to form a JOA. This discretionary governmental power could easily influence the editorial orientation of a paper hoping to enter into a JOA. See Lucas A. Powe, Jr., *The Fourth Estate and the Constitution: Freedom of the Press in America* (1991), 219. For example, at the time Knight-Ridder and Gannett were seeking approval from Attorney General Edwin Meese for a JOA between their Detroit papers, Knight-Ridder editors at the *Detroit*

Free Press and the *Miami Herald* reportedly ordered restrictions on criticism of Meese until after he ruled (James D. Squires, *Read All about It! The Corporate Takeover of America's Newspapers* [1993], 123–24).

31. See Powe, *The Fourth Estate and the Constitution*, 226.

32. Leathers v. Medlock, 111 S. Ct. 1438, 1447 (1991) (Marshall, J., dissenting). Note that this still is not quite equivalent to the neutrality interpretation, which would also prohibit discriminating in favor of the media as a whole.

33. 297 U.S. 233 (1936).

34. See Minneapolis Star v. Minnesota Comm'r of Revenue, 460 U.S. 575, 579–80 (1983) (describing the historical background of the *Grosjean* case).

35. See ibid. "Ganging up" is apparently pretty bad. In voting to deny the First Amendment claims of leaders of the American Communist party, Justice Jackson argued that "there is no constitutional right to gang up on the government" (Dennis v. United States, 341 U.S. 494 [1951] [Jackson, concurring]). Jackson's claim should be contrasted with the assumption that the Constitution protects the right to associate.

36. 460 U.S. 575 (1983).

37. See ibid., 578. From another perspective the exemption and tax were even-handed—all papers received the same exemption, although the result was that those papers whose tax liability would have been less than $4,000 avoided all liability under this tax while the larger papers had their liability reduced by $4,000.

38. See ibid., 591.

39. 481 U.S. 221 (1987).

40. 111 S. Ct. 1438 (1991).

41. See ibid., 1445, 1447.

42. Ibid., 1442.

43. *Arkansas Writers' Project*, 481 U.S., 227–28 (footnote and citations omitted).

44. See, e.g., ibid., 228 (stating that objectionable "types of discrimination can be established even where . . . there is no evidence of an improper censorial motive").

45. See Minneapolis Star & Tribune v. Minnesota Comm'r of Revenue, 460 U.S. 575, 579–80 (1983).

46. Ibid., 586 (footnote omitted); see also 589n.12 (noting again that the state is not prohibited from taxing the press as it does other businesses); 590n.14 (observing that since even profitable newspapers sometimes sell for less than the cost of paper and ink, and instead obtain necessary revenue from advertising, the use tax on inputs may be more burdensome than the sales tax).

47. *Arkansas Writers' Project*, 481 U.S., 229n.4 (stating that whether *Arkansas Times* was the only magazine that paid the tax or whether two others also paid did not have to be decided, because in either case it was clear that the burden fell on a limited number of publishers).

48. See ibid., 229–30.

49. See ibid., 234; see also 234–35 (Stevens, J., concurring in part and concurring in the judgment).

50. See ibid., 231–32. If any aspect of *Minneapolis Star* and *Arkansas Writers' Project* failed to survive *Leathers v. Medlock*, it may be the view that a pure revenue-raising purpose will never justify a tax which singles out the press or some portion of the press for special treatment. This was the only purpose that supported the tax on cable systems. A narrower rule consistent with the cases would be that, although purely revenue-raising purposes will not justify special tax *burdens* on the press, *exemptions* of some elements of the press from a general tax like the one in *Medlock* may be permissible unless chosen on the basis of content.

51. See C. Edwin Baker, "Neutrality, Process, and Rationality: Flawed Interpretations of Equal Protection," *Texas Law Review* 58 (1980): 1029, 1094 (arguing that the Court's examination of the fit of the law and a proposed purpose is usually a means for determining what purpose should be attributed to a law); C. Edwin Baker, "Outcome Equality or Equality of Respect: The Substantive Content of Equal Protection," *University of Pennsylvania Law Review* 131 (1983): 933, 972–84 (arguing that "contextual purpose" or "meaning," not the lawmaker's subjective intent, usually is and should be the constitutional concern).

52. *Arkansas Writers' Project*, 481 U.S., 232.

53. A. J. Liebling, *The Press* (1975), 32.

54. See Capital Broadcasting Co. v. Mitchell, 333 F. Supp. 582 (D.D.C. 1971), *aff'd without opinion*, 405 U.S. 1000 (1972).

55. See, e.g., Bates v. State Bar, 433 U.S. 350 (1977); Virginia State Bd. of Pharmacy v. Virginia Citizens Consumer Council, Inc., 425 U.S. 748 (1976); Bigelow v. Virginia, 421 U.S. 809 (1975).

56. Central Hudson Gas & Elec. Corp. v. Public Serv. Comm'n, 447 U.S. 557, 571–72 (1980).

57. Posadas de Puerto Rico Assocs. v. Tourism Co., 478 U.S. 328 (1986).

58. Austin v. Michigan Chamber of Commerce, 110 S. Ct. 1391 (1990). See also Board of Trustees v. Fox, 492 U.S. 469 (1989) (rejecting use of least restrictive alternative test in commercial speech cases and only requiring a reasonable fit between ends and means); Metromedia, Inc. v. City of San Diego, 453 U.S. 490 (1981) (majority of Court willing to allow a ban on commercial billboards).

59. Cincinnati v. Discovery Network, Inc., 113 S.Ct. (March 24, 1993). Although not bearing on the type of regulation discussed in this book, this decision suggests an increase in the protection offered the distribution of commercial speech over that suggested in Metromedia v. San Diego 453 U.S. 490 (1981); and the decision opens up such interesting questions as whether a city could ban commercial handbilling while permitting noncommercial handbilling, a distinction possibly justified if commercial handbilling is more of a problem and is more likely to proliferate when unregulated, if regulation of commercial handbilling results in a significant diminution of the problem, or if the constitutional requirement to permit

186

noncommercial handbilling reflects the unique importance of handbilling for some noncommercial, expressive endeavors.

60. See, e.g., *Bates*, 433 U.S. 350; *Virginia State Bd. of Pharmacy*, 428 U.S. 748; *Bigelow*, 421 U.S. 809; cf. Steven Shiffrin, *First Amendment, Democracy, and Romance* (1990) (arguing that the dissenter should be the central image of free speech); Steven Shiffrin, "The First Amendment and Economic Regulation: Away from a General Theory of the First Amendment," *Northwestern University Law Review* 78 (1983): 1212. Given Shiffrin's emphasis on the dissenter as being central to the First Amendment, his recommendations for a more nuanced approach to commercial speech are probably consistent with the regulations of advertisers proposed in this book.

61. Many of the best commentators on the First Amendment argue that commercial speech should never have been protected. See, e.g., Baker, *Human Liberty and Freedom of Speech*, 194–224; Thomas I. Emerson, *The System of Freedom of Expression* (1970), 311, 414–17; Alexander Meikeljohn, *Political Freedom* (1965), 87; Frederick Schauer, *Free Speech: A Philosophical Inquiry* (1982), 103; Archibald Cox, "Forward: Freedom of Expression in the Burger Court," *Harvard Law Review* 94 (1980): 1, 28, 33; Thomas H. Jackson and John C. Jeffries, Jr., "Commercial Speech: Economic Due Process and the First Amendment," *Virginia Law Review* 65 (1979): 1, 30. But cf., e.g., Martin Redish, "The First Amendment in the Marketplace: Commercial Speech and the Values of Free Expression," *George Washington Law Review* 39 (1971): 429.

62. 297 U.S. 233, 245–49 (1936).

63. Murdock v. Pennsylvania (City of Jeannette), 319 U.S. 105, 125–26 (1943) (Reed, J., dissenting).

64. Leonard W. Levy, *Emergence of a Free Press* (1985); David A. Anderson, "The Origins of the Press Clause," *UCLA Law Review* 30 (1983): 455. But cf. Zechariah Chaffee, Jr., *Free Speech in the United States* (1941), 17–18n.33 (newspaper letters citing the danger of a Stamp Act, like the one in Massachusetts, as showing the need for constitutional protection in the proposed Bill of Rights); Leonard W. Levy, "On the Origins of the Free Press Clause," *UCLA Law Review* 32 (1984): 177, 209 (referring to two anti-federalists who had concerns about the effects on a free press of Congress's power to tax, one of whom expressed fear that Congress might use " 'a cursed abominable Stamp Act' " to " 'abolish the freedom of the press' " and invoked this concern to argue for a Bill of Rights).

65. Edmund S. Morgan and Helen M. Morgan, *The Stamp Act Crisis* (1953).

66. Carol S. Humphrey, " 'That Bulwark of Our Liberties': Massachusetts Printers and the Issue of a Free Press, 1783–1788," *Journalism History* 14 (1987): 34, 37 (quoting Isaiah Thomas from the *Essex Journal*, Apr. 19, 1786, and the *Massachusetts Gazette*, Apr. 24, 1786).

67. Ibid.

68. See, e.g., Mills v. Alabama, 384 U.S. 214 (1966) (invalidating prohibition on election-day editorial endorsements).

69. See Miami Herald Publishing Co. v. Tornillo, 418 U.S. 241 (1974).

70. See, e.g., FCC v. National Citizens Comm. for Broadcasting, 436 U.S. 775, 814–15 (1978) (upholding cross-ownership rules); National Broadcasting Co. v. United States, 319 U.S. 190, 226–27 (1943) (upholding the broadcast licensing system established by Congress against First Amendment challenge); Committee for an Independent P-I v. Hearst Corp., 704 F.2d 467, 483 (9th Cir. 1983) (upholding the Newspaper Preservation Act), *cert. denied*, 464 U.S. 892 (1983). The regulation at issue in *Tornillo* is best seen as a burden imposed on particular editorial decisions, on content, not as a structural regulation of the media.

71. In 1978, total advertising expenditures in this country were divided as follows: newspapers, 28.9%; magazines, 5.9%; business and farm publications, 3.4%: television, 20.4%; radio, 6.9%; direct mail, 13.6%; outdoor, 1.1%; miscellaneous, 19.8%. See Kurian, *World Press Encyclopedia*, 2:986. Of these categories, direct mail may be gaining most. The Newspaper Association of America reported that in 1991, daily newspapers received 24% of total U.S. advertising expenditures, television obtained 22%, while 19% was spent on direct mail (*Facts about Newspapers* [1992], 1). The point is that advertising is not necessarily tied to the "press." Therefore, a tax only on advertising could be treated as a general economic regulation.

72. Although the broader tax would prevent the shift of advertising from newspapers to other media, there would still be some shift of resources away from advertising in general.

73. In addition to its policy merits, the broader tax might reduce predictable opposition to the tax plan from the press. Karl-Erik Gustafsson reports that in Sweden, where an advertising tax finances a subsidy program somewhat similar to the one proposed here, the initial proposal was to impose a 10% tax on all advertising in the press. In response to the Center party's suggestion, this was reduced to 6% for newspaper advertising, while staying at 10% for the rest of the press. But newspapers, which continue to oppose the advertising tax, successfully demanded that the media advertising tax be extended to a general advertising tax "so that it would not be in an unfavorable position compared with other advertising media" (Gustafsson, "The Press Subsidies of Sweden," in Anthony Smith, ed., *Newspapers and Democracy* [1980], 115–17). A more recent study states that the tax rate in Sweden is 10% on all advertising except in newspapers, where it is 3%. See Göran Hedebro, "Communication Policy in Sweden: An Experiment in State Intervention," in Patricia Edgar and Syed Rahim, eds., *Communication Policy in Developed Countries* (1983), 137, 143.

74. Note that existing case law does not support this ground for invalidation. Moreover, the current tax treatment of advertising as entirely a current business expense rather than a depreciable investment in good will causes the current tax system to provide a large "special" subsidy for advertising.

75. See Lewis Publishing Co. v. Morgan, 229 U.S. 288 (1913) (upholding law

against First Amendment challenge). Actually, an earlier law limited second-class postage to newspapers that met criteria designed to exclude papers which were primarily advertising vehicles; this also amounts to a restriction on advertisers' use of economic power to affect content.

76. 418 U.S. 241 (1974).

77. 326 U.S. 1, 22–23 (1945); see also National Broadcasting Co. v. United States, 319 U.S. 190, 224–27 (1943) (upholding the FCC's chain-broadcasting rules).

78. Associated Press v. United States, 326 U.S. 1, 20 (1945).

79. *Tornillo*, 418 U.S., 256.

80. Ibid., 257.

81. Ibid., 258.

82. See, e.g., Buckley v. Valeo, 424 U.S. 1 (1976) (upholding identification requirement). The lack of a serious constitutional problem with compelled statements that are presumably factual may relate to the tantalizing statement of Justice Brennan, joined by Justice Rehnquist, that the decision in *Tornillo* "addresses only 'right of reply' statutes and implies no view upon the constitutionality of 'retraction' statutes [that] . . . require publication" (*Tornillo*, 418 U.S., 258).

83. 425 U.S. 748, 771–72n.24 (1976).

84. See, e.g., Red Lion Broadcasting Co. v. FCC, 395 U.S. 367, 400–401 (1969) (upholding fairness doctrine), *cited as authority in* Metro Broadcasting v. FCC, 110 S. Ct. 2997 (1990); cf. Syracuse Peace Council v. FCC, 867 F.2d 654, 669 (D.C. Cir. 1989) (eliminating fairness doctrine on statutory grounds), *cert. denied*, 493 U.S. 1019 (1990).

85. See Columbia Broadcasting Sys. v. Democratic Nat'l Comm., 412 U.S. 94, 131 (1973).

86. See Columbia Broadcasting Sys. v. FCC, 453 U.S. 367, 397 (1980).

87. See 47 U.S.C.A. § 303a(b) (West 1991).

88. Although Lenin's usage is best known today, this popular phrase was the title of arguably the most influential novel in nineteenth-century Russia, Nikolai Govrilovich Chernyshevsky's *What Is to Be Done*, first published in 1863.

☆ *Index* ☆